SOLVING
THE MINISTRY'S
TOUGHEST
PROBLEMS

Volume II

SOLVING THE MINISTRY'S TOUGHEST PROBLEMS

Volume II

From the Editors of:

MINISTRIES:
THE MAGAZINE FOR CHRISTIAN LEADERS

Editor	Stephen Strang
Senior Editor	Howard Earl
Associate Editor	E. S. Caldwell
Editor-at-large	Jamie Buckingham

Solving the Ministry's Toughest Problems
Volume II
Copyright 1985
Strang Communications Company
190 N. Westmonte Drive
Altamonte Springs, FL 32714
ISBN # 0-930-525-01-9
First Printing, September 1985

Introduction

What incredible days these are for Spirit-filled ministers! During the first half of the 20th century the message of the fullness of the Holy Spirit was relegated to the wrong side of the tracks in most places, and clergymen of mainline churches viewed these storefront churches with scorn. Then perceptive observers among them took note of the phenomenal gains made by Pentecostals in Latin American countries, as well as recognizing their consistent growth patterns in North America.

Then suddenly and unexpectedly the baptism of the Holy Spirit descended on openhearted clergy and laity in the Episcopal Church in 1960, followed by growing numbers of Lutherans, Presbyterians and others in mainline Protestant churches. No denominational leadership orchestrated what was occurring, although committees were assigned to investigate the scriptural veracity of what was happening.

For the most part, these committees concluded that the gifts of the Spirit could in fact be received by present-day Christians and that ministers and lay people claiming such spiritual experiences should be retained within their churches. But the bottom line seemed to be toleration, not enthusiastic endorsement. No denominations produced publications to assist newly Spirit-baptized local pastors. Hence, the need for a periodical such as *MINISTRIES: The Magazine For Christian Leaders* that would provide these pastors with insights and helps unavailable anywhere else.

Even among Pentecostal denominations a need existed for a journal that could speak to their ministers as part of the entire spectrum of the Spirit-filled churches, instead of addressing only departmental concerns within their organizations. Again, *MINISTRIES* met the need.

Perhaps the most dramatic development in the Pentecostal/Charismatic phenomenon has been the proliferation of thousands of churches whose doctrinal stances are remarkably similar, yet they are not formally affiliated with one another. Some of these independent Charismatic churches have enjoyed spectacular growth, and their leaders are willing to share secrets of success and warnings of pitfalls with other pastors—if an avenue of communication is available. And *MINISTRIES* provides that channel.

Going a step beyond a magazine format in 1984 our editors compiled some 60 relevant *MINISTRIES* articles with timeless merit into a book titled *Solving the Ministry's Toughest Problems, Volume I.*

The warm reception that greeted that first volume paved the way for this book. In fact, our anticipation of the possiblity that another book would be compiled played a part in the types of articles selected for publication in the magazine. We typically asked, "Will this article make a strong chapter in Volume II?"

You hold in your hand the results of that question being asked again and again. In this volume 58 chapters are categorized under seven headings:

- Solving Pastoral Problems
- Solving Administration Problems
- Solving Personal Problems
- Solving Communications Problems
- Solving Music Ministers' Problems
- Solving Ministry Problems of Women
- Solving Home Group Problems

As you can see by a casual examination of these pages, practical concerns rather than philosophical theories prevailed in the selection of the topics for this book. Yes, philosophical concepts are included in several thought-provoking chapters, but most of the contents can be described as practical. This book is not designed as a textbook for seminary students, rather it is intended as a helpful handbook for those involved at various levels of Charismatic church leadership—those who are grappling with day-to-day ministry-related problems.

We make no claim that all the tough problems the ministry faces are solved here. Not even all the questions have yet been asked. And even if all existing problems had been treated as we went to press, new ones would have emerged since. But a significant amount of solutions to the tough problems that ministers struggle with can be found in the pages of this book.

The editors of *MINISTRIES* magazine—Associate Editor E. S. Caldwell, Senior Editor Howard Earl, Editor-at-large Jamie Buckingham, Assistant Editor Deborah D. Cole and I—are pleased to provide you with what we believe is a helpful, practical book. The greatest reward for our labors will be the knowledge that it ministered something to you that enhanced your ministry.

STEPHEN STRANG
Editor/Publisher
MINISTRIES *magazine*

Contents

Section II   Solving Administration Problems

Section III   Solving Personal Problems

Section IV   Solving Communications Problems

Section V   Solving Music Ministers' Problems

Section VI   Solving Ministry Problems of Women

Section VII   Solving Home Group Problems

Foreword

Ministers, by our nature, are problem solvers. That's our calling. A church without problems would have no use for a minister. Of course, there's no danger of that happening. Churches are composed of people. People have problems. The more "spiritual" the church, the greater the problems. Spirituality means we are moving toward God. That causes problems. Spirituality means we're developing relationships with each other. That really causes problems. It's the task of the shepherd to help people solve their problems.

But who solves the problems of the minister?

That's why we've published this book. Not just to solve "the ministry's" toughest problems—but to help the minister solve his problems as well.

The people who have written this book are experts in solving problems in specific areas. Most are seasoned leaders with many years of training and experience. Their methods have been tested over a period of time. They have a deep respect for the Bible and a sincere love for God. They are sensitive to the direction of the Holy Spirit. We selected them to help you solve your problems.

JAMIE BUCKINGHAM
Melbourne, Florida

Solving Pastoral Problems

1

Is a Pastor Called to Lordship or Servanthood?

By Jerry Horner

Jerry Horner is the dean of the School of Biblical Studies at CBN University in Virginia Beach, Virginia. He has served as chairman of the theology department of Oral Roberts University and Southwest Baptist University. He received the B.A. degree from Union University in Jackson, Tennessee, and M.Div. and Th.D. degrees at Southwestern Baptist Theological Seminary in Fort Worth, Texas, and has served as pastor and interim pastor of churches in Tennessee, Texas and Missouri.

Church dissension is as old as the Church itself, and disruptions in the fellowship of the local congregation may generally be traced to differences in personality, doctrine or policy. The Charismatic renewal of recent years has fostered the establishing of thousands of local churches made up of Christians from varied denominational backgrounds brought together by a common experience with the Holy Spirit.

These interdenominational fellowships range from small groups meeting in homes or rented halls to thousands gathered in huge auditoriums. Despite all the efforts to be "diligent to preserve the unity of the Spirit in the bond of peace" (Eph. 4:3), and notwithstanding the commonality that led them to lay aside denominational variances, such churches have not been exempt from the same schismatic tendencies that have threatened the more traditionally structured churches.

Of particular danger to independent churches, though certainly not confined to them, is a misunderstanding of the authoritative role of the pastor. There is a treacherous teaching in some Charismatic circles that the pastor is an autocratic chief who lords it over the congregation committed to him. Nothing can be done of any importance in the church unless he is present. The desires of the people in all matters are subordinated to his own, and he himself is subject to no one. He administers all the finances, appoints all the church officials (if such are deemed necessary), names the teachers and makes all decisions concerning the ministry of the church. Sometimes no meetings for prayer or Bible study, even in private homes, are allowed unless the pastor is present. This amounts, of course, to a "one man rule" concept of authority.

Such autocratic clericalism represents nothing but a travesty of New Testament ministry, and is destructive of the church, defiant to the Holy Spirit and disobedient to Christ. The pastor is certainly called to speak for God, and his very presence should remind people of God. However, he must constantly bear in mind that he is not God, and must always be on guard against acting as if he were. The church is in trouble when its pastor considers that he owns it and acts accordingly, arbitrarily excommunicating anyone who dares to disagree with his policies.

Distortion, and often disaster, comes when the pastor forgets that he is called not to dominate, but to serve.

The Third Epistle of John speaks of Diotrephes, a ruling elder in a local church who liked to put himself first. He made excessive and improper claims to authority, and used his authority to threaten excommunication if his demands were not met. His very words were malicious. In the face of such a situation John bypassed the ruling elder, and wrote to a church member of spiritual quality in order to commend him for engaging in a practice contrary to the dictates of Diotrephes, and to encourage him to continue. The spirit of Diotrephes ought to remind us that we are called not to lordship, but to oversight.

Too much harm is done when the top-dog syndrome causes the pastor to act like an evangelical guru, accountable to no one, making arbitrary decisions, and pleading the famous text, "Touch not mine anointed." It has been my observation that the untouchables soon become the unteachables, and that kind of superstar status is fraught with a variety of dangers. The subject-to-none pastor might rebuke his people when they are wrong, but who rebukes him when he is wrong? Has 1 Timothy 5:19, 20 been deleted from the Scriptures? Ministry must never be thought of in terms of status, but rather in terms of function. In the New Testament church, as we shall see, are found both leadership and authority, but no kind of hierarchical structure.

Clergy and Laity

No doubt the problem of authority has been abetted by a rigid distinction between clergy and laity, a distinction concerning which the New Testament church knew nothing, either in form, language or theory. On the contrary, the ministry was coextensive with the entire church, and it is impossible to find any biblical authority for reserving special functions solely for the ordained ministry. The sharp division between priest and people in the Old Testament is missing in the New Testament, which teaches that we are all priests alike. *Hiereus*, "priest," is never used in the New Testament for someone who holds a distinct office in the church.

If we were to ask any first-century Christian about the difference between a clergyman and a layman, we would draw a blank. Nowhere does the New Testament recognize two classes of Christians, the professional and the amateur, and the terms "clergy" and "laity" are never used to separate the ordained ministry from the rank and file of church members.

The word "clergy" comes from the Greek *kleros*, meaning "lot" or "inheritance." In its essential New Testament meaning, *kleros* refers to the "lot" or share in the inheritance of God which belongs to all those in Christ, not merely a small section of them. For instance, God the Father "has qualified us to share *(touklerou)* in the inheritance of the saints in light'' (Col. 1:12, NASB). Simon the sorcerer had ''no part or portion *(kleros)* in this matter'' (Acts 8:21, NASB). Paul testified that the risen Lord sent him to the Gentiles ''that they may receive forgiveness of sins and an inheritance *(kleron)* among those who have been sanctified by faith in Me'' (Acts 26:18, NASB). Not until the third century was *kleros* used for those who held office in the church, in distinction from the rest of God's people.

The term ''layman'' comes from *laikos*, which the Greeks used to refer to the uneducated masses. This word is altogether absent from the New Testament. However, its cognate *laos*, which means simply ''people,'' is used for the whole company of God's chosen ones. All together ''are a chosen race, a royal priesthood, a holy nation, a people *(laos)* for God's own possession'' (1 Pet. 2:9, NASB). Once again, not until the third century was *laikos* commonly used in the context of the church. In the biblical sense of the words, then, all clergy are laymen, and all laymen are also clergy.

The Function of Authority

What is written above in no way denies a distinction in the New Testament between the general body of Christians and those called by God to a particular kind of ministry within the body of Christ. Neither is it oblivious to the clear evidence of what we call the ordained ministry, nor to the authority given to those in this group. The New Testament definitely establishes authoritative roles and calls for submission to those in authority. What we must determine, then, is not the fact of authority, but its proper function.

Authority in the local church is a shared authority. When ruling authority or governance in the local church is discussed, elders are almost always mentioned in the plural. The only exceptions are in 1 Tim. 3:2 and Titus 1:7, which deal with the qualifications of a bishop (elder). However, neither passage implies the existence of a singular leader in a church.

The only hint of monarchical episcopacy in the New Testament is the telling comment about Diotrephes, who, as we have seen, wanted to dominate (3 John 9). Nowhere else is there the slightest suggestion of a one-man rule or ministry. There may indeed have been a presiding elder, but always, even in the smallest and youngest churches (see Acts 14:23; Phil. 1:1; 1 Thess. 5:12), there was a shared responsibility, whereby mutual encouragement, protection and correction could be realized. The writings of the early church fathers indicate that the same pattern continued until the tragic division between priest and people developed in the third and fourth centuries.

Authority in the local church is a caring authority. Much abuse of authority would be avoided if the person in authority understood and accepted his biblical role. There are two main verbs used in the New

Testament which describe the nature of pastoral authority. The first is *proistemi*, which has a root meaning of "to stand before," hence "to be the head of," "to lead." It is interesting, however, that the word always emphasizes not leadership with power but with the responsibility of concern, care and giving aid.

This meaning may be seen in Romans 12:8, where Paul exhorts leaders to carry out their responsibilities "with diligence," a word *spoude* which indicates earnest care (cf. 2 Cor. 7:11, 12; 8:16). A similar use of *proistemi* is found in 1 Thessalonians 5:12, 13, where the emphasis is not on the authority of the pastoral office, but on the labor of leaders exercising care and guidance over those in their charge. In 1 Timothy 3:4, 5 managing (*proistemi*) one's own household and taking care of the church of God are equivalent expressions; that is, "to manage" (AV, "to rule") is the same as "to take care of."

In 1 Timothy 5:17, Paul defines worthy rulership (*proistemi*) not in terms of the exercise of power, but specifically as laboring "at preaching and teaching." Unfortunately, when the separation between clergy and laity became more pronounced in later years, the word was used almost exclusively for the administrative function of elders, thus emphasizing the prerogatives of the pastoral office rather than its function of care.

The second verb used for authority in the church is *hegeomai*. This word is used in a general sense of governorship, but particularly describes local church leaders in Hebrews 13:7, 17, 24. The context reveals the nature of their leadership. Christian leaders are to be remembered and their faith imitated, bearing in mind that they "spoke the word of God to you." (v. 7, NASB). They are also to receive obedience and submission, "for they keep watch over your souls, as those who will give an account" (v. 17, NASB; cf. 1 Cor. 16:16).

It is clear, then, that the New Testament prescribes a church eldership or oversight (Acts 20:28; 1 Pet. 5:2). Such oversight involves some kind of rule or management. But the emphasis is not so much on the exercise of power as on service to be exercised generally through watching over men's souls, and in particular, through the teaching of God's Word and by example.

The Pattern of Authority

There is no question that pastoral authority is prescribed in the New Testament. But to describe that authority in terms of office and status, of power and control, is to wander far afield from basic biblical teachings. The pastor's authority does not demand submission because of his position, but because of his service. Thus, Paul exhorts the Christians at Thessalonica to "appreciate those who diligently labor among you, and have charge over you in the Lord . . . because of their *work*" (1 Thess. 5:12, 13, NASB). Churches need officials committed to service far more desperately than those who are interested in impressing people with their ability to rule.

Sometimes I wonder if ecclesiastical titles are a hindrance rather than a help in the work of the ministry, inasmuch as they set the bearer apart not only from the world at large but from the people for whom he is responsible. Not only so, but they remove him further from his appointed role as servant.

It seems that Jesus and the New Testament writers deliberately eschewed the use of terms which might denote a select and privileged class within the church characterized by domination over others. They chose instead words like *diakonos* and *doulos*, secular words describing the menial tasks of a slave. Paul affirmed that our Lord took upon himself the form of a *doulos* (Phil. 2:7), and Jesus himself declared that he was among us as a *diakonos* (Luke 22:27).

The word *diakonos* is a functional word, designating a person who renders acts of service to other people, particularly waiting at tables. This humble word is utterly incompatible with a hierarchical structure, and reminds us that the Church of the New Testament denies pomp and status for its officials and acknowledges greatness only in terms of service.

This feature of the ministry is amply illustrated by Paul's horrified reaction to the exaggerated deference paid to church leaders by the Corinthian Christians. With stinging sarcasm he cries out, "What then is Apollos? And what is Paul?" (1 Cor. 3:5,NASB). He deliberately uses the neuter pronoun, speaking of himself and Apollos in derogatory and almost scornful terms. In effect, he is asking the Corinthians: "What on earth do you think we are, that you regard us with such ridiculous homage?" Then he answers his own question in a fashion almost denigratory: "We are only servants *(diakonoi)* whom God has been pleased to use." He continues the use of the neuter in v. 7, when he declares that "neither the one who plants nor the one who waters is anything."

In the same context, Paul referred to himself and other church leaders as Christ's *huperetas*, a word used originally for rowers in the lower tier of a war galley, under-oarsmen (1 Cor. 4:1). From that it came to mean: anyone who does something under somebody else as a subordinate or an underling. So Paul does not push his superiority, but acknowledges his subordination. He was a minister, not a master.

In contrast to ecclesiastical celebrities seeking superstar status, genuine servants of the Lord have to be willing to subject themselves to the pitiless gaze of a ridiculing world, to be regarded as fools, and to be considered as the world's rinsings and scrapings.

Whereas *diakonos* is functional, *doulos* is a word indicating relationships. It means quite literally a slave, one who is owned by another

24

person, with no rights or independent status whatever. Peter and Paul, apostles though they were, apply it to themselves. James and Jude, half-brothers of Jesus, delight to call themselves *douloi*. In fact, it is a characteristic description of Christians (1 Pet. 2:16; Rev. 1:1). While the word usually expresses one's relation to Christ, Paul also used it to describe his relation to his converts (1 Cor. 9:10; 2 Cor. 4:5). This graphic word ought to shame into silence arguments about the status and validity of ministries.

The Pattern of Jesus

The highest ministry of all is that of servanthood, and Jesus set the pattern for us to follow in that regard. In his teaching, he completely reversed the common understanding of leadership. There is certainly no denying that the pattern and glory of His ministry was service.

Jesus acted out the lesson of the royalty of service in graphic fashion at the Last Supper when he washed the disciples' feet. Relentlessly, in words recorded in John 13:12-17, he pressed home to them the revolutionary idea that greatness is measured in terms of service.

It is a confession of our own failure to follow the example of our Lord when we reflect on the fact that we are more prone to wear the robes of the ruler than the apron of the servant.

Although he does not describe the foot washing, Luke's account of the Last Supper indicates that the action of Jesus arose out of a quarrel among the disciples over precedence and status (Luke 22:24). Like many of us, they would fight for the throne of authority but not for the towel of servanthood.

Christ's teaching in response to this attitude is unmistakable, both here and following the request of James and John for places of honor in the kingdom. You may recall that the other 10 were indignant at the brothers. The reason for their displeasure is not difficult to see, in light of the dispute later at the supper. They wanted the throne themselves.

Note the patient but pointed instruction of the Lord: "You know that the rulers of the Gentiles lord it over thee, and their great men exercise authority over them. It is not so among you, but whoever wishes to become great among you shall be your *diakonos*, and whoever wishes to be first among you shall be your *doulos* (Matt. 20:25-27, NASB).

The contrast is striking. Pagan leadership is marked by lordship and authority. Christian leadership is characterized by service, even slavery. This lesson needs to be heeded by contemporary church leaders: passion for domineering power must be transformed into passion for *diakonia*.

The choice between lordship and servitude confronts every pastor. Paul faced that choice and wrote, "Not that we lord it over your faith,

25

but are workers with you for your joy'' (2 Cor. 1:24, NASB). Peter faced it and admonished, ''Nor yet as lording it over those allotted to your charge, but proving to be examples to the flock'' (1 Pet. 5:3).

The pastor, then, is not a lord but a servant, not a boss but a fellow worker and example.

In paying undue deference to church leaders, the Corinthians were claiming to belong to Paul or to Apollos or to someone else (1 Cor. 1:12). Paul in response taught that the opposite was the case. If anybody belonged to anybody, it was the leaders who belonged to the people. ''All things belong to you,'' including Paul and Apollos (1 Cor. 3:21, 22).

That teaching has an application today. It is more proper for a congregation to say ''my pastor'' than it is for the pastor to say ''my congregation,'' for the pastor belongs to the church, and not the church to the pastor. The church is not to be regarded as an estate to be farmed for the pastor's own profit nor a garden to be trimmed to his own taste.

The English expositor and pastor Charles Bridges recognized this truth, as seen in these words first published in 1830:

''The great Shepherd, indeed, who gave Himself for, gave us to, the flock, and there is no more responsible thought connected with our work, than the obligation of giving ourselves to our people, so that they shall be led to prize us as a gift from Christ. Oh! That we might be able to tell them 'We belong to Christ, and He has given us to you; we owe our whole selves entirely to you; we are your servants for Jesus' sake; we have given ourselves to the work, and we desire to be in it, as if there was nothing worth living for besides: it shall form our whole pleasure and delight. We will consecrate our whole time, our whole reading, our whole mind and heart to this service.' '' *(The Christian Ministry,* p. 106.)

But our great example is Jesus. The pattern and glory of His ministry was service, and we can and must make that pattern our own, because, in truth, our ministry is an extension of His. Christ would have had refrangible credentials if He had desired to rely on status and authority. But He never entertained such a thought, because to Him the authority of the servant lay simply in the fact of His service.

Surely the church would be strengthened if Christian leaders followed in this revolutionary path of their Lord, a way so contrary to the natural man that it cannot fail to point God's people to the beauty of service, and thus provide an impetus for their own sacrificial service.

Pastors don't need to declare and defend the authority of their office. They simply need to discover and practice its true function.

The greatest control the pastor can gain over the congregation is not the power of strong-arm tactics, but the power of foot-washing service, and that in itself arises from superior self-forgetfulness.

2

How Can a
Minister Succeed?

By C. M. Ward

C. M. Ward, chancellor and former president of Bethany Bible College in Santa Cruz, California, is one of America's foremost evangelists and radio/television speakers. A former pastor, Bible college instructor and editor, he also was radio evangelist for "Revivaltime," the international radio voice of the Assemblies of God. He has written 23 hardback volumes of radio sermons, authored over 250 booklets and has recorded the entire Bible on cassette and 8-track tapes.

There are three components—sower, seed, soil. It is not feasible to grow cotton in Alaska. The climate controlling the soil is not suitable. This is an important lesson to learn in the ministry. Toward what are you best suited, and where most productive? Make your calling sure!

An evangelist may have an extraordinarily successful meeting on the West Coast and a flop in Tennessee. He preaches the same message. He employs the same publicity. He uses the same methods. The prevailing culture—the soil—is different.

The most successful ministries are those which realize this fact, and exercise the courage and discipline to stay in the locale best fitted to them.

James was most successful in staying in Jerusalem—"see how many thousands of the Jews there are who believe." Paul was most successful preaching to a Gentile world. Phillip's success was in Samaria.

I have experienced this as a pastor. I found better results using fewer evangelists and singers and inviting to return those who displayed an empathy with my locality.

Pastors can get out of "sync." Sometimes they are lured by promises and adventure from faraway places. Then they are unable to repeat the growth they knew in the places they left.

It is an exception to the rule that a great missionary will decide to change his direction and accept a pastorate. The high hopes usually flounder. Administrative ministry seldom blossoms in the evangelistic field. I must determine as early as possible where I fit best. There is success in contentment.

Cultures change. Boston thinking, humor, habits, folklore, legends, pride are quite different from those of New York. Even the language is different. It takes an extraordinary Yankee to find genuine response from a Georgia audience.

Even athletic teams usually do better in home arenas. To have the crowd with you is a tremendous incentive.

Jesus favored Galilee rather than Judea.

Stay with what you do best! As a rule, all preachers want to sing and all singers want to preach. This unrest can bring difficulty to a service.

The late Dr. Charles Price returned to the same camp meetings every year. The late Katherine Kuhlman found a terrific market for her ministry in Pittsburgh.

Jesus said, "Find the place where you are *received!*" (see Matt. 10:11-14).

Preachers, to their sorrow, yield to seductions of pleasant weather, modern and expensive parsonages, more fringe benefits, and move. Congregations and preachers are disappointed with the results. They chased the myth that success is highly transferable. I must not ignore the *soil*.

Different fish spawn in different waters.

Barnabas did well at Antioch but not elsewhere. Luke was a medical doctor turned writer, but not used in any miracle ministry. Peter might have been a bust in Corinth. He was the key in Jerusalem.

Usually the early years of a preacher are experimental. By the time he or she reaches 40 there should be an imperative within that points to what he or she *must* do, and where best it can be accomplished.

"I come to do Thy will." That prerogative can be found in the individual. It is more sacred than destiny. It is the margin between profit and loss in life. God has a *place* and a *work* for me. I can discover these as easily as a horticulturist discovers an area for citrus or an area for corn.

I need not be frustrated if I accept contentment, what the Eternal determined best for me.

Martin Luther was adaptable to his time in history. Not everyone is a William Booth who can start a Salvation Army. There are too many copycats. Instead of yielding, preachers insist that they duplicate someone's unique ministry and success. It isn't likely.

My father, the late elder A.G. Ward, was a master of exposition in the Song of Solomon. I have very little insight into it.

Find what *works* best for you and do not be ashamed to use it. Great professional baseball batteries (pitcher and catcher) determine this as early in the game as possible. The curve may not be working at all. It does not have the snap. It isn't finding the corners. The fast ball is unbeatable on the occasion. It has zing. It is rising or falling. So the pitcher and catcher will go with what is *working*.

The preacher will find times when teaching is the "in" thing. Attendance soars. You would like to change the pattern for your own relief. If you do, you ignore the "hot market" and empty your auditorium.

It's presumptuous to preach the doctrine of hell in mid-summer when the heat is over the 100-degree mark. It's not a good time to lead the congregation in ''Rescue the Perishing'' on Christmas Sunday morning. Bad judgment brings loss.

Some preachers are great weepers. Jeremiah was. They would never be given an A-plus for homiletics, but the compassion and wet handkerchiefs build overflow crowds.

Tulips are for the spring. Mums are for the autumn.

An Isaiah is not an Amos. John is not a Nathaniel. Discover who you are and where you belong!

3

How Can Prayer Shape a Church?

By Larry Lea

Larry Lea founded Church on the Rock in Rockwall, Texas, with 13 members. Within five years the church had a membership of over 7,000 with a pastoral staff of 21 and more than 340 home CARE (cell) groups in a town of about 10,000 people. Pastor Lea is the author of *Could You Not Tarry One Hour?*, a book of revolutionary teaching on how to pray. Lea also conducts prayer clinics in churches across America.

Do you face the dilemma of too much church business and not enough prayer? Most pastors do. Let me suggest a prayer goal that changed my life. The power of prayer is the key to all that has been accomplished at Church on the Rock during the past four years. I realize this afresh every morning as I look at a circle of more than 100 intercessors who line the perimeter of our sanctuary.

This 6 a.m. prayer meeting came into being simultaneously with the birthing of the church. That took place on an icy day in January 1980 when 13 committed people gathered in the back room of a skating rink. Today, more than 4,000 meet each Lord's day for worship here in a Texas town of 8,000, located 35 miles east of Dallas. Growth like that cannot be achieved through human endeavor; it can only be attributed to the Holy Spirit's drawing power in response to intercessory prayer.

To me, prayer is the highest call of all. That's why I consistently emphasize it. I am happy to report that people respond to that emphasis. Some 500 people pray at least 60 minutes daily for the success of God's Word through the ministries of our church.

I didn't give prayer the priority place it deserved when God first called me, even though deep down I knew the call to prayer must be primary in a minister's life. As a student in Bible college God spoke to me through His Word, showing me that a man must be called to pray if he truly is to answer a call to preach.

The following seven years of my life were exasperating because during those years I usually felt defeated by my lack of discipline in a prayer life. Maybe the most dangerous part of my struggle was that everything looked successful. From 1972-1978 I served as the minister of youth and evangelism at Beverly Hills Baptist Church in Dallas. During those years, this exciting church grew from 400 to 4,000. Our youth group topped 1,000, and monthly I preached to more than 3,000 young people in an evangelistic crusade setting. Simultaneously, I was finishing a master's program at Southwestern Baptist Theological Seminary in Fort Worth, Texas. Amid all this, the call to pray loomed as an illusive goal which I never seemed able to reach.

Outwardly all seemed great; inwardly, I felt like "dead men's bones." I was mastering the busy work of Martha while desiring the eternal work of Mary. Sitting at Jesus' feet and hearing His voice was my heart's desire. Yet the discipline to put away my church business for the quality time He required seemed unreachable. I cried out to God in desperation and failure, and He opened a way of escape.

After the sudden death of my pastor in 1978, I was called to become senior pastor of Beverly Hills Baptist Church, the church I loved and served as youth pastor. It seemed only logical and right to continue to minister in such an environment of growth and success. Nevertheless, at this juncture in my life, the Lord taught me an invaluable lesson. He showed me that sometimes His will appears contrary to what is logical and right.

During those days I met B. J. Willhite, then pastor of First Assembly of God in Kilgore, Texas. While I was preaching a revival in this small assembly, I learned that Pastor Willhite had been rising for prayer before 5 a.m. for 30 years. The revival in Kilgore lasted seven weeks and more than 400 people were saved. But this revival was as much for me as for those who were saved.

I began to rise early with Pastor Willhite and, for the first time in my life, day after day prayer became my central focus. While in prayer, God's Spirit opened my heart not to pursue the pastorate at the large city church but to resign my position, move to Kilgore and learn to pray.

To all of my friends I had made a tragic mistake in not pursuing the pastorate of that large church. To me, for the first time since God's initial call to pray, I began to answer the highest call of all. So for the following 18 months, my wife, our three children and I lived with my mother and father who resided in Kilgore.

The vision that produced the Church on the Rock came to me during those months of prayer. Today's early morning prayer meetings could be called a continuation of what was being built into my life while in prayerful fellowship with Pastor Willhite. And now, as pastor of prayer, B. J. Willhite administrates the extensive prayer ministry of the Church on the Rock.

Why Pray an Hour?

Once, when I was at my busiest for God, a word was dropped in my heart from Jesus' question to His sleepy disciples: "Could you not tarry one hour?" This word concerning one 60-minute prayer time haunted my faulty prayer life until finally conviction gave way to surrender, and spiritual victory ensued. I do not know why Jesus asked, "Could you not tarry one hour?" Nor do I know why my heart was *so* convicted to seek God as a discipline for one hour daily. All I know is, when in 1978 I prioritized the first hour for God, everything began to change.

In October 1983, I flew to South Korea, to study church growth at Yoido Full Gospel Church. After Paul Yonggi Cho gave his first message (on prayer, of course), he said, "Now let us pray for one hour." Some 250 ministers and I knelt for an hour of prayer. For three months at Church on the Rock I had preached, "Could You Not Tarry One Hour?" For five years one hour daily had been my minimum prayer goal. Could it be now in Korea that Cho was about to confirm what was going on in my life and my church?

After praying for one hour with Cho, we went out to sit in the sun for a photograph session with the entire group of ministers. I was asked to sit by Cho. When the picture session was finished, Cho very calmly took my hand, looked into my eyes and said, "Something supernatural happens when you pray one hour." I said nothing, my mouth just dropped open!

What to Pray?

Someone might ask, "What do you pray about for an hour?" First, let me clarify, I'm not talking now about study or meditation. I'm talking about an hour spent primarily in petition, supplication and thanksgiving.

"What to pray" is an excellent question. It seems that gets at what the disciples asked Jesus in Luke 11:1 when they said, "Lord, teach us to pray." My little tract "Could You Not Tarry One Hour?" deals with a basic question about prayer: Can we or should we proceed in further petitions until we have prayed what the Master commanded us to pray?

I challenge you to take Matthew 6:9-13 and spend an hour with the Lord. Praising your way into His presence will cause you to petition your way into His power.

My teaching series went line-by-line through "the Lord's Prayer," taking each phrase and asking the Holy Spirit to breathe in life. For example, when praying, "Our Father, which art in heaven," we examined the important truth of the fatherhood of God. From "hallowed be thy name," I taught the redemptive names of God in the Old Testament, climaxing with the all-encompassing name of Jesus. From "thy kingdom come, thy will be done in earth as it is in heaven," I shared promised answers to petitions for family, church and nation.

If you allow the Holy Spirit ample time to address each phase of each phrase in this prayer, an hour a day will become a minimum. I realize this teaching may seem very elementary to some people, but it became a victorious prayer formula for me. The formula goes like this: the Master's prayer command, plus the leadership of the Holy Spirit, equals a victorious hour in prayer.

Why Did Jesus Pray?

For Jesus the highest call was the call to prayer. If anything can be gleaned from the Gospel writers' accounts of our Lord, it is that the power source for His life and ministry was prayer.

Early in His earthly ministry, we find Jesus ministering in Capernaum. Well into the night He poured out healing and deliverance to the broken of that place. Mark 1:32-34 records, "And at even, when the sun did set, they brought unto him all that were possessed with devils. And all the city was gathered together at the door. And he healed many that were sick of divers diseases, and cast out many devils; and suffered not the devils to speak, because they knew him." No doubt, Jesus was spiritually, emotionally and physically exhausted after such activities. Then we see His secret, "And in the morning, rising up a great while before day, he went out, and departed into a solitary place, and there prayed" (Mark 1:35).

The disciples followed Jesus and found Him at the place of prayer. They saw the divine link between prayer and power. They asked, "Lord, teach us to pray." Whether He was raising the dead, cleansing the leper, opening blind eyes, feeding the multitude, or preaching the kingdom, they saw one distinct pattern. Pray, then preach! Pray, then heal! Pray, then obey!

The priority Jesus places on prayer is graphically illustrated in Matthew 21:12-16, a passage identified as the cleansing of the temple. Notice the progression of concepts about the Lord's house in these verses:

1. A house of purity, verse 12.
2. A house of prayer, verse 13.
3. A house of power, verse 14.
4. A house of perfected praise, verses 15, 16.

In this action Jesus shows the intent of God's heart. To lead us from purity to prayer; from prayer to power; and from power to perfected praise is the heart of the Master's work in our churches.

Jesus' life on earth was nothing more than a walk in the Spirit from one prayer place to another. Finally, His disciples followed Him to Gethsemane where He received instruction and strength to suffer. In Luke 22:40 He came to "the place." This was not a random place but a designated prayer spot. He had "the place" for seeking the face of His Father. How we need a place which is designated "the place."

After Jesus finished His role on earth as a suffering servant and risen Lord, His primary ministry of prayer continued. Hebrews 7:25 states, "Wherefore he is able also to save them to the uttermost that come unto God by him, seeing he ever liveth to make intercession for them." With His redemptive work finished at Calvary, His high priestly ministry of intercession continues at the right hand of the Father. For

Jesus, prayer is the highest call of all.

What Does Prayer Bring?

The first supernatural thing that happened to me when one hour became a way of life was simply an awareness that I was free from the guilt of prayerlessness. From that point revelation began to come sweetly!

When Jesus said in John 20:21, "Peace be unto you: as my Father hath sent me, even so send I you," all the disciples knew to do was form a prayer meeting and wait for revelation. Then came *Pentecost!* Then came *preaching!* Then came *people!* With the people came the *problems!* Nevertheless, the apostles didn't break the pattern. They said in Acts 6:4, "But we will give ourselves continually to prayer, and to the ministry of the word." Notice the order of their priorities: prayer first, then the ministry of the Word. Today, in general, our priorities are the people first, our preaching second and prayer as an addendum plea for help! I contend the power of preaching the revealed Word (a word living in us by the Holy Spirit's revelation) is directly contingent on prayer. You have as much inspired revelation as you have determined intercession.

Leonard Ravenhill once said, "At Pentecost, Peter preached one sermon and saw 3,000 saved. Today, we preach 3,000 sermons and see one saved!" What's the difference? The difference is simply that Peter preached out of the flow of revelation that was birthed in prayer.

Think of it this way: Revelation comes only from God; therefore, I must be vitally linked to Him in order for the flow to continue. That's where prayer comes in. Prayer is the discipline that vitally links us with God.

Moses prayed 40 days then came the revelation of the Ten Commandments. Isaiah was in the temple, no doubt interceding for the nation of Israel, when the heavens opened wide. Ezekiel was seeking God when he saw the wheel in the middle of the wheel. Daniel had fasted and prayed when he saw an angel like unto the Son of Man.

Where was John when "The Revelation" was released? One might answer that John was in awful exile for crimes he never committed. I answer, "John was *in the Spirit* on the Lord's day." Suffice it to say, revelation for service comes only through intercession.

First John 5:4 says, "For whatsoever is born of God overcometh the world: and this is the victory that overcometh the world, even our faith." The converse of that truth would read, "That which is not birthed by God will not overcome the world." Could this be the simple explanation why so much that we do does not truly succeed? Could it be that if we wait and allow the Spirit of God to give clear direction concerning the next step in ministry that indeed that step would overcome the world?

Pray and Obey

I wish I could claim originality for our slogan for church growth. In April 1981, while attending a church growth conference at Word of Faith Temple in New Orleans (Charles Green, pastor), I first met Cho. I was one of a thousand preachers at the convention and didn't dream of a personal interview with him. But on the last night of the convention, I told my wife and associate pastor that I felt something very unusual was about to happen to me that night. All during the service that evening the Holy Spirit seemed to prompt my spirit to be alert. Then Cho ended the service, but nothing unusual had occurred. Suddenly, Charles Green appeared from behind the auditorium stage beckoning me to come with him. Along with my wife, associate pastor and his wife we wound our way through the back halls of the civic theatre. Pastor Green later said he felt a compulsion to get me with Cho that night.

When finally confronted with Cho, I asked the only sane question that came to mind, "How did you build the greatest church in history?" His answer was brief and to the point: "I pray and obey!" From that time to this, "pray and obey" has been the watchword of Church on the Rock.

Although our church has now developed a functional cell system ministry with 140 groups (approximately 3,000 people), I do not recommend approaching home ministry (or any ministry) without prayer. Then, out of obedience to a commitment birthed in prayer, you can proceed with confidence.

This is how our cell ministry was birthed. Seeing we—four elders and I—could not successfully shepherd 300 people in 1981, we sought the Lord in His Word for a real solution. We were convinced the home ministry was the *what to do,* so we sought the Lord daily on *when* and *how* to implement this biblical revelation.

Three basic revelations came to us before we implemented the home cell ministry:

1. The pastor and elders had to be convinced that God had spoken to us to proceed. Also, we had to be willing not only to start the program but to lead it throughout the church's life.

2. We had to make a commitment to training leadership. To join our church, a person must go through a 10-week "Finding the Rock" course. This course includes basic Christian foundations and reveals the vision of the church. We added two more courses to train our leaders. The second three-month course deals with how the leader relates to other members in the body of Christ, emphasizing his response to spiritual authority. The third course is designed to teach the practice of leading a home group meeting.

We call our cell meeting the "Care" ministry of the church. Care represents an acrostic for Contact And Relate Everyone.

3. We had to identify the purpose of the "Care" ministry. That purpose was to establish a network of personal ministry to minister to each person individually in the body and to teach each group to be a light in a dark world. More simply, our dual purpose is fellowship and evangelism as co-equal priorities for each group.

With these three purposes established, we shared with the congregation (then about 1,500 people) the vision of "Care" ministry and began with church-wide participation and commitment. We are continually training leaders and starting new groups. We started with eight groups three years ago; today, there are 140 and counting.

We are thankful for what God has done and continues to do through our cell ministry. It is overcoming the world because it was birthed in our spirits by prayer. But I believe it would be a mistake for you to take my cell system if you did not seek God and hear clearly His will and way for your church. No matter how biblical the plan may be, if it is not originated, energized and undergirded with prayer, it will not overcome the world.

4

What Are the Qualifications for an Effective Ministry?

By E. S. Caldwell

E. S. Caldwell is associate editor of *MINISTRIES: The Magazine For Christian Leaders*. He served the Assemblies of God as promotions coordinator for the Division of Home Missions and publicity director for the radio-TV department. He pastored 23 years in Idaho and Missouri. He is a graduate of Northwest College of the Assemblies of God and also attended Northwest Nazarene College.

I heard what sounded like the thunderous roar of Niagara Falls inside a church in Seoul, South Korea. I was attending the second service on a Wednesday evening in Yoido Full Gospel Church (formerly Full Gospel Central Church) pastored by Paul Yonggi Cho. That multivocal roar came from the combined sound of more than 10,000 people praying in tongues at the same time—not shouting, but praying aloud in a conversational level.

As the rushing, thunderous sound surrounded me, my mind raced back 14 years to when I first heard the pounding waters of the 3,010-foot wide Horseshoe Falls cascading 158 feet downward. That was magnificent. This was majestic! It seemed uncanny that the two sounds were so similar.

How did I know they were praying in tongues instead of their Korean language? Frankly, I wasn't certain until I asked Miss Lee, the coordinator of the seminar. "Mostly the people are praying in the Spirit," she informed me.

Visualize the scene with me. The vast arena contains eight sections of pews fanning out in curved rows beneath a high, domed ceiling. The back of each pew contains a shelf where the worshippers can place hymnals or Bibles. The Koreans sit while they pray, their arms extended forward and slightly upward. Many of them rock gently back and forth. Their intensity is evident—eyes squeezed shut, concentration apparent. They are talking to God in languages He has provided. Communication with Deity immerses every fiber of their beings. Spiritual dynamism charges the atmosphere. This is prayer in concert elevated to the nth degree.

Can the platform regain control of this torrent? Yes, and with amazing ease—a single stroke of a bell on the pulpit. One silvery chime penetrates the air and within seconds the voices hush, ready to respond to the next phase of the service. Suddenly everyone is singing the familiar old hymn, "Near the Cross." Then it's "Amazing Grace," and foreigners like me discover "how sweet the sound" when we hear it in the Korean tongue.

Next, it's time to say in unison the Apostles' Creed (this summary of Christian doctrine is included as a part of every service on Sunday,

Wednesday and Friday and every cell meeting, whenever in the week each of the 21,000 cells meet).

Cho is at the pulpit. He informs the congregation that foreign visitors are present. He invites those attending the Church Growth International Seminar to stand. We are clustered in two sections of the balcony. As soon as we are on our feet, Cho urges his congregation to pray for the 252 visitors from seven parts of the globe.

The Koreans stand, 10,000 strong, each extending both arms toward us and their prayer begins. This time it's different—it's like the sound of a mighty rushing wind. And accompanying that sound comes a physical sensation—something resembling electrical energy swept from the Korean multitude up, over and through the assembled visitors. I've never before felt anything quite like that rolling surge of power. And when I had opportunity I asked other participants if they too experienced what I had felt. "Like nothing I've ever felt before," said Dale Galloway, pastor of the New Hope Community Church in Portland, Oregon. Similar comments were made by others, whether Baptist, Church of Christ, Lutheran, Nazarene or Pentecostal.

That first on-site visit to the world's largest church (389,321 members as of July 31, 1984) made all of us ready to listen attentively to its pastor. You simply have to be there to grasp the magnitude of what God continues to accomplish in that church. You have to believe with your own eyes when you see all-day, mass-production baptismal services in its Jerusalem Chapel, counting 8,208 immersions in July alone.

And so when the seminary sessions get underway, on the 11th floor of the CGI building, you listen attentively to the slight-built, soft-spoken, keen-eyed senior pastor. He's discovered something that's worth knowing.

Qualifications for Ministry

In the first session, Cho lists 10 qualifications for an effective ministry. Summarized briefly, they are:

1. *You must be a man or woman of visions and dreams.* On the day of Pentecost, Peter quoted what God said through the prophet Joel: "I will pour out my Spirit upon all flesh...and your young men shall see visions, and your old men shall dream dreams" (Acts 2:17). So visions and dreams are the "language" of the Holy Spirit. If you are not a man or woman of visions and dreams, you are finished so far as church growth is concerned. "I first dreamed of 150 in my church, then 300," said Cho. "Then in 1964 the Holy Spirit told me to visualize 3,000—and to act as though this was now true.

"Show me your vision, and I'll show you your future. Seeing comes ahead of possession. God said to Abraham, 'What you see, you will possess. Romans 4:17 says that 'God...calleth those things which be not as though they were.' "

41

By the help of the Holy Spirit get visions and dreams. You must fast and pray. Remember, your dream is the vessel through which God fulfills your desire.

2. *You must be a pastor who has a clear goal.* When you set a goal, you really need the Holy Spirit's help. "I usually set a five-year goal," Cho said, and he recommended that ideally a pastor should plan to stay in a church for the rest of his life. When setting goals one should ask: Can I believe this? Is it achievable? Is it concrete? Making the goal clear is important because it gives you a sense of direction, it provides a means to motivate your people, it helps you persevere and it enables you to measure your progress. And when you arrive at your goal, you can have a success image.

3. *You must be men and women of powerful faith.* Cho cautioned that in any project the leader expect a "death experience," because only after death could there be a resurrection. He said that when he announced his plan to expand the present sanctuary seating capacity from 10,000 to 25,000, he faced great resistance. Many elders left the church.

And about this time, some leaders in the Korean Assemblies of God branded him a heretic and began action to withdraw his credentials. At issue was the advice Cho offered an only son whose father attempted suicide because the Christian youth refused to offer ceremonial food in respect for his deceased mother. Some denominations condemn the practice as idol worship; others say that it is just paying respect to deceased parents. In this instance, Cho advised the youth, who was contemplating withdrawing from the Church: "Brother, your father won't understand, so why don't you carry out that ceremony, respecting your mother, and still come to church? Then, by and by, bring your father, too. Then when he gets converted, he won't be too much concerned about the ceremony?"

A tape recording of only that excerpt from Cho's Wednesday lecture on 1 Corinthians 8 was the "damning evidence" with which the Korean denominational officials intended to oust their most successful minister. Cho responded to his jealous contemporaries: "Before you officially chase me out of the denomination, I'll just turn in my resignation." The officials called in the secular and religious press and announced that Cho was a heretic. And a writer was hired to produce a book that defamed Cho. It was a terrible situation, but in the three years since, Cho has been exonerated. He was selected by Korean lay Christians to serve as one of the main centennials of Protestant Christianity in Korea (1,200,000 attended the event in August 1984). Now the secular press and television praise Cho as an authentic representative of the Christian Church.

"Never budge or waiver when you have a vision," says the pastor who prevailed after overcoming a firestorm of unwarranted attacks.

He commented that in America some pastors are dominated by laymen. But a church board should be supportive of the pastor's vision.

4. *You must be a man or woman of prayer.* Church growth does not come by gimmicks and pushing buttons.

Before you come to the pulpit, the battle should already be won. "I must pray at least three hours for one message," says Cho. And he adds, "When I have many people praying, I am not afraid of anything."

5. *You must be men and women of desire if you want to see church growth.* To have success, you have to have a fervent heart.

6. *You must have a good relationship with your people.* But as a pastor you will be tempted between home visitation and visitation with God. In Acts 13, the church leaders ministered to the Lord *before* they ministered to the people. God has a tremendous need for fellowship because God is *love.* "Until you have a deep fellowship with God," says Cho, "He will not bless you."

"I cannot personally visit with the members of my church; they are too many," he says. "But I can visualize them. I see them clearly, then I pray for them. I can minister to them in prayer even though I am on another continent."

Many of these people are prospering. Some 3,000 are now successful businessmen. When they first came to the Lord, they were poor.

7. *You must be an absolutely honest person.* When you make a mistake, you must honestly confess it and ask forgiveness. If you try to justify yourself, you will lose your friends.

8. *You must be men and women of morality.* A pastor is in the vortex of temptation. Money is a temptation to some. Pride tempts others. And members of the opposite sex are also a temptation. Never yield to temptation.

It takes 30 or 40 years to become a successful pastor, and all can be lost in one fall. "I travel with elders and deacons so I will be protected and have witnesses of my moral conduct," Cho remarked.

9. *You must study continually.* Cho says that he makes a practice of reading books written by successful people. He also reads news magazines and devotional books. He recently learned the Japanese language—a three-year project. Now he preaches in Japanese on weekly telecasts aired in Japan.

10. *You must learn how to delegate.* Cho had to learn this the hard way. In 1964 he was singlehandedly pastoring 3,000 people, and collapsed with nervous exhaustion. His illness lingered for 10 years—until the cell system, with the delegation it requires, was completely established.

During that time he learned to delegate his work to associate pastors (he now has 316). He also learned how effective and loyal women could be in ministry assignments (two-thirds of his associate pastors are women, and the same proportion of his 21,000 cell leaders are female).

In the 10 years Cho was somewhat incapacitated, his church grew from 3,000 to 18,000. The Lord did not allow him to recover until he had learned to delegate responsibility to his associates and cell leaders.

During 1984 each of his 21,000 cell leaders has a goal of winning 10 people to the Lord. By winning only two families, that goal can be met. In 1983 one cell leader brought 320 people to the Lord for salvation. Simple arithmetic shows that 10 converts multiplied by 21,000 cell leaders equals 210,000 converts in a single year. And the leaders are on target.

Other Highlights

I attended a cell group of the ninth floor of a modern high-rise apartment. Wives from the complex came with their leather-bound hymnals and Bibles. They sang, they recited the Apostles' Creed, they studied the printed Scripture lesson, they prayed. It was a well-rounded spiritual event in which everyone participated. A friend of mine attended a cell group in a more primitive setting—a house without plumbing. He reported that eight of the women in attendance were not yet converted, but they were well on the way to accepting the message of the gospel.

Cho says his goal is to have 50,000 cells, with the potential for half a million conversions a year!

As a minister, the less work you do, the more successful you will be. A general does not fight on the front lines, he lays out strategy. Then the people of your church can be motivated, involved and fulfilled.

Cho says that if you don't "lose your job," you are not a successful pastor.

In other sessions, Cho discussed pulpit ministry, signs of revival and a detailed explanation of his cell system.

Then there was the unforgettable experience enjoyed by seminar members who attended the Friday all-night prayer service. And on Sunday we attended one of the seven magnificent worship services—complete with a symphonic orchestra accompanying glorious anthems sung by one of the seven choirs. Worshippers were packed in everywhere, including 13 chapels, each with TV screens watched by 500 to 1,000 people. Awesome!

On Monday we visited Fasting Prayer Mountain, located 45 minutes north of Seoul. The ark-shaped chapel seats 10,000—5,000 in benches, 5,000 on the floor. On the lower level there are two additional chapels, each platform displays the same giant banner you saw in the central church—the words of Mark 16:15 in Korean and English: "GO YE

INTO ALL THE WORLD AND PREACH THE GOSPEL TO EVERY CREATURE.'' Four services a day minister year-round to those who set aside chunks of time to fast and pray. And for those who want seclusion, there are 152 one-person concrete prayer grottos inconspicuously placed throughout the tree-shaded landscape. These mini-bunkers provide a power greater than any artillery for restraining the onslaught of communist armies encamped but a few miles to the north. As a prayer mountain pastor put it, ''With our prayer, North Korea cannot attack South Korea.'' You know you walk on holy ground!

Pastors who visit South Korea will learn lessons that will not be fully grasped anywhere else. These lessons are especially beneficial for pastors from a superpower, high-tech nation like America. The only question is: *Can we be humble enough to learn?*

5

What Is the Gift of Faith?

By Elmer L. Towns

Elmer L. Towns is dean of the School of Religion, Liberty University, Lynchburg, Virginia. He has taught in Christian colleges for 27 years and authored 46 books relating to church growth, theology and the Sunday school. Towns has received degrees from three theological seminaries and two universities.

As I studied some of the largest churches in America, I came to the conviction that the faith of the pastor was one of the main reasons for the church's growth. However, I did nothing with this conviction until I heard Peter Wagner state that the spiritual gift of faith was the common denominator he found in the pastors of the largest churches. Wagner went on to explain that some of these pastors were extraordinary preachers, while others were average speakers. He saw the same difference in administration, counseling and teaching, but he felt *all* the pastors of large churches had the spiritual gift of faith. Finally, I visited the 10 largest churches in the world and there concluded that the pastor's faith was the common denominator that caused the growth of the world's largest churches.

I examined over 120 books on spiritual gifts and found almost no comprehensive study on the spiritual gift of faith. It was usually discussed briefly in the material dealing with spiritual gifts, but most usually was covered in a paragraph or at most a few pages. Whole books and dissertations are given over to the discussion of the spiritual gifts of tongues, miracles or healings, while the spiritual gift of faith has been neglected too long. I contend that the spiritual gift of faith is one of the foundational abilities for church growth or any work for God; and those who "move mountains" for God have done so by exercising the spiritual gift of faith.

The gift of faith is a spiritual gift that is bestowed upon certain believers to edify the body of Christ. The gift of faith is the use of faith that gets extraordinary results. Kenneth Kinghorn observes in *Gifts of the Spirit,* "while all Christians possess the grace of faith, not all Christians possess the gift of faith."

Kurt Koch says in *Charismatic Gifts,* "The faith that comes as a gift of the Spirit is the daring and conquering faith that 'removes mountains.'" In *Gifts of the Spirit,* Leslie Flynn makes the observation, "The gift of faith, listed by Paul in 1 Corinthians 12:9, is more than saving faith." Therefore, I conclude that the spiritual gift of faith is not synonymous with saving faith, even though it is generally confused with saving faith, but it is *more than* saving faith.

The spiritual gift of faith has been generally described as ''faith of miracles'' by Donald Gee, ''special faith'' in *The Living Bible,* ''wonder working faith'' by B. F. Underwood, ''daring faith'' by Koch, and ''the gift of prayer'' by John MacArthur.

But even when the authors who write about the gift of faith recognize that it is special, they do not generally agree on a definition. Perhaps their disagreement arises from the fact that: little is said of the gift of faith in Scripture; the Church has largely ignored the gift of faith and its practice; and Christian writers have not researched the topic thoroughly.

Three Views

There seem to be three different approaches to understanding and interpreting the gift of faith, yet no one has classified these differences. First, some interpret the gift of faith as an instrument that can be used in Christian service, as one would use the Bible, prayer or preaching to accomplish the work of God. This is called the *instrumental* view, which appears to be the traditional or historical Christian view. It is listed first because of its historical priority.

Second, the gift of faith is interpreted as the ability to see or perceive what God desires to accomplish. The person with the gift of faith sees what God wants accomplished, then uses every resource available to accomplish his vision. This is called the *insight* or *vision* view, because the gift of faith is seeing what God can do in a situation. This seems to be the recent interpretation and is held by most evangelical Christians who are now writing on spiritual gifts.

Third, the gift of faith is the ability to move God to intervene divinely in a crisis that faces the work of God, or to intervene supernaturally in the work of God so that He accomplishes what the person with the gift believes will happen. This view is called the *interventional* interpretation. It is held mostly by Pentecostals, who believe that miracles are occurring in the work of God, and by some pastors identified with large churches (plus other leaders with dynamically growing churches) who may or may not believe the day of miracles has passed, but still believe they have experienced the intervention of God in their Christian service.

Describing this third view Horton says in *The Gifts of the Spirit:* ''The operation of miracles is more an act, as when the waters were opened by Moses and Elijah; while the operation of the gift of faith is more a process...Faith, the gift, is equally miraculous with all the other gifts, but we might say that its power or manifestation is of greater duration than those of the gifts of healing or miracles.''

Perhaps the three interpretations of the gift of faith are three progressive steps in expressing faith in God. The three views are different points on a continuum. Those who believe the first step, *instrumental faith,* have used faith as an instrument (Eph. 6:16), but they do not necessarily deny the work of God in the next two steps. They just have not grown or continued to a higher level of usefulness.

The same can be said of the second interpretation of the gift of faith, for its proponents have used faith as a vision to see what God can accomplish. The third position does not interpret the gift of faith differently, but includes the first two aspects in its definition, then adds the interventional factor.

The gift of faith goes beyond the normal use of faith that is available for Christian work in the present world. The gift of faith is involved in intercessory prayer, but is "abundantly more" than God answering prayer. Those who exercise the gift of faith pray; but the gift of faith is more than praying in faith (James 5:14), or "asking in faith" (James 1:6). God seems to give them unexpected results because they exercise faith whether or not they pray. Sometimes the gift of faith is exercised through prayer; at other times, the Christian will accomplish results by saying to a mountain, "Be thou removed" (Mark 11:23).

The gift of faith is more than living by faith (Hab. 2:4, Rom. 1:17, Gal. 3:11, 2 Cor. 5:7). When a Christian is living by faith, he is applying the principles of the Word of God to his life with the result that he lives a godly life that is pleasing to the Lord. Living by faith involves the personal life of the believer as he exercises trust in the Lord. But in contrast, the gift of faith involves Christian service where "mountains are moved" and problems are solved. The Christian exercises faith to change the circumstances (solve a problem, supply a need, stop a force, or provide protection) so that the work of God goes forward.

The gift of faith goes beyond the normal biblical methods and principles available to the Church. God has provided that certain principles should be followed in Christian work, such as evangelizing people (Mark 16:15), being a witness (Acts 1:8), gathering people together (Deut. 31:12), and praying for God's blessing on the work (Acts 4:31). These and other principles are available for Christian work, but there are times and circumstances when the work of God is halted.

Even when the normal principles of Christianity are applied, barriers (called mountains, Mark 11:23) continue to face the work of God. At this time, a person with the spiritual gift of faith can exercise it to remove the problem or to change circumstances.

At times, the gift of faith is exercised simultaneously with other ministries and the outside observer may mistakenly think something other than faith has solved the problem. As an illustration, a person may exercise faith to cause a church to grow. To do this, the person uses advertisements and displays powerful preaching to motivate people to invite their neighbors to attend church. The primary solution to church growth came through the exercise of faith, the secondary solution came through motivational preaching and proper use of advertising.

The gift of faith may be related to circumstances that lead to a solution of a problem or changing circumstances. A pastor may exercise faith to build a new auditorium, yet the congregation has no apparent finances available. God could give the church a large gift or someone could die and leave the church enough in the bequest for construction of new facilities. There are many illustrations whereby God used ordinary circumstances in response to the exercise of faith, so that unexpected timing or unexpected sources provided solutions to the problems in a church. As such, it was an unusual intervention by God, even though He used secondary sources.

The gift of faith may solve a problem or alter circumstances apart from the expected flow of circumstances. God may solve a church's problem through such an outstanding display of events that observers may interpret the solution to be supernatural or miraculous. However, the miraculous is only perceptual. This could be the outpouring of money from such a large number of people, including those not expected to give, that the supply is labeled "a divine supply."

The gift of faith goes beyond the normal tools that Christians use in Christian service. These tools, also called "means of grace" by sacramental churches, are the influence of the Bible, the Holy Spirit's work (convicting, illuminating, guiding, filling or empowering), the influence of a godly life, the ministry gifts (preaching, teaching, counseling, etc.), the use of the church office (pastor and deacons), the use of baptism and the Lord's Table, or involvement in the church by attendance, service and fellowship. When a person exercises the gift of faith, he does more than obey the Lord in employment of the above named "tools" or "means of grace."

The exercise of the gift of faith is an intentional effort on the part of the person who desires to change the circumstances of the work of God or solve a perplexing problem.

At times, the person may do two or more things at one time, such as motivate people to be baptized (preaching), yet his exercise of faith is the primary motivating cause that resulted in getting people scripturally baptized. Therefore, faith and preaching work together to bring revival to the church, or are evident when many people carry out the Great Commission in their neighborhood. To one it may be an evident display of faith, to the next it is the evidence of a person's gift of preaching or teaching (the observer may not be aware that the person is exercising the gift of faith).

The gift of faith is not always dependent upon exact doctrine or mature knowledge of doctrine. I have interviewed the pastors of the 10 largest churches in America, and the 10 largest in the world. I have reported conversations with Paul Yonggi Cho, pastor of the Yoido Full Gospel Church, Seoul, South Korea, and with Jack Hyles, pastor of First Baptist Church, Hammond, Indiana.

Cho told me the primary reason for the spectacular growth of his church is the baptism of the Holy Ghost, which results in an endowment of power, eradication of the old man and speaking in tongues. Jack Hyles denies the biblical interpretation of the Pentecostal experience and does not believe tongues are for this dispensation. Obviously, one or both men have painted the other (or themselves) into a theological corner.

I believe both Cho and Hyles are filled with the power of the Holy Spirit and that God is blessing both churches in spite of the fact they radically disagree in their approaches to the Holy Spirit. But both men believe in the fundamentals of Christianity. To justify the apparent conflict, use the term "blessability." God blesses those who place themselves in a positive position to His formula that brings success in church work. God does not punish His workers, nor annul their usefulness for wrong doctrine until their variance negates their positive influence.

Those who have the gift of faith transcend doctrinal boundaries. As a matter of fact, the basis of God's blessing is not based on being doctrinally literate, doctrinally correct, or doctrinally complete. The new babe in Christ can exercise faith and "move mountains." All he needs is "faith as a grain of mustard seed" (Matt. 17:20).

But on the other side of the issue, the greatest display of faith is evidenced by those who have grown in their exercise of faith, so that they are more mature in Christ. And, of course, maturity is dependent upon growth in doctrine and understanding.

Then, too, there probably is a limit to the tolerance by God of false doctrine. Perhaps God condescends to those who hold differing doctrines until a person accumulates too much doctrinal static or interference for him to be identified as a Bible Christian and hence, his doctrinal weakness limits his effectiveness for service. Probably, God has His "point of counterproductivity" so that when a person crosses an invisible point of no return, He no longer responds to the person's exercise of faith. Considered in God's denial of this person's faith is his yieldedness to truth, pursuit of truth and attitude to those of another doctrinal persuasion.

The gift of faith should not be confused with holiness of life, nor separation from sin. Those who feel the blessing of God is dependent upon the separation of the person from sin are perplexed when they hear that another person who gives confession to being a Christian is engaged in something they called sin.

Since the Christian life is a continuum, the question could be asked, "At what point in the continuum does the person become pure enough to exercise interventional faith?" Obviously, there is no point where the gift of faith begins its operation. When the person begins his ministry, faith may be exercised in a small capacity. A person may grow in the gift of faith as old habits and sins are pruned by the Holy Spirit. Even though the two actions are separate, they have a correlation through maturity and total experience.

God does not bless a person's ministry because of legalism, nor does a person have the gift of faith because of cleaning up his life. Some may claim that repentance of a particular sin is a criterion for God's interventional activity in their church work. They are wrong; it is faith that motivates God to intervene in the circumstances of a church.

However, some have repented of certain sins, hoping that by "cleaning up their life" God would intervene in their church work. Obviously, repentance can lead to greater faith, but repentance is not the thing that moves God to work in a church.

God is pleased by faith (sometimes expressed in repentance) and blesses the church because of faith. God has recognized the act of faith and solves the problems, so that the work of God goes forward. But their repentance was not the casual factor that brought about the result, the intervention of God. It was their faith.

Practical Applications

The gift of faith must now be analyzed for its practical implication, especially its influence on church growth. The following observations are made on the basis established previously that the gift of faith is ministry oriented, can grow in usefulness, and is exercised in relationship to human responsibility.

Announce a solution to problems facing the ministry. Jesus advised His disciples to "say unto this mountain, Be thou removed" (Mark 11:23). Since a mountain was a barrier or obstacle to the work of God, a first step in removing problems in the Lord's work is to announce what is desired.

Paul described this process, "And though I have all faith, so that I could move mountains" (1 Cor. 13:2). This seems to be an illustration that the early Church understood, that is, that they were to remove problems by a statement that reflected their faith that God would solve the problems.

Paul made statements that God would solve problems that faced him. Paul announced that the boat should not leave Crete: "Ye should have harkened unto me, and not have loosed from Crete" (Acts 27:21).

He further publicly announced the results he expected from God: "I exhort you to be of good cheer: for there shall be no loss of any man's life among you" (Acts 27:25). This illustration does not clearly identify the gift of faith, but it surely was an expression of faith.

Some might explain that Paul spoke in faith because the angel appeared to him the previous night (Acts 27:23). But the angel confirmed what Paul had previously communicated as a statement of faith in solution to the problem. Hence, the situation has all the characteristics of one who exercises faith to announce a solution to the problem.

Setting goals or announcing specific plans for the ministry. The gift of faith involves a continuum with three points. First, relying on the instruments of God to accomplish the ministry; second, having vision to see what God could accomplish; and third, to motivate God to intervene so the work will prosper. These three aspects are practically applied by setting goals for church growth or making specific plans that will prosper the ministry and produce growth.

Paul planned to visit the churches of Greece to receive an offering and take it to Jerusalem: "Now concerning the collection for the saints, as I have given order to the churches of Galatia, even so do ye" (1 Cor. 16:1). There was no qualification in the plan such as, "if you have the money," nor did Paul have a contingency plan, "if the money comes in." Paul makes a confident statement that the money would be received, and "then will I send to bring your liberality to Jerusalem" (1 Cor. 16:3).

The illustration of faith in Hebrews 11 reflects those who made plans and acted upon them. Noah built an ark (v. 7), Abraham went into an unknown country (v. 8), the parents of Moses preserved his life (v. 23), and Moses rejected Egypt to choose life with Israel (vs. 24-27).

Of course, the ministry has prospered where people did not set goals, nor did they make specific plans, nor did the people exercise faith. Such was the case when God delivered Peter from prison. Apparently, the people were not praying in faith because the church seemed surprised and even doubted Peter was released (Acts 12:15). In many such cases, God seems to work in spite of the lack of faith of Christians.

Also, Paul announced at least one goal that was not apparently accomplished: "Whensoever I take my journey into Spain" (Rom. 15:24). Some pastors have announced attendance goals that were not met. Therefore, a leader should be cautious when announcing goals or solutions to problems. Paul may have spoken in selfish desire, and some pastors set goals for church growth for human motives, not divine guidance. But on the other hand, perhaps the gift of faith works through the leader's desire concerning church growth goals. He is simply articulating what God desires to accomplish. Perhaps he announces the goal but God uses someone else to accomplish the project, or the goal is accomplished later in life, or after the leader dies. As an illustration, Paul apparently did not go to Spain, but the gospel was carried there by others.

In any case, the leader must never assume omniscience. Everything he says may not be said by faith, and what he says may not be the will of God. James warns the Christian, "Go to now, ye that say, To-day or tomorrow we will go into such a city, and continue there a year and buy and sell and get gain" (James 4:13). James cautions, "Ye ought to say, If the Lord will, we shall live, and do this, or that" (James 4:15).

Whenever a leader exercises the gift of faith and states a goal or announces specific plans, he ought to do so with the attitude that everything is qualified by the will of God. Since the will of God is reflected in the Word of God, the goals and plans that are closest to Scripture are closest to the will of God.

A positive attitude in the ministry. If the leader exercises faith in the proper way, then he will have confidence in God. The writer of Hebrews observed, "Now faith is being sure of what we hope for and certain of what we do not see" (Heb. 11:1, NIV). When this attitude is carried into Christian service, the leader will minister with confidence. Paul announced, "I can do all things through Christ who strengtheneth me" (Phil. 4:13). This confidence was based on the power of Christ, and is not explicitly related to the gift of faith.

At another place, he confidently notes, "Thanks be unto God, which always causeth us to triumph in Christ" (2 Cor. 2:14). In both of the above references, there is not a direct, traceable cause and effect relationship between the gift of faith and confidence. But, when one exercises the gift of faith by stating a goal or solution, he cannot doubt. Jesus tied faith and confidence together: "shall not doubt in his heart, but shall believe those things which he saith shall come to pass; he shall have whatsoever he saith" (Mark 11:23).

Recognize the human factor in exercising the gift of faith. The gift of faith is not the same as the gift of miracles. In an evident miracle, God is the source and channel that produces a supernatural intervention or transcending of the natural laws of the universe. In the gift of faith, God works through the human instrument and He limits Himself to the human expression of faith. Whereas God is the source of the Christian work, the human is the channel through which He works.

Earlier, the illustration of Paul's statement in relationship to the shipwreck was noted as a possible exercise of the gift of faith. Paul said what should be done (remain in Crete, v. 21). Then Paul made a statement to remain with the ship (v. 31), and eat (v. 33). With the statement of faith and God's providential care, the people were responsible for certain duties. They ate, rowed, swam and were generally responsible to carry out the deliverance that was provided by God.

In the area of church growth, the pastor may set attendance goals or make a statement of faith that he will establish a church. But then accomplishment of the results is also the responsibility of the leader. He must follow proven principles to accomplish his goal.

Only Faith Moves God

The gift of faith is a special ability to see what God can do in a certain project, to trust God to bless the work so that a project is accomplished and on some occasions, to move God to intervene in the natural flow of circumstances so that problems are solved, goals are reached and protection is given to those needing it.

The gift of faith is more than living by faith and is not the fruit of the Spirit called faith ("faithfulness," NIV). Whereas the fruit of the Spirit involves Christian character, the gift of faith involves ministry such as preaching, teaching or evangelism. The gift of faith is an ability that is available to those in ministry. Finally, the gift of faith does not seem to be a prominent ability so that a person has the title *faith,* as in *pastor* or *evangelist.* The gift of faith is not merely foundational to all Christian service, because certain individuals have the ability to use faith in their ministry in an unusual and unique way.

Most of the qualities possessed by men relate to themselves or their relationship to others, such as love, joy, peace or patience. But of all the qualities available to men, faith is that one asset that pleases God and moves God to intervene in the affairs of men in an unusual or unexpected way. And those who have the gift of faith seem to personify that ability to the greatest degree. "If ye have faith as a grain of mustard seed, ye shall say unto this mountain, Remove hence to yonder place; and it shall remove; and nothing shall be impossible to you" (Matt. 17:20).

6

How Does a Denominational Minister Pastor a Mixed Flock?

By Clarence Yates

Clarence Yates, before retiring in 1985 from active ministry, had served in pastoral positions in the United Methodist Church for 43 years. During the last 11 years of his pastorship he ministered to a church that included both Charismatic and non-Charismatic members in its congregation. Yates saw this congregation grow and prosper through his obedience to the Holy Spirit.

When I came as pastor of this church 10 years ago, I found a small, but articulate and active group of Charismatics who were struggling to find their identity within the structure of United Methodism. The church had more than 50 years of tradition within the structure of our denomination. While it was fairly conservative in its theology, it was not particularly evangelical.

I brought to the church a strong evangelical emphasis and an openness to the Charismatic influence. I was helped in my approach by the writing of Robert Tuttle who emphasized that we must be Charismatics not in the classical Pentecostal sense, but within the parameters of Methodist theology.

One of my main struggles at the beginning of my pastorate was to keep my flock from moving into the classical Pentecostal camp. While we have succeeded in accomplishing this goal, nevertheless, I am constantly being pressured by new Charismatics to move toward the more classical position.

My purpose has been to create a balance between the Charismatics and non-Charismatics, thus producing a New Testament church in the 20th century. One of my problems has been criticism, both overt and covert, from my peers and ecclesiastical leaders who don't fully understand or appreciate the Charismatic position in United Methodism. Thus, while only a small percentage of my church would be called "Charismatic" in the true sense of the word, yet our church is labeled "Charismatic" throughout my conference.

I have members who would be delighted to see our Sunday morning worship service be Pentecostal in nature. My purpose is to help create an atmosphere of worship that is open and responsive to the Holy Spirit, yet maintaining the traditional worship structure of United Methodism.

One way we have succeeded in satisfying the varying desires of traditional Charismatics and those who are non-Charismatic is in offering small group ministries where the people are free to express their classical Pentecostal desires, or to be traditional and conventional evangelical United Methodists. Thus, we attract to our church both those who are looking for Charismatic emphasis and those who desire to have a warm-hearted evangelical approach.

That we have succeeded at least to some degree in this goal is indicated by the fact that in the last 10 years our membership has doubled from 1,400 to 2,800 and our average Sunday morning attendance has increased from 400 to nearly 1,400.

We endeavor to accomplish our goal of ministering to these diversities by three emphases:

● We emphasize the Giver rather than the gifts, while accepting the validity of all the gifts of the Holy Spirit as listed in the New Testament. Our emphasis is on the Person and work of the Holy Spirit.

● We emphasize the need to be a people of prayer. The entire thrust of our ministry and of all our decisions as a church is based upon prayer. Over a year ago we initiated a weekly 24-hour prayer vigil from 7 a.m. Friday to 7 a.m. Saturday. We also encourage those who will to make this a day of fasting as well as prayer. Our goal is to make Thursday also a day of 24-hour prayer vigil, and ultimately to have someone praying in our chapel every hour of every day of the week.

● We emphasize not only the gifts of the Spirit but also the fruit of the Spirit as listed in Galatians 5:22, 23.

Being pastor of a mixed flock is perhaps more difficult than being pastor of a traditional denominational church, but it is infinitely more rewarding.

7

How Does an Independent Minister Pastor a Mixed Flock?

By Jerry Mason

After pastoring Hunter Memorial Community Church, east of San Diego, California, from 1982 to 1984, Jerry Mason moved to Prescott, Arizona, with his wife and son where he is devoting his time to freelance Christian writing. He has a B.A. degree from San Diego State University and an M.A. degree from the University of California, Davis.

Jesus taught and pastored 12 disciples who were very diverse in their backgrounds. Peter and Andrew were businessmen from Capernaum. Matthew was a tax collector in the same city. It's a safe bet that the three had confronted each other in less than favorable circumstances before they met Jesus. But Jesus called them to walk together.

James and John, along with their mother, caused no small stir in their desire for prominence. Jealousy among the disciples was easily inflamed.

Simon the zealot had an obvious bias about the need for Israel to throw off the yoke of Rome. It is logical to imagine he did his best to convince Pastor Jesus about his bias.

Yet the Lord held His diverse company together.

How frustrating it must have been, however, to teach clearly and repeatedly to a group who couldn't understand, as Philip confessed; or who, like Thomas, wouldn't believe without additional proof.

The responsibility of a pastor, or shepherd, includes keeping the flock together. Jesus' responsibility was none too easy then, and it is none too easy today as He leads His church, using as sheepdogs men called pastors. I believe that we sheepdogs can create as much frustration for the Shepherd as the sheep do for us. Yet the job of bringing Jesus' flock together can be done.

Jesus shepherded a mixed flock—with divergent aspirations and abilities.

The American system of Christianity has attempted to bypass the problems of blending flocks through denominational choices. Here people can choose the church system which best suits their personalities and inclinations. But denominations cannot be instituted everywhere. In many rural areas there are too few people to attempt such divisions.

Thus the Lord led me, from a background of Lutheran, Independent Fundamental Churches of America, Wesleyan, Baptist, Christian and Missionary Alliance and Assemblies of God identifications, to pastor a flock in the dry mountains east of San Diego, California. It was a community church which had no denominational affiliation in its 26-year history. Those who were in the church when I came leaned toward the fundamentalist and non-Charismatic persuasion. But the Lord led me to welcome and encourage those of Charismatic and Pentecostal backgrounds into this flock.

And it has been a carnival ride. God has spoken with the word of knowledge and the word of wisdom as those who feel uncertain of such things have listened. They have seen the Lord heal sickness on many occasions, even though some questioned aloud whether gifts of healing are operative today. I tried to listen to the Lord through apprentice prophets while soothing their fears that gifts of the Spirit might never flow freely in our mixed flock.

For a time Satan gained a foothold of divisiveness and caused the uncertainty of some to deepen.

Through it all, I learned to respect the stance of the fundamental Christians. I saw God use their conservatism to protect the flock from wolves and to discern the best routes through trials. Simultaneously I learned much about the gifts of the Spirit as the Lord led me.

My task in great measure was to listen carefully on two fronts. Yet the Lord never led me to take sides.

Rumors and "confidential" gossip pulled at every loose thread of our seams. The factious conduct of one man led to his expulsion from our assembly. This drew many of us together and caused a few to leave in anger. But the expulsion was agreed to by church workers on both sides of the gifts-of-the-Spirit dividing line.

The church board and I decided to disfellowship a man because of wife and child abuse, alcoholism and cultic leanings. He had also scorned both counsel and warnings. I took a Sunday morning service, at the board's recommendation, to explain the action to the congregation. Because the man was highly factious, the board chose to put him out without opportunity for public rebuttal.

Jim and Sheila (not their real names) were friends of the man. During the presentation of the church's actions, they protested. Jim stood up and, interrupting me, heatedly said that I was wrong about the man and unbiblical for preventing him from sharing his side. He then walked out. Sheila stood at that time and began flailing her arms in the air and shouting accusations at me. She whirled completely around in the sanctuary aisle and dramatically promised to "take my fasting and prayer elsewhere."

It was a painful and embarrassing experience. My job of remaining calm and continuing the service was a challenge. But the Lord came to my rescue. He had led a previous pastor of the congregation (from many years earlier) to visit on that Sunday morning. His gentle and wise words revealed that the purpose of the Lord through such upsetting events was for our growth.

Several months later Sheila sought my counsel. Her marriage was in trouble and her physical health was very poor (among other weaknesses she suffered from anorexia). She confessed eyewitness knowledge of wife abuse by the disfellowshipped man (I'd had other such witnesses). She also expressed her desire to return to our fellowship. And she began attending services.

I sought out the church board and friends of Jim and Sheila, and prayed about the matter. I was led to encourage Jim and Sheila to make a public statement of their changed thinking and to submit to church leadership. This they did not do. Sheila said she would publicly apologize, but she felt that she could not submit herself to the church. Jim never agreed to any of it. Sheila quit attending our services.

Today I can see that our board dealt in wisdom and love with issues of importance. I received correction from them on occasion, and I believe that it was appropriate and led by the Holy Spirit. And they listened faithfully to the teaching and preaching in which the Spirit led me.

The board saw the needs of the congregation differently, at times, than I did. And individual members, with all their varied perspectives, also saw things differently than I.

Denominational backgrounds and loyalties were numerous. Methodist, Baptist, Pentecostal, Assemblies of God, Church of Christ, Catholic and Lutheran influences are each found in two or more families within our gatherings. More than once I have been told in private, "It's not your fault, but I just won't be joining you in church in the future." Yet most people did join in.

Because the church leadership had no outside denominational authority to turn to, we reached within our melting pot for counsel. Together we prayed to the head of the church. Jesus was faithful.

The church was created to be a blend, yet some ingredients insist on maintaining their original character. Thus, Jesus has occasionally increased the heat under the pot.

Our gatherings included those who desired to see people "dancing" and being "slain in the Spirit" sitting next to others who seemed troubled when we sang from any book other than the traditional hymnal. I was regularly being encouraged to see one viewpoint or another or hearing rumors that someone was leaving because I didn't see his viewpoint. Ironically, I could see and respect all their viewpoints.

How can a pastor effectively lead Christ's diverse people and maintain harmony among fellow church leaders? How can a pastor cope with a congregation which doesn't really seem to want to unite, but seems to prefer their own ways of religion? Frankly, I believe that such questions have a way of misdirecting our thinking. Regardless of our divisions, "Christ himself is our way of peace" (Eph. 2:14, LB). We are to focus our attention on Jesus, who loves them, covers them, forgives them and protects them.

Jesus said that His flock would be diverse. And He prophesied that they would hear His voice and that "there will be one flock with one Shepherd" (John 10:16, LB). Regardless of our cajoling or commanding, this coming together of the diverse people of the church cannot happen unless Jesus speaks. He said, "My sheep hear my voice, and I know them, and they follow me" (John 10:27).

The eyes of every pastor can be turned to the one Shepherd of the entire flock. Then we can do the things we see Him doing. Our job is frightening when we are looking at wolves. It is frustrating when we're looking at sheep. It is confusing when we're looking at other sheep dogs. But it is so very glorious when we are looking to the Shepherd.

Church leaders try so confidently and weakly, so blusteringly and reservedly to hold believers together in a day of divisions. Within today's Christianity there are limitless Pauls, Apolloses and Peters to follow in preference to a united body of Christ. So how can we cope with such forces of dissension within our assemblies? I have five specific observations.

First, denominational divisions are no stronger than any other divisions between brethren. The previous pastor in my church had more trouble holding control than I did, although there was no theological separation within the flock at that time.

If our purpose is to control, then we are dictators rather than pastors. Our purpose is to help direct sheep under the guidance of our Shepherd. Therefore, all separations between brethren, whether political, financial or denominational, are alike and each is potentially harmful. We must, by the power of Jesus, the head of the church, pull down strongholds that separate brethren.

Second, Christian leaders are usually trained into denominational preferences. When we teach parishioners who think differently from us, there is something in our consciences that demands a no-compromise stance. And there is something in their consciences which calls for no-compromise when they listen. This can create great tension among brethren.

This problem of a non-compromising heart sometimes results from pride rather than clear biblical mandates. It is important to determine things which genuinely cannot be compromised. And it is equally important to learn when to speak out and when to remain silent on such things. There were many truths which Jesus kept to Himself for three years because, He said, "You cannot bear them now" (John 16:12, RSV).

Men may have a difficult time working together across denominational lines. But God has no problem crossing such barriers. Jesus in

His flesh breaks down walls of division. God adheres to His righteousness, yet He reaches down to sinners, not through compromise but through grace. Therefore, "let your speech always be with grace, seasoned with salt, that ye may know how you ought to answer every man" (Col. 4:6).

Third, "love covers a multitude of sins" (1 Pet. 4:8). If love can cover sin, no doubt it can cover denominational differences. Our responsibility is always to love our sheep.

Fourth, the true Shepherd, Jesus, is the only One who can effectively call His sheep. So many voices are calling out today that there is much confusion among the flocks. But when Jesus calls, they will hear His voice because He knows His sheep, and they will follow Him. If we receive guidance from Jesus, the sheep will follow that guidance; they do listen to Him.

As the sheep follow their Shepherd, the sheep dog can run about keeping things in order at the Shepherd's direction. If we wait on Jesus to call His sheep, most of them will move, with little anxiety required of us.

Fifth, God does not normally bypass the authority structures to which churches have bound themselves. Therefore, we can rest in the authority structure to which we have been called. Church boards will be used by God if we will submit ourselves quietly to God in their presence. If we do not restfully trust God to work through His church, we are likely to be in defiance of God's accepted program.

The product of two years of ministry to a mixed flock has been a growing together of each "side." Each has been given freedom to respond to God rather than to the dictates of a theology. There has been a greater desire to study the Scriptures by the body as a whole. And gradually there has developed a deepening spirit of community prayer.

8

How Do You Handle the Question of Re-Baptism?

By Francis MacNutt

Director of Christian Healing Ministries in Clearwater, Florida, Francis MacNutt was one of the first Catholics to become involved in the Charismatic renewal. The former priest and his wife, Judith, have two children. He is the author of three best-selling books, *Healing, The Power to Heal* and *The Power That Heals*. An honors graduate of Harvard University, MacNutt earned a Ph.D. in theology from Aquinas Institute of Theology.

F or many years, as a Roman Catholic priest, ministering mostly to Catholics in their own setting, the question of believer's (adult) baptism by immersion was a purely theoretical one. None of the parents who brought their babies to me for baptism at the age of six weeks, or thereabouts, experienced any uncertainty about their actions. It was only later, as Catholics began to mingle more freely with Protestants, and when many Catholics experienced the baptism of the Spirit and began to attend meetings of groups like the Full Gospel Businessmen's Fellowship, that they were faced with questions they found difficult to answer.

Increasingly I found that many Catholics were being "rebaptized"— often during a trip to the Holy Land under the leadership of an evangelical leader. When they stopped at the Jordan, they would join the rest of the group and step into the river to be baptized by the leader.

In 1969 one Catholic priest in New York State went so far as to be baptized by an Assemblies of God pastor in the Niagara River, much to the consternation of his bishop and the Catholic people who heard about it.

As I see the situation, most priests and ministers from denominations that believe in infant baptism do not realize how serious the pastoral problem is, unless they work actively outside their own Christian fellowship. In the United States, at least, many members of mainline Christian denominations have left their churches and joined evangelical groups that hold to the necessity of their being baptized as adults by immersion. Countless others have remained within their religious churches, but have been "rebaptized," leaving them disturbed and confused in their identity.

Often people have come to me at conferences and proclaimed: "Praise God! I used to be a Catholic (or an Anglican, or a Presbyterian), but now I'm a Christian!" Among other things, this usually means they have repudiated their infant baptism and been rebaptized.

I don't think the leaders of the mainline churches have any idea of what a real problem this is, since their members usually get "rebaptized" quietly (they certainly wouldn't talk to their pastors about their plans and slip away to join another church with no formal notice.

I remember one large Lutheran Charismatic conference in Minneapolis where I was invited to speak. There were about 8,000 people in attendance—about half of them Lutheran and half of them Roman Catholic. I wanted to point out to the Lutheran pastors on the platform that there was a problem about ''re-baptism'' that they needed to confront, so I asked the people to raise their hands if they had ever seriously thought about seeking re-baptism. I thought that perhaps a thousand would raise their hands but, to our amazement, half the crowd raised their hands. Then I went one step further and asked how many had actually gone ahead and been rebaptized. About 2,000 people then raised their hands! The pastoral problem was far greater than any of us had imagined.

Early in the Catholic Charismatic renewal, the desire of many Charismatics to be rebaptized was recognized and leaders sought to discourage their people from listening to those Protestant Charismatics who told them that their infant baptism was unscriptural and didn't count. Kevin Ranaghan, for instance, wrote an article in *New Covenant* magazine giving reasons why Catholics should not be disobedient and seek re-baptism. But still, as my informal poll in Minneapolis indicated, many accepted an invitation to step into the waters of immersion and great confusion of identity resulted.

Many Full Gospel meetings in hotels ended up in the swimming pool with 60 or so Christians from mainline churches descending into the water to be baptized by the Pentecostal speaker who had just told them they had never really been baptized.

A Solution

Not only did I hear about these problems at a distance, but I was sometimes in a situation where I had to make a decision on how to help confused Christians. As a result I believe that there is a pastoral solution to the apparent irreconcilable differences between the proponents of infant baptism and the proponents of adult baptism by immersion.

This solution came to me about 10 years ago when I was a speaker at a five-day ecumenical retreat called a Camp Farthest Out, held in the state of Iowa. About 300 people attended and, of these, about 100 were Catholics drawn to an unfamiliar setting because I was one of the speakers.

As is usual in such camps, there were special meetings for the youth. These meeting were led by a dynamic Baptist couple, enthusiastically determined to get the youth to make decisions for Christ and to be saved. Then they planned, on the fourth evening, to lead those who had made their adult commitments to a nearby river to be baptized. Since these youth leaders had had little contact with Catholics or other mainline Protestant churches, they saw it as completely normal to baptize the young people, whether or not they had been baptized as infants.

Some of the Catholic young people were so innocent of the theological problems involved that they came to me in great excitement and asked if I would come with them and baptize them since I was the Catholic priest. I started to argue with them and tell them that they were already baptized, but I had a sense that, if I didn't join them, they would probably go to the river with the other young people anyway. So I told them that I would pray about it and let them know what we could do.

In prayer I realized that there were several very real positive values in "believer's baptism" and that, as a church, we needed to do something positive about the situation rather than merely forbid rebaptism.

In the first place, many church-going Christians need to make an adult commitment to the Lord; they need to have a conversion experience. In churches that believe in infant baptism the ideal is that their members will know the Lord to their fullest capacity at every stage of the way—that the nurture of a loving family will help the child know the Lord throughout his life.

But while many Christians will say that they have known the Lord as far back as they can remember, others have told me that, although they went to church all their lives and attended Catholic high schools and colleges, they never really knew the Lord. They say they were spiritually dead until they accepted an altar call given by a Protestant preacher, say, at the age of 40. Then they knew Jesus for the first time and experienced an insatiable desire to learn more about Him by reading the Bible.

When this rebirth happens they almost always desire to symbolize that experience by being baptized. They want to die with Christ and rise with Him again in baptism. Let the theologians explain it as they will, but this coming to life in Christ is not simply repentance or conversion from sin. It seems to be a real new birth—a coming to know Jesus for the first time as well as a committing of one's life to Jesus for the first time. (For Catholics this needs to be sacramentalized in a way other than the sacrament of penance. The appropriate symbolism is some form of baptism.)

Furthermore, I find that even those who have lived a fully Christian life from childhood frequently desire to reenact their baptism, since, as babies, they were not aware of what was going on. They want to experience that initial sacrament—baptism—and they want to experience the initial reception of the life of God within them and the washing clean of sin. This means, too, that they want to be immersed in water to experience the fullest symbolism of going under the water to die with Christ and then to rise up again as a new creation (2 Cor. 5).

Thinking and praying about this I realized that all these desires were praiseworthy, for something was missing in infant baptism. Certainly the person's conscious decision was missing, as was the experience of being washed clean of sin and receiving new life. The desire to receive all this was very good!

But to believe this, is it necessary to condemn infant baptism? Rather, should there not be a way to preserve the values of infant baptism along with the values of adult baptism by immersion without condemning either one of them?

Those churches that condemn "re-baptism" do so because it calls into doubt the reality of infant baptism and its values. Those Christians who ordinarily "re-baptize" aggravate the situation because they doubt the reality of infant baptism. That is precisely why they "re-baptize." Historically, both groups have had to attack the other, to defend the values they held dear in baptism.

Infant Baptism Values

The values of infant baptism are also very true and real. In the first place, it can be pointed out that infant baptism was never attacked in the early church when any practice at variance with apostolic tradition would certainly have been attacked. The Christian tradition for infant baptism seems very strong. In ages when most children did not live long enough to make an adult Christian commitment and receive baptism as adults, parents would necessarily be concerned about Jesus' words about the necessity of being baptized to receive eternal life.

The Charismatic renewal has helped me understand even more fully the value of infant baptism (which I never doubted), for what I see more and more is that the action of God's grace is the most important element in our lives—far more important than anything we ourselves can do. In the healing ministry, in which I am involved, I can spend hours praying with someone, but, obviously, unless God is working, the person will not be healed. Usually, I need to do something—that is, to ask God to do something—to heal the person. But "it is all God's work" (2 Cor. 5:18, Jerusalem Bible).

I think those who deny the value of infant baptism fail to see that the key element in baptism is not in the human decision, but in what God will do for and in this little infant even before the child is able to will or to understand. John the Baptist leapt in his mother's womb when Jesus, within Mary, came into his presence. Various prophets, like Jeremiah, were called from their mother's womb: "Before I formed you in the womb I knew you: before you came to birth I consecrated you; I have appointed you as a prophet to the nations" (Jer. 1:5).

We know that God can touch people without merit or action on their part. My own experience in praying with people for the inner healing of their past has shown me, in ways more dramatic than I ever would

71

have believed as a young priest, that people are affected very early in their lives by forces for good or evil. At least four times I have been praying for individuals to be healed of harmful emotional experiences in their past, only to have them—without any suggestion on my part—suddenly start to relive their time before birth. They would assume the curved-in fetal position and start shouting something such as "I'm not going to come out! I'm not going to be born!" and I would have to then ask Jesus to free this person from what had happened even before birth. I have realized that a child, even before it is born, knows whether it is loved or rejected. A fascinating book by psychiatrist Dr. James Verny, *The Secret Life of the Unborn Child* (Summit Books, New York), offers strong evidence that the unborn child is already responding to the communication of love, especially from the mother:

"After following two thousand women through pregnancy and birth, Dr. Monika Lukesch, a psychologist at Constantine University in Frankfurt, West Germany, concluded in her study that the mother's attitude had the single greatest effect on how an infant turned out. All her subjects were from the same economic background, all were equally intelligent, and all had the same degree and quality of prenatal care. The only major distinguishing factor was their attitudes toward their unborn children, and that turned out to have a critical effect on their infants. The children of accepting mothers, who looked forward to having a family, were much healthier, emotionally and physically, at birth and afterward, than the offspring of rejecting mothers" (pp. 47-48).

The above question is typical of the evidence Dr. Verny offers throughout his fascinating book to the effect that even unborn infants are responding in some mysterious way to the communication of love—or its lack. This evidence from the medical world simply reinforces my own experience in praying for the inner child in an adult to be healed; occasionally, in deliverance prayer, when I have prayed that a person be freed of demonic influence, I have found that this evil influence became attached to the child even before birth (e.g., when the child's mother was involved in witchcraft).

At one point, I questioned the wisdom of the prayers for exorcism in the Roman Catholic baptismal rite for infants, but I now see the wisdom of asking God to free an infant from all harmful or demonic influences, as well as to pour His own life into the child. As I would understand it now, the sooner the life of God can be infused into a child and the child be healed of harmful influences, the better. The healing that takes place is not just poetic or symbolic; it is very real.

A sign of this would be the amount of physical healing that takes place in baptism. Michael Scanlan, president of Steubenville University, tells me that he sees more physical healing take place during baptisms than at any other time. Agnes Sanford also wrote about her husband, an Anglican minister:

"My own husband has often been called to baptize a 'dying' baby. Not one of them has ever died. So he is now sure that the interposition of the sacrament of baptism, together with his own person between God and the baby, is sufficient to recharge any child with life" (*The Healing Light*, p. 93, Macalester Park Publishing Co., St. Paul, Minnesota, 1947).

I myself have often prayed for babies before they were born and I have encouraged pregnant mothers and their husbands to pray for their unborn babies, and our experience indicates that this prayer makes a big difference. We pray that God pour His life and His love into the child to the full extent of its capacity—to fill the baby with a desire to be born and a great love of life— to keep the baby free from all sickness and accidents and harmful influences.

The common experience of those parents who pray, with the father laying his hands on the mother's stomach, is that these children, when born, are considerably happier, more peaceful and more healthy than their own children who were born before they learned to pray in such a way.

In short, it is very important to pray for a child that God make it His special child and fill it with His presence long before the child is able to make any kind of adult commitment.

To prove scientifically that these advantages of prayer are real is difficult, but my faith, reinforced by my experience and that of countless other parents, convinces me that the child, before reaching the age of an adult faith commitment, is far more subject to God's grace than even the proponents of infant baptism have ever dreamed or imagined.

No Compromise

Thus, there are strong practical reasons for infant baptism, as well as for adult baptism. These strong reasons have led their proponents into confrontation and even into the setting up of new divisions in Christendom. But can't there be a way of reconciling these two positions, so that the spiritual advantages of both types of baptism can be preserved—without theological compromise?

Getting back to my practical dilemma with the young people at the Camp Farthest Out: I had to act. If I refused to baptize them in the river at the same time the Baptist youth minister was baptizing the Protestants, but had simply laid down the law and told them they were already baptized and that they should go back to their rooms and stay, most of them would have listened politely and then gone on and joined the group at the river that afternoon. Their parents were coming to me, deeply concerned because the children were for the first time in a predominantly Baptist environment and were being convinced that they had not really been baptized. "Do something," they were saying, "to convince our children to be loyal to the Catholic Church. We brought them here trusting that they would be safe, because you were one of two main speakers." (The other speaker at this camp was Ruth Carter Stapleton, Jimmy Carter's sister.)

Moral dilemmas such as this make you sympathetic to the desire of churches to remain apart, to protect their flocks from doctrinal confusion by contamination. Such separation and the forming of protected enclaves is the simplest solution, but I believe that ordinarily it prevents us from discovering the synthesis of Christian truth that we need to draw us togehter. Where I used to believe that I didn't need other Christian churches, I now find that they often have seen some areas of Christian truth more clearly than I, and that I need these other groups, precisely in their otherness.

Proponents of adult baptism are not wrong; we need to see that. Nor are proponents of infant baptism wrong; others need to see that. We do not want a watering down of truth to bring us together at the lowest common denominator. We need to come a level higher, whcre both truths can be joined without compromise to either position.

At any rate, at that camp in Iowa I felt trapped. If I said, "No, I won't go to the river and baptize you," I would lose most of the young people. Even if I sat down with them and explained the reasons for infant baptism, the pressure of their peers— coupled with the arguments of the Baptist youth minister and the excitement of a trip to the river— would have drawn most of them.

But I couldn't say "yes" without confusing them in their Catholic identity and leading them to believe that I agree with the youth minister that they needed to be re-baptized.

So I prayed and asked the Lord to show me a way out that would help the young people and be faithful to the truth as I saw it.

And the answer came. So simple, as answers from the Spirit of God usually are. It was this: I would tell the young people that I believed that they had truly been baptized when they were little, but that I also understood that they wanted to enact the conversion that many of them had truly experienced in this camp and to experience what they had missed in their infant baptism. So, what I proposed was that we all go to the swimming pool at 10 o'clock that night, when all the activities of the camp had ended. I told them to bring their parents and there, in the pool, I would immerse each of them three times and proclaim, "Joseph Newell," (or whatever the young person's name was) "I renew your baptism, in the name of the Father, and of the Son, and of the Holy Spirit."

Without any difficulty they understood what I proposed and they all wanted it this way. I asked them not to tell anyone outside their family and closest friends what we were doing, because I feared that someone would garble the report of what we had done and it would be publicized afterwards: "Did you hear that Father MacNutt re-baptized 20 people out in Iowa?"

But, as human nature goes, the secret was too good to be kept and at 10 o'clock nearly 200 people showed up around the darkened swimming pool. I descended into the middle of the swimming pool and preached for about 10 minutes on the meaning of baptism and on dying and rising with Jesus. After telling the crowd that I was not re-baptizing this group, but was renewing their baptism, a group of adults asked to join the young people, and by the end of the evening nearly 50 people had gone under the water and renewed their baptisms.

What I discovered was that this practical solution was needed, not only that day in 1972, but on a much larger scale. Those mainline churches that believe in infant baptism need some such solution. Certainly in the United States it is a critical problem (even though most church leaders don't seem to recognize how many of their members they are losing because of it). They need such a solution not just because they might lose members if they don't take some action more positive than just forbidding it, but because adult Christians need some way of experiencing their baptism, much stronger than simply repeating the baptismal promises on the eve of Easter. They need to experience what they missed in their baptism as babies.

Too many Catholics have told me that they have been deeply disappointed in their church that never led them to know Jesus in a personal way—that they only came to know Jesus through the preaching of evangelicals such as Billy Graham, and through an altar call in a Protestant church. I can certainly understand their criticism. And, too often, I hear evangelical criticism of Catholics: "But they don't know Jesus as their personal Savior." That criticism is too often true.

The pastoral solution is, I believe, simple. In the churches that practice infant baptism we need preaching that will call the people to conversion and to an adult commitment to Jesus Christ as Lord and Savior. We can no longer presume that all our people have made such a commitment just because they were baptized, and that all they need to do is to repent, confess their sins and come back to the church. For some that is true, but others need to come to know the Lord as adults—as for the first time.

Following such evangelical preaching we need some ceremony, some chance, for people to commit their lives to Jesus—the action of the human person acting with God's grace. Then we need something to symbolize the action of God in washing them clean, making them new creatures, causing the old self to die and the new self to rise with Jesus. Why not have a ceremony, as a liturgy, where adults who have made a full commitment can come to the waters and be immersed as a renewal of their baptism? What more powerful celebration of Easter than to have, say, those people in a church who believe they are ready, commit their lives to Jesus, make a public declaration before the congregation and then be immersed as a renewal of their baptism and as a sign of what God is doing by way of giving them a new life?

So far as I know, there is no real theological problem with this solution, and it combines a belief in the validity of infant baptism with a recognition of the values proposed by adherents of believer's baptism.

This solution was forged by my own Charismatic experience in an apparently impossible moral dilemma. Every time I have been called upon to act in this way—renewing people's baptism through immersion—they have been immensely grateful and happy.

9

Which Commentaries
Should You Buy?

By Larry Hart

Larry Hart is associate professor of theology at the School of
Theology, Oral Roberts University, Tulsa, Oklahoma. He earned
degrees from Oral Roberts University and Southern Baptist Theological
Seminary. He served in the pastoral ministry for nine years in Ken-
tucky and Indiana and was chaplain at ORU.

Most pastors worth their salt are eager to obtain the best practical resources to help them carry out their myriad tasks as shepherds in God's flock. I can remember pumping the seminary professor I most respected and trusted for suggestions on the best Bible commentaries, and my own students do the same with me from time to time.

If ever there was a time when the body of Christ needed pastor-teachers who are serious students of Scripture, it is now! The present renewal needs leaders who have mastered sound principles of biblical interpretation, with skills in biblical Hebrew and Greek. Such leaders can enable and help the people they serve to read the Bible with understanding.

In Charismatic circles it is too often the case that scriptural texts are twisted and tortured in the name of "spiritual revelation." Believers too often simply accept mindlessly and passively the pronouncements of their teachers and pastors, while those very teachers and pastors have spent very little time in substantive study of Scripture. How often has a preacher claimed for a passage a supposedly Holy Spirit-revealed meaning which clearly violates all the principles of sound biblical interpretation? How many times do people approach the Bible as if it were a Rorschach (ink blot) test and project whatever meaning that fits their fancy onto the text?

Perhaps one of the reasons it is so urgent that Charismatics cooperate with the Lord as He merges them with the evangelicals is this very problem of "playing fast and loose" with the Bible. Evangelicals care passionately about "rightly dividing the Word." (Recently the International Council on Biblical Inerrancy (ICBI) published a masterful treatment of the subject of more than 900 pages: *Hermeneutics, Inerrancy, and the Bible*. They are also the theological watchdogs for historic orthodoxy. And, in my opinion, they have generally written the best commentaries.

Gordon Fee and Douglas Stuart of Gordon-Conwell Theological Seminary have provided a very helpful resource in this area, a volume entitled *How to Read the Bible for All It's Worth* (Zondervan, 1981). It is the kind of book a Christian leader with the responsibility of teaching and preaching the Bible can use with great profit as well as pass on to those he or she serves. The book contains a very helpful survey of the best Bible commentaries.

A similar service is rendered by Mark Lau Branson in his *Reader's Guide to the Best Evangelical Books* (Harper & Row, 1982). Actually, not all the books surveyed could be classified as "evangelical" or "conservative," but Branson's overview of the best in Christian books is nevertheless informative and downright fun! Have you ever wondered what books are Jack Hayford's favorites—both personally and professionally? How about those of Pat Robertson, Lloyd Ogilvie, Jerry Falwell, James Dobson, Peter Wagner, Pat Boone, Richard Foster, John MacArthur, Carl F. H. Henry or Philip Yancey? They are all listed in this volume along with those of a number of other Christian leaders.

Branson also refers the reader to two comprehensive surveys of the best Bible commentaries which I would also recommend: John Goldingay and Robert Hubbard's *Old Testament Commentary Survey* (Revised Theological Students Fellowship/InterVarsity Press, 1981) and Anthony Thistelton and Don Carson's *New Testament Commentary Survey* (Revised Theological Students Fellowship/InterVarsity Press, 1977).

We use commentaries to help us get at the precise meaning of a biblical passage. What Paul *meant* to say to the Corinthians, for example, controls what the letters *mean* to us today, what God is saying to us through them. The first prerequisite to understanding the Bible, though, is a personal relationship with its Author.

As J. I. Packer points out in his excellent volume, *Keep in Step with the Spirit* (Revell, 1984, p. 239), the Holy Spirit provided us with the Bible through His role in the processes of revelation, inspiration, canonization, preservation and translation. He also enables us to appropriate fully the Bible's message through His work in authentication, illumination and interpretation. A coldly rational analysis of the text without crying out for the Holy Spirit's help is futile. It is impossible to "substitute" the Scriptures for the Spirit or vice versa. They are inseparable. The Bible is a supernatural book—authoritative, God-breathed, infallible, inerrant. The starting point for fully understanding it is being empowered by the One who wrote it. Nevertheless, this truth does not exonerate us from the task of serious study of the Bible with all the available helps.

To begin with it must be said that the absolutely best commentary on the Bible is the Bible itself. This fact calls for a wide reading of the Scriptures—daily, weekly, monthly, yearly. In addition, we can receive tremendous help simply by using cross references. The New American Standard, New International and New King James versions, for example, have excellent cross-reference editions available. Also, a number of fine study Bibles have been provided which are tantamount to having access to numerous commentaries within the confines of one book. Very handy! The Bible is amazingly clear as it stands without any of these helps. The Reformers called this the "perspicuity" of Scripture. Even so, the Bible demands and deserves scholarly study.

John Calvin said that the two most important characteristics of a good commentary are *brevitas* (brevity) and *felicitas* (coming to the point). Look for these in your own investigation of commentaries. Both Luther's and Calvin's Bible commentaries are available today and are still tremendously helpful and relevant, precisely because they were so skilled at getting across the riches of God's timeless truth. Through the study of Bible expositors old and new we have access to a virtual gold mine of scriptural teaching. Through the printed page, commentaries enable us to sit at the feet of scores of spiritually gifted (and scholarly) teachers and preachers. Don't be afraid to explore them! Bad commentaries are like bad hairpieces: generally you can spot them quite easily!

So read the Bible—both devotionally and for a broad knowledge of what it says. Use reference and study Bibles. All along, cry out for the Spirit's help. Study the Word with some of the helps listed below.

If I could only have one book in my library in addition to the Bible, it would be *The Eerdmans' Handbook to the Bible*. I know of no more helpful or reliable a resource for understanding the Bible than this book. The first task performed in getting at the meaning of a passage is establishing the context of the passage. Scholars call this "contextual analysis," and the reason it is so important is summed up in the adage: a *text* taken out of *context* is a *pretext*. You will have gone a long way down the road of contextual analysis simply by carefully reading through the particular book of the Bible you are studying and then checking with the *Eerdmans' Handbook to the Bible* for historical backgrounds, literary questions and the like. In addition, this handbook contains a sort of chapter-by-chapter running commentary for each book of the Bible. With its numerous helps, beautiful full-color photography (one trip to Israel and you will treasure this volume even more!) and sound scholarship, the *Eerdmans' Handbook* is, in my opinion, simply unsurpassed for the purposes it serves. Eerdmans has also produced a concise version of this handbook which is especially handy for travel.

Many pastors graduate from seminaries still wrestling with the problem of how to bridge the gap between exegesis and homiletics—that is, between the study of the biblical texts and the preparation of sermons. Walter C. Kaiser Jr. of Trinity Evangelical Divinity School has written a book precisely to answer that need titled *Toward an Exegetical*

Theology (Baker, 1981). In a practical, step-by-step fashion Kaiser shows how it is done. He argues, as well, that too many commentaries are being produced that fail miserably in this area. Thus, he has written a commentary of his own on Malachi as a companion volume to further illustrate and demonstrate the principles he develops. *Malachi: God's Unchanging Love* (Baker, 1984) also contains a helpful appendix on the "Usefulness of Biblical Commentaries for Preaching and Bible Study."

Another issue (should I say problem?) that seminary-trained church leaders face is that of biblical criticism. Can these historical and literary methodologies be used constructively? With the long and depressing history of *destructive* biblical criticism controlled by naturalistic presuppositions (i.e., "miracles don't happen"), should I consult the various commentaries whose authors make use of these scholarly methods?

Years ago C.S. Lewis called for a little humility on the part of the biblical scholars with their "assured results" of historical criticism, form criticism, source criticism, reaction criticism, and the like. After all, Lewis' own contemporaries were using similar literary methods in their analysis of Lewis' own writings, and more often than not they were missing the mark. How much more biblical critics who are separated from the writings they are analyzing by 2000 years and who do not share the same cultures and languages of the Bible writers! (See Lewis, "Modern Theology and Biblical Criticism," in *Christian Reflections*, Eerdmans, 1967, esp. pp. 159-161.)

Right now the entire enterprise of biblical criticism is being called into question. For evangelical perspectives on this issue consult: *Biblical Criticism* (Zondervan, 1978) by R. K. Harrison, B. K. Waltke, Donald Guthrie and Gordon Fee; *The New Testament and Criticism* (Eerdmans, 1967) by George Eldon Ladd; *The Old Testament and Criticism* (Eerdmans, 1983) by Carl E. Armerding; and *New Testament Interpretation* (Eerdmans, 1977) edited by I. Howard Marshall.

Perhaps we will simply have to live with some ambiguity in this area of concern. Evangelicals themselves have seemingly made constructive use of these methods, and the results are often impressive. Howard Marshall's commentary on Luke and F. F. Bruce's commentary on Galatians in the series *New International Greek Testament Commentary* are two examples. (*Anything* these two brilliant evangelical biblical scholars write is worth purchasing, including their commentaries!) On the other hand, I often find myself having to separate the wheat from the chaff when I consult the works of non-conservative biblical scholars. Raymond E. Brown and Markus Barth might serve as two good examples.

Markus Barth's two-volume commentary on Ephesians and Raymond Brown's two-volume work on John, both in the *Anchor Bible* series, are impressive pieces of biblical scholarship. I have received tremendous insight—and numerous sermon ideas!—from consulting these commentaries. Brown also published *The Birth of the Messiah* (Doubleday, 1977) on the infancy narratives in Matthew and Luke, from which I have received numerous stimulating insights into the theology of these passages. And yet in picking the fruit from Brown's exegetical garden *beware of the snakes!* He can be absolutely brilliant in discerning literary forms and theological insights and at the same time be devastatingly *skeptical* of the actual historicity of the biblical events he is studying. He is too often controlled by naturalistic presuppositions in his use of the historical/literary methodologies. Markus Barth (son of the great theologian, Karl Barth) seems to me to be less "radical" than Brown, but the same concerns about the accuracy of the results of these scholarly labors still stand. So if you feel uncertain of your abilities to sort out these matters then perhaps you should avoid these kinds of commentaries or at least refrain from recommending them to the people you serve.

Positively speaking, a Catholic Charismatic scholar like George Montague can use the biblical critical methods without being controlled by skepticism toward the supernatural. His book, *The Holy Spirit: Growth of a Biblical Tradition* (Paulist Press, 1976), is a very interesting, stimulating and practical commentary on virtually every passage on the Holy Spirit in the entire Bible. He comments:

"Fundamentalism makes the mistake of thinking there is no distance between the biblical times and ours, and it distrusts the help of historical and literary sciences to bridge that distance. To some extent this reaction is understandable, for biblical criticism of the rationalist variety has not always avoided imposing its own philosophical presuppositions on the material and on the student. Somehow the truth of the matter must lie between these extremes."

Montague aspires to merge scholarship and spirituality and to a large degree succeeds.

Personally, I ride the biblical criticism horse very lightly. The results are too often too speculative for my tastes, although at times you might catch me singing to a congregation in the biblical Greek a supposed hymn of the early church in such passages as Ephesians 5:14 or 1 Thessalonians 5:16-22. (Dale Moody, the seminary professor I alluded to earlier, taught me how to do that!)

Sometimes you can find the best comments on a given passage of Scripture in books other than commentaries per se. Through the use of the Scripture index all kinds of insights—and related biblical truths— can be gleaned from New Testament theologies such as those by Donald Guthrie *(New Testament Theology,* IVP, 1981) and George Ladd *(A Theology of the New Testament,* Eerdmans, 1974).

If you are studying a Pauline epistle it is often quite helpful to look up comments on your passage in texts on Paul's theology, such as those by F. F. Bruce *(Paul: Apostle of the Heart Set Free,* Eerdmans, 1977) or Herman Ridderbos *(Paul: An Outline of His Theology,* Eerdmans, 1975). Archeological information often sheds additional light as well. My favorite source is J. A. Thompson's *The Bible and Archeology* (3rd ed.; Eerdmans, 1982). Also, there is now available the *Archeological Commentary on the Bible* (Doubleday, 1984) by Gonzalo Baez-Camargo.

If you are studying the Old Testament narratives of Exodus or Numbers, you can find numerous insights in Jamie Buckingham's *A Way Through the Wilderness* (Chosen Books, 1983). In addition, Lloyd Ogilvie and Charles Swindoll have published a number of books chock-full of exegetical and homiletical insights (see their numerous titles). It is helpful to expand your horizons in these ways in your quest for insightful commentary on the passages of Scripture you are studying.

The Bible commentary series that perhaps comes the closest to bridging the gap between "what it meant" and "what it means" (Kaiser's ideal) is InterVarsity Press' *The Bible Speaks Today*. John R. W. Stott's commentaries on the Sermon on the Mount, Ephesians, Galatians, and 2 Timothy in this series are superb.

Commentary sets on the entire Bible are usually uneven. It is generally better to select the best volumes from each rather than purchasing the whole set. The exceptions might be the *Tyndale Commentaries* and the *New International Commentaries*. Both *The Expositor's Bible Commentary* and *The World Biblical Commentary* show promise, and the old Keil and Delitzsch series is still quite valuable. *The New Century Bible Commentary* series has some fine authors, and *The Good News Bible Commentary*, just beginning, is worth examining. Word Books, under the editorship of Lloyd Ogilvie, is publishing an excellent series (especially for preachers!) titled *The Communicator's Commentary*. William Barclay's *Daily Study Bible* is a perennial favorite, and the *New Bible Commentary: Revised* is perhaps the best one-volume commentary (OT and NT) to consult.

And finally—and all importantly—*obey* the Bible! Believe it. Do what it says. Base your life on its promises. Nourish your life on its truth. Put its principles into practice. We have only scratched the surface in appropriating the Bible's liberating truth. Could this be true in part because we have been too lazy to study the Bible?

Finding the Best Volumes
Within Commentary Sets

Commentary sets covering the entire Bible usually consist of some volumes that are more effective than others. It is generally better to select the best volumes from a number of sets rather than to purchase whole sets.

Larry Hart compiled the list below, which gives some of the best commentaries for each book of the Bible.

The following abbreviations are used:

AB *(The Anchor Bible*, Doubleday); BST *(The Bible Speaks Today*, InterVarsity); EBC *(Expositor's Bible Commentary*, Zondervan); HNTC *(Harper's New Testament Commentaries*, Harper & Row).

IB *(Interpreter's Bible*, Abingdon); ICC *(The International Critical Commentary*, T&T Clark); NBC *(The New Bible Commentary: Revised*, Eerdmans); NCBC *(The New Century Bible Commentary*, Eerdmans); NICNT *(The New International Commentary on the New Testament*, Eerdmans).

NICOT *(The New International Commentary on the Old Testament*, Eerdmans); NIGTC *(The New International Greek Testament Commentary*, Eerdmans); OTL *(Old Testament Library*, Westminster); TNTC *(The Tyndale New Testament Commentaries*, Eerdmans); TOTC *The Tyndale Old Testament Commentaries*, InterVarsity); WBC *(Word Biblical Commentary*, Word).

Recommended Volumes

Genesis:
Derek Kidner, TOTC, 1967; Ronald Youngblood, *How It All Began* [Gen. 1-11], (Regal Books, 1980); Ronald Youngblood, *Faith of Our Fathers* [Gen. 12-50], (Regal Books, 1967).

Exodus:
R. Alan Cole, TOTC, 1973; Brevard S. Childs, OTL, 1974; Bernard Ramm, *His Way Out* (Regal Books, 1974).

Leviticus:
R. K. Harrison, TOTC, 1980; Gordon Wenham, NICOT, 1979.

Numbers:
Gordon Wenham, TOTC, 1981; Philip J. Budd, WBC, 1984.

Deuteronomy:
Peter C. Craigie, NICOT, 1976; J. A. Thompson, TOTC, 1974; G. Ernest Wright, IB, 1956.

Joshua:
John Bright, IB, 1956; Martin H. Woudstra, NICOT, 1981; Trent C. Butler, WBC, 1983.

Judges:
Arthur E. Cundall, TOTC, 1968.

Ruth:
Joyce G. Baldwin, NBC, 1970; Edward F. Cambell, AB, 1964; Leon Morris, TOTC, 1968.

1 & 2 Samuel:
Hans W. Herzberg, OTL, 1965; Ralph W. Klein, WBC (1 Sam.), 1983.

1 & 2 Kings:	Carl F. Keil, *Biblical Commentary on the Books of the Kings* (1876; Eerdmans reprint, 1970); William LaSor, NBC, 1970.
1 & 2 Chronicles:	Jacob M. Meyers, AB, 1965.
Ezra, Nehemiah:	Derek Kidner, TOTC, 1979.
Esther:	Joyce G. Baldwin, NBC, 1970; Lewis B. Paton, ICC, 1908.
Job:	Francis I. Anderson, TOTC, 1976; Robert N. Schaper, *Why Me, God?* (Regal Books, 1974).
Psalms:	Derek Kidner, TOTC (2 vols.), 1973, 1975.
Proverbs:	Derek Kidner, TOTC, 1964.
Ecclesiastes:	Derek Kidner, BST, 1976.
Song of Solomon:	Robert Gordis, *The Song of Songs and Lamentations* (Rev. ed.; Ktav, 1974).
Isaiah:	Edward J. Young, NICOT (3 vols.), 1965-72.
Jeremiah:	J. A. Thompson, NICOT, 1980; John Bright, AB, 1965.
Lamentations:	R. K. Harrison, TOTC, 1973; Delbert R. Hillers, AB, 1973.
Ezekiel:	John B. Taylor, TOTC, 1969; Andrew W. Blackwood, Jr., *Ezekiel* (Baker, 1965).
Daniel:	Joyce G. Baldwin, TOTC, 1978; Ronald S. Wallace, BST, 1979; Edward J. Young, NICOT, 1949.
Hosea:	Derek Kidner, BST, 1981.
Joel, Obadiah, Jonah, Micah:	Leslie C. Allen, NICOT, 1976.
Amos:	J.A. Motyer, BST, 1975.
Nahum, Habakkuk, Zephaniah:	John D. W. Watts, Cambridge Bible Commentary, 1975.
Haggai, Zechariah, Malachi:	Joyce G. Baldwin, TOTC, 1972.
Matthew:	D. A. Carson, EBC, 1984.
Mark:	William L. Lane, NICNT, 1974.
Luke:	I. Howard Marshall, NIGTC, 1978; Leon Morris, TNTC, 1974.
John:	Leon Morris, NICNT, 1970; Raymond E. Brown, AB (2 vols.), 1966, 1970; F. F. Bruce,

	The Gospel of John (Eerdmans, 1983).
Acts:	F. F. Bruce, NICNT, 1954; I. Howard Marshall, TNTC (2nd series), 1980; Stanley M. Horton, *The Book of Acts* (Gospel Publishing House, 1981).
Romans:	C. E. B. Cranfield, ICC (2nd series), 2 vols., 1975; Cranfield, *Commentary on Romans* (abridged for general readers; Eerdmans, 1984); C. K. Barrett, HNTC, 1957.
1 & 2 Corinthians:	F. F. Bruce, NCBC, 1971; C. K. Barrett, HNTC, 1971 (rev. ed.), 1974.
Galatians:	F. F. Bruce, NICGT, 1982; Donald Guthrie, NCBC, 1969; John R. W. Stott, BST, 1968.
Ephesians:	Markus Barth, AB (2 vols.), 1974; John R. W. Stott, BST, 1979; F. F. Bruce, NICNT (2nd ed.), 1984.
Philippians:	Ralph P. Martin, NCBC, 1976; Gerald F. Hawthorne, WBC, 1983.
Colossians, Philemon:	Ralph P. Martin, NCBC, 1974; Peter T. O'Brien, WBC, 1982.
1 & 2 Thessalonians:	Leon Morris, NICNT, 1959; Morris, TNTC (2nd series), 1984; F. F. Bruce, WBC, 1982; I. Howard Marshall, NCBC, 1983.
1 & 2 Timothy, Titus:	Donald Guthrie, TNTC, 1957; J.N.D. Kelly, HNTC, 1963 (reprint: Baker, 1981); John R. W. Stott, BST, 1973.
Hebrews:	F. F. Bruce, NICNT, 1964; P. E. Hughes, *The Epistle to the Hebrews* (Eerdmans, 1977); Donald Guthrie, TNTC (2nd series), 1983; Raymond Brown, BST, 1982.
James:	James Adamson, NICNT, 1976; Peter Davids, NIGTC, 1982.
1 & 2 Peter, Jude:	Michael Green, TNTC, 1971; J. N. D. Kelly, HNTC, 1969. 1, 2, & 3 John: I. Howard Marshall, NICNT, 1978; John R. W. Stott, TNTC, 1964.
Revelation:	George Eldon Ladd, *Revelation* (Eerdmans, 1972); G. R. Beasley-Murray, NCBC, 1974; Robert Mounce, NICNT, 1977.

10

What Happens When Pastors Are Leaders?

By E. S. Caldwell

E. S. Caldwell is associate editor of *MINISTRIES: The Magazine For Christian Leaders*. He served the Assemblies of God as promotions coordinator for the Division of Home Missions and publicity director for the radio-TV department. He pastored 23 years in Idaho and Missouri. He is a graduate of Northwest College of the Assemblies of God and also attended Northwest Nazarene College.

To what extent do our churches mirror the society in which they exist? I've heard pastors say, "Cho's ideas work in Korea, but they won't work here." So one of the things I wanted to learn when I visited South Korea in 1984 was whether or not the huge church pastored by Paul Yonggi Cho merely mirrored the way things were done in that country. I discovered that Cho's way of doing things sharply contrasted with traditional Korean methods.

This unexpected observation began to come into focus while I was a passenger on a bus that roamed a variety of alternative routes in Seoul.

The intended destination of the bus ride was Fasting Prayer Mountain, a few miles north of the city. The bus kept trying various roads because torrential rains the previous night caused mud slides and washouts. Maybe it was a little crazy to keep trying, but when we boarded the bus it didn't seem dangerous. And once aboard we couldn't communicate with the Korean-speaking driver, so he kept responding to road blocks by looking for yet another way to reach the destination. As a result, we Americans on board saw neighborhoods in Seoul that most foreigners miss.

Two kinds of structures were present everywhere we went throughout the winding streets of Seoul: store front shops of a nearly uniform size and miniature churches.

There must be tens of thousands of little shops in Seoul. One displayed only hand tools; the next, men's shirts; the next, steel springs; the next, lead ingots; the next, bicycles, and on and on. Each shop had a 12-foot front, and each had a colorful 12-foot sign. Each specialized in only one type of product. Typically, the store was on the ground level and the family that operated the business lived above the shop.

And there must be thousands of churches in Seoul. In fact the city of 10 million population does have 4,000 Christian churches. Wow, that's a lot! But consider this—the vast majority of those church buildings are about the same size as those shops.

Why are the churches so little? I think I found the answer two days later when another bus finally took us through the countryside to Prayer Mountain (the first driver had to give up after exhausting every possible passage—and seeing another bus upended in the flood).

It's fairly easy to spot a typical Korean mini-church—look for a brick building about the size of a two-car garage with what appears at first glance to be an army surplus transmission tower perched like an iron skeleton of a steeple on the tile roof. About midway up the tower you will see a four-sided sign displaying the church name to passersby. Atop the tower stands a cross.

Every hamlet, every cluster of homes along the bus route was punctuated by one of those pint-sized houses of worship. Since typically Koreans don't own automobiles, nearly every settlement had its own place to assemble for Christian services. I estimated that most of the families in a hamlet could be packed into the meeting house.

It made sense for those churches to be scaled down to the size crowd that could reach them on foot. But why build tiny churches in the big city?—Look out, here comes the old "but we've always done it that way." People moved from the farm to town and built a church the same size as they attended back home.

Besides, a typical Korean business is just big enough to provide the basic income the owner-family needs to survive. And the church building is about the same size—just big enough so that a dozen tithing families can about meet the needs of a pastor and his family (after all, the government advocates no more than two children).

Now I saw it in sharp focus—societal forces in Korea shaped the way the church functioned. And for 80 years Christian missionary endeavors limped along as unimpressively as in many other parts of the globe.

Then came Cho.

Cho is to Christianity in Korea what Safeway was to merchandising groceries in America in the 1950s. The word *supermarket* was coined to describe the innovation that virtually wiped out the mom-and-pop grocery stores and drug stores that once were a part of Americana.

The Holy Spirit gave Cho a plan for church growth that in 20 years resulted in the largest congregation in the world—and it was done in a city that typically housed its churches in buildings not as big as your parsonage.

To put it bluntly, Cho stood against society's way of doing things.

He's not the only innovator. Downtown Seoul is the home of the 10-story Lotte Department Store. It's a magnificent building with elevators, escalators and clerks, clerks and more clerks.

I walked in moments after the doors opened. The entire sales force stood at attention while the loudspeaker blared the national anthem. They bowed to me. (What did I do? I bowed back.)

I wondered how on earth the store's management could afford this huge staff—10 floors of them! Later on I found the answer—Koreans come by the bus load to spend their money on all the goods to be found, from the groceries on the first floor to the variety of restaurants on the top floor. From top to bottom the entire building was jammed with shoppers.

While business boomed at Lotte Department Store, it continued to move at a snail's pace in all those little shops throughout Seoul. Owners eked out an existence.

Lotte Department Store and Yoido Full Gospel Church have something in common. Both have rejected the notion that the way it's always been done is the only way it can be done. They stood against societal forces.

Koreans come by the bus loads to Yoido Full Gospel Church all day every Sunday. They also come by taxi, bicycle and on foot. And in those mini-churches what happens? Well, pastors still eke out an existence.

There's a lesson here for American churches—and for churches in many other parts of the earth: "Don't let the world around you squeeze you into its own mold" (Rom. 12:2, Phillips). A church can and should be willing to innovate, under the Holy Spirit's guidance, in order to fulfill its part of the Great Commission.

No one faults a small church in a small community doing its very best to minister in the restricted population it serves. But a small church that stays small when it is within a city full of people should carefully examine itself.

Churches that want to stay small can stay small—that's the way it works in Korea, and that's the way it works here.

11

What Is the Solution to Ethical Misconduct?

By Bob Mumford

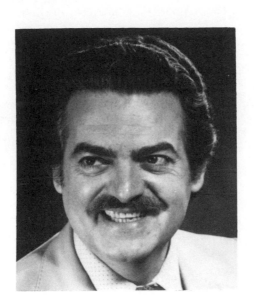

Bob Mumford is a pastor and elder of Gulf Coast Covenant Church and also serves as a member of the executive committee of Integrity Communications in Mobile, Alabama. Mumford has served as dean of Elim Bible Institute and spent 31 years as a pastor involved with international leadership and conference ministry. He also is the author of several books, including *The King and You*, *Take Another Look at Guidance* and others.

The apostle Paul was the spiritual father of the Galatian church. He was concerned for their well being and he said these words: "Let us not become boastful, challenging one another, envying one another" (Gal. 5:26).

Within these words can be found the roots of the sins of pastoral ethics.

The word "boastful" is interpreted in the Greek Lexicon: "attempts to achieve unfounded respect." That is creating images and all that goes with it.

"Challenging" is: "inviting to challenge or combat." And "envying" is: "being pained at what someone else has."

Keeping those words in mind, I would like to make four observations.

The highest calling in the New Testament is to know how to be a brother or sister. If it is not the *highest* calling, then it would be a high calling, far more challenging than any of us realizes.

It is the desire in my heart to see the meaning of "my brother" or "my sister" restored.

I was sitting with a group of pastors and they were asking me questions about what I was doing, what I was seeing, and so forth. Finally, I said, "One of the things I feel God is saying is that He is seeking to restore to us the meaning of the word 'brother.' "

I turned to one of the pastors, a young handsome man, and said, "Do you call your church a church family?"

He said, "Yes!"

Then I said, "Is it one?"

He couldn't answer me. His eyes filled with tears, and they began streaming down his face. To call it a church family and for it to be one are two different things.

As soon as I say the words "my brother" or "my sister," there is inserted into the relationship a strange dynamic we need to understand.

If a man drives up in a Mercedes 450SEL, silver, with steam-heated door knobs and he is an insurance salesman, it doesn't bother me. But if he drives up in a 450SEL, silver, with steam-heated door knobs and says, "Hi, brother," I go through some changes. "What's he doing with God's money? Why is he spending it on that? Who does he think he is? You cannot be a Christian and drive a 450SEL.'' That is what's going on inside. If he wasn't my brother I wouldn't care what he drives. The moment he says, ''Hi, brother,'' some mysterious dynamic enters into the thing. That mysterious dynamic is called *sibling rivalry!*

I have two sons. I learned about sibling rivalry from them, with great pain. One of my sons loves to work on cars, he is a carpenter, a mason—he loves to work with his hands. The other one is a philosopher. He is clean, he doesn't like to sweat, let alone get dirty. When you say work, he breaks out in little pimples. These two kids could not be more different, and there exists a rivalry between them.

Here's where I learned this particular lesson. Every father knows that children hide their peas under the napkin. Right? But my oldest boy would say, ''Dad.''

''Yes, son?''

''Eric is hiding his peas under the napkin.''

Then Eric would go crazy—he would absolutely go bananas. ''Why don't you leave me alone! What are you doing? Then we'd go through this whole big session and I would try to restore the peace and put it all back together.

One day a very interesting thing happened. My oldest son Bernard brought a friend home for dinner. During the meal I noticed that Bernard's friend didn't eat his peas—he hid them under the napkin. The strange thing was that Bernard helped him. Do you see what I mean? There is something going on between two brothers that isn't there between two friends!

When I say, ''Hi, brother,'' I have to be prepared for the rivalry, boasting, challenging, envying. There is something of a dynamic there. It's why brothers in the church have bitten and eaten and devoured one another for so many years.

Sibling rivalry is the prodigal and the elder brother. I'm glad the prodigal met the father on his way home before he met the elder brother. His brother would have sent him packing, wouldn't he? He would have said, ''Daddy isn't home. You don't live here anymore. Get out of here!'' Because that's what happens between two *brothers*.

Cain and Abel. Moses and Miriam. Miriam said, ''Who do you think you are? Do you think you're the only one God speaks to?'' Can't you see Moses' sister reading him the riot act? No one would have had the courage except his own sister. You know you can't punch out your own sister.

Isn't it an amazing phenomenon? The problem is not easy to solve. If you're the insurance salesman, I don't care what kind of house you live in. I don't care how much money you make. I don't care how many people you have working for you. But if you're the pastor in

93

the next church to me: "That's my brother. Who does he think he is? Look at that. Remodeling. Everybody knows they're broke. How can they remodel that house? They're making debts, that's what they're doing."

Why should I worry if you're remodeling? Why should the kind of car you drive or where you go for a vacation bother me? I'm not worried where the neighbors next door go for their vacation.

My second observation is:

Human response does determine church history. By that I mean, whether or not we are able to work it out and be together as brothers and sisters will affect the history of the church. Continual fighting and bickering will change the direction of history.

I believe God's will rules over all, but I believe that if you sat down today and read Phillip Schaff's six volumes of church history, you'll discover that much church history was affected by two brothers that couldn't get along, such as Augustine and Pelagius or Luther and Zwingli.

You say, "Well, it was a doctrinal disagreement." Wait a minute. If I don't like you as a person, it's not difficult to find six Bible reasons for not walking with you.

I recently read an article that pointed out the fact that the bishop of Constantinople and the bishop of Rome divided, not so much doctrinally, but because they didn't like each other. I've been here long enough to know that when one bishop doesn't like the other bishop, then all of church history can be affected by a relational problem.

"Ask of Me and I shall give the heathen for your inheritance." If, as brothers, we do not know how to handle the inheritance when God hands it out, what will happen? Will the family fight over it? Suppose the Lord says, "I'm going to give you Minneapolis." Who is He going to give it to? The Lutherans, of course. But there are some other "brothers" who wouldn't like that very much.

I was on my way to Africa and needed to make out a will. I wanted to make it very simple and uncomplicated and told the lawyer what I wanted. Well, he said, "Mr. Mumford, you don't understand. If you make a will and don't make it clear, your children will fight over the will."

I said, "Not my children."

He laughed.

I said, "I'll be back. I've got work to do." I went home and sat my children down and talked to them.

My third observation is in the form of a question:

Are you a son or daughter of my Father? It's a basic question. This is the question that I am continually forced to ask myself. If you are a son of my Father then my conduct toward you, as my brother, must change. It's the Father's heart that is pained by sibling rivalry. It's the Father's heart that is injured by my wrong actions toward you.

When someone says, "the brotherhood of man," I have a struggle buying that because not every human being has faith in the God of the Bible. I can buy the Fatherhood of God. That makes me more comfortable. The Fatherhood of God includes all who have entered His family.

When I see that you are my brother, I have to watch the fact that a dynamic is present and that my conduct has to change.

My fourth observation is internal:

I personally must have a place to rest. "The Lord is the portion of my inheritance and my cup. Thou dost support my lot. The lines have fallen to me in pleasant places. Indeed, my heritage is beautiful to me" (Ps. 16:5,6).

Every brother or sister could honestly find a place to rest here. My Father will watch over the inheritance and make sure you get your part. You don't have to strive for it, compete for it. You don't have to step on your brother in order to get it. You don't have to be involved in the rat race. When you win the rat race, that makes you the number one rat.

I don't want to compete with my brother in an illegal way. Good competition is fine. I'm not talking about the good kind, I'm talking about the illegal kind, the boasting, the envying, the sibling rivalry that provokes the kind of breaking of ministerial ethics that is across our nation and around the world.

I live for the day when I not only suffer with those who suffer, but *rejoice* with those who rejoice. You know, as well as I do, it is easier to suffer with those who suffer, than to rejoice with those who rejoice.

I can choose my friends. I can choose my enemies. But I can't choose my brothers. My Father chooses them. When the prodigal came home, the elder brother said to his father, "This, *your son....*" The father said, "No, that's *your brother.*"

Many times when I complained to God, "This, *your son...,*" the Lord has said, "No, that's *your brother.*"

Solving Administrative Problems

12

How Do You Plan Successfully?

By Don McMinn

Don McMinn is minister of worship and praise at Allandale Baptist Church in Austin, Texas. Among his published articles is "Strategic Planning in the Local Church" which appeared in the April 1984 issue of *Search* magazine.

A dramatic account of personal planning and goal setting was recorded in the March 24, 1972, issue of *Life* magazine. At the age of 15, John Goddard set down 127 "goals" which he wanted to accomplish in his lifetime. He accomplished 103 of these goals by the time he reached 47 years of age.

Included in these "life-purposes" were to: climb Mt. Kilimanjaro, Mt. Ararat, Mt. Fuji (and 14 others); become a physician; retrace the travels of Marco Polo and Alexander the Great; study the Hopi Indians; land and take off from an aircraft carrier; type 50 words a minute; learn French, Spanish and Arabic; circumnavigate the globe; milk a poisonous snake; fly in a blimp; climb Cheops pyramid; read the entire Encyclopedia Britannica, and achieve 110 other goals, similar in variety and scope.

It would be interesting to discover what prompted Goddard, at the naive age of 15, to consider and record the direction and goals of his entire life. (I would also like to tap in on the determination and resoluteness with which he pursued and accomplished these goals!) Needless to say, if he had not *planned* to achieve such specific objectives, he would have fulfilled few of them.

There are very few purposeful events that occur in life that are not first planned. Some may be planned at a dinner table while enjoying a cup of coffee, others in an intricately involved planning session at the office or at a conference. Regardless of where or how plans are made, planning is important and it must be viewed as a necessary and worthwhile endeavor.

Without effective planning, your life and ministry are destined to be controlled by the wiles of circumstances. Those who do not plan seldom reach their potential unless they achieve under the auspices of someone else's planning efforts.

I suppose a certain amount of anti-planning bias will always exist. Many Christians even refer to James 4:13 as support for their lack of conscientious planning: "Come now, you who say: 'Today or tomorrow, we shall go to such and such a city, and spend a year there and engage in business and make a profit.' Yet, you do not know what your life will be like tomorrow."

In the margin of my Bible, I have written, "Planning without God—v.13." In this passage James is simply denouncing the sin of presumption; it is an attitude he is warning against. In verse 15, James says, "Instead, you ought to say, if the Lord wills, we shall live and also do this or that." He concludes the chapter with the words, "Therefore, to one who knows the right thing to do, and does it not, to him it is sin." In essence, it is possible to know the will of God (with obvious reference to the future), and once you discover His will, it is sin not to perform it!

I have met very few ministers who would outright reject the concept or practice of planning. Very few would take the position that planning is of no value, and a micro-minority would be bold enough to say that planning is ungodly and contrary to Scripture. However, not enough ministers plan on a consistent basis, particularly personal planning. Few ministers speak against planning but too few engage in it.

Several years ago my wife and I contracted with a builder to have a house built. Several months were spent reviewing and revising architectural plans and drawings. Before the first footing was poured, we knew exactly where each outlet was going to be, the shape of the kitchen cabinets, and the color of the interior stain.

We should consider foolish a man who would build a house without a specific set of plans. "Where do we want the concrete poured?"

"Oh, just over there will do."

"Where should the walls be framed in?"

"I guess wherever they will fit on the slab that has been set."

Sound ridiculous? What is truly ridiculous is that many people will be more conscientious about building their house than they will about planning their lives.

What is even more tragic is that most of our churches and Christian organizations suffer from similar results of non-planning. Einstein once characterized our generation as one in which there is an efficiency of means but a confusion of ends. We have never been more busy or more efficient, but we have lost track of where we are going.

Planning is not an attempt to foretell the future. Planning is an attempt to regulate and shape the future and to prepare to negotiate unforeseen circumstances to one's advantage. Planning always involves decision-making. Planning does not attempt to make future decisions but rather considers the futility of present decisions. Good planning contemplates how a current decision is going to affect the future environment.

Have we seriously considered the implications of Isaiah 37:26? "Have ye not heard? Long ago I did it, from ancient times I planned it. Now I have brought it to pass." This is God speaking. We are getting an inside view of how He runs the universe—God plans! There is something

101

divine about planning; it is something God considers important; it is the key factor in negotiating His will with the factor of time. Planning is not an option, it is an imperative!

Planning to Plan

Once planning is accepted as a necessary function, adequate resources must be allotted, particularly time and energy. It is important to understand that one must "plan to plan." A certain amount of time in the daily schedule must be reserved to engage in the planning process. That seems like an obvious requirement which does not need to be suggested but it is probably the major factor leading to insufficient and ineffective planning. It is not that we question the importance of planning or that we are unschooled in planning techniques; the problem is simply that we do not plan to plan.

Planning is a form of work. It is not a matter of "Let's get our planning over with and then we'll start working." When you are planning, you are working.

Having been raised in a family of manual laborers, it took a while for me to associate "work" with functions other than "hands on" labor. Planning is not only a type of work; it is probably the most efficient type of work. The following chart shows a work ratio that demonstrates the importance and efficiency of planning.

Relative to my personal ministry, I devote the entire last week in December for strategic planning. During this week, I attempt to get a perspective on the broad concerns. Once every two months, an entire day is given to accessing and updating plans. Plans for a new week are developed every Sunday evening. Each day's activities are defined during morning devotions. These designated times are essential. They must be protected and cultivated!

It might be good to clarify at this point the difference between personal planning and planning for your ministry or organization. I have often seen men establish elaborate plans at the office but never carry over the discipline to their private lives. Both are important. I usually organize my personal planning charts under the following headings. (Included are a few specific examples from my 1984-85 charts.)

Financial

- Abide by '84 budget.
- Secure lot to build new house in '85.
- Start a college fund for children.
- Remain debt-free.

Professionally

- Write two articles.
- Take a course at the university.
- Attend two conferences.

- Study six major choral works.
- Begin book on choral articulation.

Personal

- Read one book per month.
- Develop three new close friendships.
- Secure and learn to use personal computer.
- Begin physical conditioning program.

Family

- Plan one family vacation.
- Develop goals for girls (ages 4 and 6) and help them reach goals.
- Spend one night a week alone with wife.
- Develop family hobby for pastime.

Personal Ministry*

- Lead 12 people to Christ.
- Teach continuous witnessing training course.
- Lead five families into our church.
- Disciple four men.

Note: These are plans exclusive of my work at the church.

That is, if I were a layperson instead of a minister, I would still have these personal ministry plans.

As minister of praise and worship at my church, my ministry planning charts for last year included:

- Complete music ministry personnel chart by October.
- Begin music conservatory in September.
- Produce "Living Christmas Tree" in December.
- Work sub-planning charts for music ministry. (This would include plans for all choirs, orchestra, ensembles, etc.)

Obviously, each of the above plans was broken down into numerous and often detailed and lengthy goals and strategies.

When I was conducting research for my doctoral dissertation I discovered an intriguing term which gave me a whole new outlook on planning. The term is *a priori* and it is a type of logic which moves from general to specific. It begins with a large entity and breaks it down into smaller segments. The opposite is *a posteriori* which begins with specifics and attempts to combine them into a whole unit.

It is the difference between opening the hood of an automobile and disassembling the parts of the motor (general to specific) as opposed to going to a junk yard and attempting to assimilate a motor out of various spare parts (specific to general).

Applied to planning, *a priori* logic means that we first establish broad, far-reaching goals and then we break down those large goals into smaller and smaller units. Unfortunately, we often have to grab onto what is around us (smaller units of achievement) and hope they will somehow fit together into a larger purpose (though they usually do not).

To give another example, it is the difference between a college student selecting a degree program and then systematically passing all the courses required for that degree and a college student who takes courses "at random" and then at the end of four years, tries to make them fit into a degree program.

To oversimplify the issue, there are two types of planning: strategic and operational. General Robert E. Wood, ex-chief executive officer of Sears Roebuck and Company distinguished between the two types of planning and emphasized their relative importance when he said, "Business is like a war in one respect; if its grand strategy is correct, any number of tactical errors can be made and yet the enterprise proves successful."

Strategic Planning deals with the broad purposes and objectives of an organization, its character and personality. It usually covers a long time spectrum and the entire scope of an organization, and is a concern of top management.

Operational Planning deals with short-range goals and decisions, usually covers a short time span, and is a function of lower management. An organization (or person) can overcome mistakes made on an operational level as long as its main strategy is sound. However, if the primary strategy of an organization is faulty, it is destined for failure, even though its day-to-day operations may be adequate.

In every organization there must be adequate thought put into both types of planning. Too often we get so involved in daily activities that we lose sight of where we are going; or perhaps we have never even considered where we are going, in which case, we are only concerned with day-to-day existence. We never visualize a larger perspective. On the other hand, some may dream dreams of grandeur but never break the vision down into more manageable working units. As a result, they are never able to accomplish the "big things in life" because they cannot visualize how these broad goals must be broken down into smaller, more achievable activities.

Successful Planning

Planning is the key to success, but not all planning is successful. To go through the motions of planning does not mean that we will automatically reap the benefits normally derived from the process. There are several key factors in successful planning:

1. *Planning must be flexible.* The life of an organization moving through time is like a canoe trip down a large river. Regardless of how conscientiously plans are made, there is a constant need for monitoring and correction if the final destination is to be reached.

Plans should never be "set in cement." This flexibility factor has become more important in recent years because of the speed at which our society and environment is changing. Plans made a year ago could very well be antiquated and inappropriate. Therefore, planning must not be seen as a one-time event but rather as a continuous process.

Proverbs speaks to this planning characteristic: "The mind of man plans his way, but the Lord directs his steps" (Prov. 16:10); "Many are the plans in a man's heart, but the counsel of the Lord, it will stand" (Prov. 19:21).

If the future appears to be unusually uncertain, contingency plans may need to be developed simultaneous with primary plans. Specific "trigger factors" would then be identified and monitored.

2. *The execution of plans must be monitored and controlled.* Some type of system should be developed to ensure that performance conforms to plans. Unfortunately, it is not sufficient to develop plans, delegate their execution, and then forget them. Successful planning necessitates monitoring these plans until they are completed, or in the case of perpetual plans, the task of monitoring must be a constant process which is built into the system.

A specific project may be followed until it is completed, but a plan as broad as the mission or main objective of an organization will need to be observed for the life of the organization or until the plan changes. How often a church will set as one of its major objectives, "To Evangelize the Lost," but through the years that church will lose its impact on the lost community. Plans must be monitored and controlled.

3. *The planning process should involve those who will be responsible for the execution of plans.* People support what they help to create. When we are "handed down" a directive, we are generally much less enthused about the idea than if we had been included in its inception and refinement. If at all possible, we should include in the planning process those who will be responsible for the plans.

This is the inherent strength of M.B.O. (Management by Objectives) developed by Peter Drucker in the mid-50s. M.B.O. not only insists that every manager has clearly defined objectives, but that the managers must set their own objectives or be intricately involved in the objective-setting process.

By imposing "our" plans on someone else, we run the risk of miscommunication and perhaps a halfhearted attempt to implement these plans.

4. *Plans must be adequately clarified and communicated.* How often have you sat through a productive planning session, left the meeting enthused about results and yet nothing ever materialized? There is an essential link between planning and implementation; the link is clarification and communication.

In the course of a planning meeting, thousands of words, thoughts and suggestions make their way to the surface. When these are narrowed down, modified and finalized, the result should be a concise, written statement of plans.

A planning meeting that does not result in a set of plans is a waste of time. Not only should the plans be written down but it should be determined and recorded who is responsible for executing the plan, when the plan should begin and end, what resources will be allocated to the projects and what restraints will affect the plan (these would include personnel, finances, use of facilities and equipment, etc.).

Likewise, plans must be communicated in a positive, clear fashion. Often this can be done by merely distributing a planning sheet to the appropriate persons. Other situations necessitate a personal meeting between the planners and those whom the plans will affect.

More elaborate means of communication would involve brochures, a slide presentation, or even short trips. Generally, plans that are broad in scope and ones that affect many people necessitate more involved communication. More time should be allotted for communication.

5. An "open system" approach should be the mindset for good planning. If an organization is going to succeed, it must have an open system approach to planning. An open system is sympathetic to its environment; it allows external entities to influence the decision-making and planning processes.

A closed system attempts to exist with no regard to concerns outside itself. Obviously, a closed system will soon become outdated and inefficient.

In a ministry situation, there are certain absolutes such as doctrine, Christian principles and ethics which remain constant regardless of changes in the environment. However, our approach to ministry is in constant need of revision and these revisions should be made looking outward and not inward.

God—The Master Planner

For Christians, the bottom line of this function called planning is *seeking the will of the Lord.* A planning session is nothing more than a seeking-the-mind-of-the-Father session.

For one full day our church staff participated in a most rewarding planning meeting. We left the meeting having solidified our church's major thrust for 1985. The strategic direction of our church came first; the operational plans came later.

One staff member shared that through prayer the Lord had laid on his heart Mark 8:22-26. It is the story of the blind man who, having been touched once by Jesus, saw men "like trees, walking about." Upon receiving a second touch, he saw clearly; he saw men as men. The point is, we too often see people as "trees walking," temporal, expendable items, and we find ourselves in need of a second touch to see "people as people."

Another staff member shared the burden of "relationship evangelism" as the key to "fruit that remains." Along with this is the development of a mindset among our people that they are to share Christ in the sphere of influence in which God has placed them.

Still another staff member contributed the fact that our denomination would be using the slogan "Five in '85" quite extensively during the year.

After consideration of all input and several hours of brainstorming, the following was solidified:

People as People—our slogan and mission for the year. We will develop in our members a new perspective on the lost community.

Five in '85. Our objective is to encourage and train our body to bring five people (friend, relative, associate, neighbor, acquaintance) to Sunday school during the year. The ultimate goal is to have these five people join our church.

It sounds simple but it will work! Our entire church is now focused in one direction.

God's people, more than any other, should conscientiously devote themselves to planning. In order to maximize God's investment in our lives, each of us should plan for our life, the life of our family and the life of our church. And the sooner we start, the better.

The story is told of a French marshall who asked his gardener to plant a new sprig in his estate. The gardener objected, "But it will take a hundred years for the sprig to grow into a mature tree!"

"In that case we have no time to lose," replied the marshall. "Plant it now!"

Begin a systematic approach to planning and begin it now. You will be pleased at the outcome.

13

How Do You Establish a Pastor's Income?

By Stephen Strang

Stephen Strang is editor and publisher of *Charisma* and *MINISTRIES: The Magazine For Christian Leaders* and president of Strang Communications Company.

I know most pastors are not paid well from experience—I was a preacher's kid. My dad served several small congregations in Missouri and Iowa. It seems that church boards back then had the philosophy that if the Lord would keep the pastor humble, they would keep him poor. Part of the reason, I'm sure, was that the working-class Pentecostal congregations that Dad served were made up of people who were trying to get by on low salaries, too. Today the economic level in most of those churches is much higher—but the mentality is often the same. Let's keep the preacher in modest straits financially lest he get proud; or worse yet, lest he make more money than we do.

By now I have the attention of every preacher. I don't know a single pastor who doesn't think he is worth more than he's being paid.

But at the same time, I've seen preachers who are as stingy as the church boards they deplore. It's like the barnyard pecking order. The strongest chicken pecks on the next strongest chicken in the barnyard, who pecks on the next chicken in line, and so on.

In our denomination circles, some preachers were as stingy with the next group in line as they felt their own church boards were with them. The next group in pecking order happened to be Bible college professors. The apparent rule of thumb in our denomination was that Bible college professors' salaries had to be kept below the income of the average pastor in the sponsoring district. I know that from experience, too, because when I was a teenager, Dad left a pastorate to become a Bible college professor.

I've also seen the pecking order take place in how pastors pay their own staff members. Often if the church is large enough to have a multiple staff, the pastor has a pretty good salary. But when it comes to paying staff members, well, that's different.

I used to work for a huge Pentecostal church with a staff of more than 40. The pastor of the church had served many small congregations over the years and had been underpaid for most of his career. Finally, when success came, it came big. So this pastor enjoyed a very generous salary.

But when it came to hiring staff members, church leaders reminded them they were working for "a ministry." Translated, that meant, "We pay lower salaries than the outside but the outstanding working environment in this huge church will more than make up for it."

Not only that, raises were very modest. In fact, during the five years I was on that staff, my raises did not keep pace with inflation so my salary actually went down.

Ironically, that pastor loved to quote the scripture, "Thou shalt not muzzle the ox that treadeth out the corn. And, The laborer is worthy of his reward" (1 Tim. 5:18). But his favorite verse seemed to be, "Let the elders who rule well be considered worthy of double honor, especially those who labor in preaching and teaching" (1 Tim. 5:17, RSV), to show, I'm sure, that his salary should be double that of the other pastors who didn't get to teach in the Sunday services. I wonder if this pastor or others who might share his thinking ever considered the scripture: "With the same measure that ye mete withal it shall be measured to you again" (Luke 6:38). Or, "It is more blessed to give than to receive" (Acts 20:35).

All of this is background to lead up to my introduction to an emphasis on pastors' salaries. I believe it is an extremely important topic and not much is written about it. Because of this, we commissioned a survey of *MINISTRIES* readers several months ago. We selected 300 names randomly from our readers.

In working on this, and after growing up in a preacher's home and serving on a church staff, I've come to some conclusions about what some pastors are paid. I believe they are paid too little, so I have some suggestions for church boards or anyone who is a decision-maker for a pastor's salary.

Every congregation ought to pay its pastor as well as the congregation can afford, given economic conditions and living costs in the area. Not only is this doing for others as you would have them do unto you, but it's just common sense that when you pay well, you "get what you pay for."

If the church pays good salaries, it will generally get a higher caliber of leadership. That's because the church can attract gifted men who can make a decision about whether or not to accept the church's call based on God's will. They won't have to try to determine whether it's God's will despite the fact that they can hardly raise a family on the meager salary that's offered.

At a very minimum, a church ought to pay a pastor as much as the average church member makes. It is not fair to expect the pastor to get by on less than the average church member lives on. If there isn't the money to pay the pastor that well, I think the church has some other problems that need to be solved immediately. The church ought to cut back in some other areas so they can pay the pastor more.

The Church of God (Cleveland, Tennessee) sets a scale for what churches should pay their pastors. The scale lists 13 church sizes, from 50 or fewer members to 950 or more. The weekly salary at the bottom of their scale is $272.00 plus $59.00 for expenses. At the top, the salary is $502.00 plus $163.00 for expenses. In addition, where funds are available, the church is urged to pay the pastor's utilities, health insurance and retirement, and to pay as taxable income an amount equal to one-half of his Social Security tax.

A church board and pastor ought to agree ahead of time how the pastor's salary will compare to the growth of the church. As the congregation prospers numerically and financially, the pastor's pay ought to increase, too. Even though pastors ought to be in the ministry because they feel the call of God and not because of the lure of a high salary, it's just common sense that they will be more motivated in their day-to-day actions if they know they will be rewarded if they work hard and if they are successful at what they do.

The opposite is also true. The pastor can be unmotivated if he feels he is working very hard yet is having to struggle financially and is powerless to do anything about it. Also, he can't be as effective a pastor if he is constantly worried about his own personal financial problems. A minimum should be that the church would review the pastor's salary annually and would at least adjust it for the cost of living.

A church should put only deeply spiritual men in the decision-making role of the pastor's salary. There is no better way for the congregation to control the pastor than by controlling the purse strings, especially on the pastor's salary.

Satan is constantly trying to bombard the body of Christ and Christ's representatives in the local church. He'll use even this very non-spiritual aspect of the church's life—setting the pastor's salary—as an opportunity to cause hard feelings and to discourage the pastor. Many pastors end up moving to different congregations because they feel an obligation to their own families. Keeping a good pastor is important. The truly great churches in America that have seen substantial growth over the years are the ones that have had real consistency in leadership.

The last point is directed toward pastors. Often they approach the church board with an appeal that their bills are too high and they need a raise. This is the worst way to approach the subject. They should tell the church board that under their ministry the congregation has made some substantial strides forward. They might even want to list them. They ought to say that their ministry is worth more to the congregation than when they came and they ought to get a raise.

14

What Are Pastors Being Paid?

By Linda Howard

An author of three books and numerous articles for Christian publications, Linda Howard also served as editor of a magazine and is administrative assistant in the youth department of Tabernacle Church in Melbourne, Florida. Mrs. Howard has a degree in managerial science and with her husband authored *Aerospace Technologist* for NASA.

H is voice crackling with emotion, Mr. Morgan rose to his feet, clinging to the back of the pew. "I'm 76 years old and I've never made more than $10,000 a year my entire life. My wife and I have raised four children. The Lord always saw that our needs were met. The preacher doesn't need a raise. He makes too much already." The congregation, spiced liberally with older parishioners, nodded their heads in agreement and voted down the pastor's five percent cost-of-living increase.

When the steel mills went to half-time in 1980, the little town in Pennsylvania faced financial disaster. Many of the steel workers who attended the thriving Charismatic Christian Life Center were laid off. The rest of them went to half-time and took a cut in pay. The board met and voted to continue giving the pastor his salary even though the building bond program was a constant drain on the already strained budget.

When the young pastor heard the news, he reconvened the board and asked to be put on half salary. "My people are living with a cut in pay," he concluded, "so can I." Supernaturally, the Lord provided for the needs of the clergyman and his family.

While boards and budgets continue to determine the salaries of most pastors and clergy, there seems to be no set criteria for determining what is an equitable amount a pastor should receive. Even worse, little information is available to pastors or congregations to help them determine a common basis and criteria upon which to base the salary. Even the Scriptures, without a careful study, seem nebulous and vague.

In commissioning the pastors' salary survey, these and other objectives were kept in mind. J. Foy Johnson, district superintendent of the Peninsular Florida District Council of the Assemblies of God stated: "We do not have any kind of current information on this as most of our ministers are very tight-lipped on sharing this kind of information.

"Some churches are extremely thoughtful and generous. The size of the church has little to do with the salary package of the pastor. Some churches are stingy and unrealistic in their pastoral remuneration."

Scientifically Accurate

Believing a basis for salary appropriation was a necessary step to determining our goal, a NASA scientist and professional engineer licensed by the state of Florida, Frank S. Howard, was commissioned to produce a scientifically accurate survey. The questionnaire was formatted to meet the requirements for obtaining accurate and workable information. The questions were studied, reformatted and reviewed.

MINISTRIES sent out 300 randomly selected forms requesting the recipient to complete and forward the information back to us within one week.

To obtain scientific accuracy, it was required that the input data be normally distributed, that there be a wide range of pastors' salaries presented and that a variety in the sizes of churches be represented. Forty-five usable responses were received. The surveys received met all the necessary requirements needed for accurate statistical analysis.

The information submitted on the forms showed a concern and interest by the pastors to give accurate, complete data. It was observed that pastors receiving the largest salaries filled out the most complete forms. Pastors who were paid significantly less than the median (average) salary indicated they knew less about the income of their parishioners and generally did not complete the survey forms.

"Data analysis showed no abnormalities or dishonest answers in the input. Either would have biased the calculation results," said Howard. Pastors' salaries ranged from $9,840 to $43,000 with an average of $25,239. It was noted that 68.27 percent of the pastors' salaries fall within the range of $17,078 and $33,401.

Within 16 different denominations represented, 14 of the respondents were non-denominational and 13 were Assemblies of God. The other denominations from which information was drawn varied from Southern Baptist to Episcopal. Church sizes ranged from 40 attending a typical Sunday morning worship service to 3,000 attendees each Sunday.

Four old-line denominational churches were over 100 years old. Ten additional congregations were 50 years or older. The great-granddaddy was an Episcopal congregation 135 years old. Ten churches had been in operation for less than five years. The baby was a non-denominational congregation which was only one year old.

The churches' annual incomes showed a large variation. The minimum income was $13,000. The largest church income was $2 million. The average income was $169,680. Only nine of the churches employed one staff member who was the pastor. On the average, the churches employed 3.9 staff members. There were a total of 179 employees on staff at the 45 churches surveyed.

The average age of the pastors surveyed was 40.68 (almost 41) years old. The youngest was 29; the oldest, 60. They proved to be well-educated with an average of 4.95 years of education beyond high school.

The churches responding to the survey gave a total of $734,859 to missions in the last year. The minimum amount given was $150. The maximum was $160,000. The respondents reported a total of 1,824 conversions and 1,582 new members in 1983.

Key Is Average Member's Salary

It was determined that the pastors' salaries were most closely related to the average salaries of the people in the pastors' congregations. There was no significant correlation between the pastor's salary and any of the other data on the form. The pastor can and should expect to earn a corresponding salary to the average income of his parishioners.

"That's what the Scriptures teach," said one minister who has been a pastor for more than 20 years. In both the Old and New Testaments, examination proves that the priest and bishop were to make a salary consistent with the prosperity of the people. When the tithe was initiated in the Mosaic Law, the Israelites were instructed by God to give one tenth of their earnings to support the priest and the Levites. When the people prospered, the minister prospered.

Paul reaffirmed this teaching in 1 Corinthians 9:7-11, NIV:

"Who serves as a soldier at his own expense? Who plants a vineyard and does not eat of its grapes? Who tends a flock and does not drink of the milk? Do I say this merely from a human point of view? Doesn't the law say the same thing? For it is written in the Law of Moses: 'Do not muzzle an ox while it is treading out the grain.' Is it about oxen that God is concerned? Surely he says this for us, doesn't he? Yes, this was written for us, because when the plowman plows and the thresher threshes, they ought to do so in the hope of sharing the harvest. If we have sown spiritual seed among you, is it too much if we reap a material harvest from you?"

The average church budget distribution allots 35.28 percent of income to salaries. The pastor received 15.2 percent of that amount.

Pastors receive 69 percent of their income from their base salary, 20 percent from other benefits (housing allowance, utilities, etc.) and 11 percent from outside sources other than the church.

Fringe Benefits Unfair

In the area of benefits (retirement, hospitalization insurance, life insurance, etc.), pastors were found to be treated unfairly. Only 33 percent receive any retirement benefits. Almost all pastors (96 percent) are allowed to keep honorariums they receive for additional speaking engagements but only 13 percent are given severance pay. Seventy-eight percent of them are given freedom to travel but only 20 percent are reimbursed for improvements made on a church-owned parsonage.

With the growth of the non-denominational church, a retirement plan can present a problem. The Southern Baptist Annuity Board gives their denomination's pastors liberal and secure retirement benefits.

In Assemblies of God congregations, Johnson said, "We recommend to our churches that they consider a generous salary-benefit package for their pastors, taking into consideration" such benefits as housing, hospitalization, auto allowance, entertainment allowance and an incentive plan. They recommend annual review and adjustment, and they urge the church to participate with the minister in a retirement plan.

To take up the retirement gap, some church boards are using innovative methods. "Our church is independent and doesn't have access to a cooperative retirement program," said the board member of a small church discussing the problem of retirement for pastors. "We have set up an Individual Retirement Account (IRA) in our pastor's name. Each pay period the church and the pastor put in matching funds. It has worked well for us."

"Overall," reports Howard, "pastors should be paid proportionately but many of them are underpaid. The study showed that independent pastors are the best paid with an average of $26,110 a year. The Assemblies of God pastor receives the smallest average salary. Other denominational pastors fall in the middle receiving an average of $23,900 annually.

"This study clearly indicates that the benefits each pastor receives should be examined by almost every congregation," said Howard.

Mistreating God's Servants?

The lack of pastoral salary and benefit considerations by church members was amplified to Howard in an incident which occurred several years ago.

"Because I've been ordained by our local congregation," Howard relates, "I've been asked to conduct several marriage ceremonies. One of the weddings was in a small town about 30 miles from our home. My wife and I traveled to the dress rehearsal on Friday night. The father of the bride took great pains to show me his 35-foot sailboat, docked outside his back door. They lived on a waterfront lot. He took me into his garage and showed me his Corvette.

"The next day we went back to their town for the wedding and the reception. All together the wedding festivities and travel took more than eight hours. When we were leaving, the bride handed me an envelope. She told me my honorarium was inside. 'Daddy wanted to see it before I gave it to you,' she said, wearing a pleased smile.

"The mother of the bride walked us to the door. 'I put our honorarium in an envelope. Did my daughter give it to you?'

"We assured the mother she had and left. When I opened the envelope, it was empty. The father of the bride had obviously intercepted the honorarium which had been intended for me.

"The Lord spoke to me, 'This is the way many people treat My servants.' I've never forgotten the Lord's word. It changed my attitude about what my pastor receives."

In 1 Corinthians 9:14, NIV, Paul admonished, "The Lord has commanded that those who preach the gospel should receive their living from the gospel." Our survey shows that in addition to lacking an adequate benefits package, many pastors are not able to live on an equal par with their parishioners the way the Lord ordained in the Scriptures.

15

How Much Political Involvement by Churches Does the IRS Allow?

By James Guinn

James Guinn is a certified public accountant with the firm Guinn, Smith & Company in Irving, Texas, a firm that has provided C.P.A. services to over 250 religious organizations, helping more than 100 non-profit corporations receive tax-exempt status from the Internal Revenue Service.

Guinn earned a bachelor of business administration degree from Midwestern State University in Wichita Falls, Texas, and worked for Arthur Andersen & Company, one of the largest international public accounting firms.

Many times, especially in a major election year, churches and religious organizations have a tendency to want to become involved in the political process. Under certain circumstances some activity is permissible. However, involvement in these areas may be a very "dangerous" area for Internal Revenue Code Section 501(c)(3) organizations.

Internal Revenue Code Section 501(c)(3) precludes exemption for an organization which participates or intervenes in (including the publishing or distributing of statements) any political campaigns on behalf of any candidate for public office.

The first point to be noted is that this is an absolute prohibition. The intervention does not have to be substantial in terms of time or money to cause loss of exemption. Since there is no definitive rule, any intervention could result in loss of the organization's exempt status and denial of deductions to donor for gift, estate and income tax purposes. Regulations state that intervention in campaigns includes, but is not limited to, the making of oral statements or the publishing of written statements for or against any candidate.

Pertinent sections of revenue ruling 78-248 are quoted to illustrate the IRS position regarding political intervention, as follows:

"Whether an organization is participating or intervening, directly or indirectly, in any political campaign on behalf of or in opposition to any candidate for public office depends upon all of the facts and circumstances of each case. Certain 'voter education' activities conducted in a non-partisan manner may not constitute prohibited political activity under section 501(c)(3) of the code. Other so-called voter education activities, however, may be proscribed by the statute. The following situations are illustrative:

"**Situation 1**—Organization A has been recognized as exempt under section 501(c)(3) of the code by the Internal Revenue Service. As one of its activities, the organization annually prepares and makes generally available to the public a compilation of voting records of all Members of Congress on major legislative issues involving a wide range of subjects. The publication contains no editorial opinion, and its contents and structure do not imply approval or disapproval of any members of their voting records.

"The voter education activity of Organization A is not prohibited political activity within the meaning of section 501(c)(3) of the code.

"**Situation 2**—Organization B has been recognized as exempt under section 501(c)(3) of the code by the Internal Revenue Service. As one of its activities in election years, it sends a questionnaire to all candidates for governor in State M. The questionnaire solicits a brief statement of each candidate's position on a wide variety of issues. All responses are published in a voter's guide that it makes generally available to the public. The issues covered are selected by the organization solely on the basis of their importance and interest to the electorate as a whole. Neither the questionnaire nor the voter's guide, in content or structure, evidences a bias or preference with respect to the views of any candidate or group of candidates.

"The voter education activities of Organization B are not prohibited political activity within the meaning of section 501(c)(3) of the code.

"**Situation 3**—Organization C has been recognized as exempt under section 501(c)(3) of the code by the Internal Revenue Service. Organization C undertakes a voter education activity patterned after that of Organization B in situation 2. It sends a questionnaire to candidates for major public offices and uses the responses to prepare a voter's guide which is distributed during an election campaign. Some questions evidence a bias on certain issues. By using a questionnaire structured in this way, Organization C is participating in a political campaign in contravention of the provisions of section 501(c)(3) and is disqualified as exempt under that section."

An additional situation is as follows:

A church publishes a magazine in which the views of opposing candidates for a political office are printed. Items that could be interpreted to be intervention are:

1. Prominence is given to one candidate over the other by a magazine article location, use of color, photos, typesetting, etc.

2. Not all candidates for the office are given space in the magazine.

3. Prior and subsequent oral statements by church leaders, with regard to issues discussed in a church magazine by a particular candidate, that would indicate the "favored" candidate.

For example, two candidates' views regarding abortion are printed, one is pro-abortion and one is anti-abortion. If the church leader then makes oral statements that biblical teaching is anti-abortion, then the church has pinpointed the candidate for which the members should vote, and could be construed to be intervening in political campaigns.

Many religious leaders at times "walk a tightrope" with regard to political intervention, especially in the area of oral statements. However, it is a dangerous gamble with the stakes being loss of exempt status.

The more appropriate approach in light of IRS regulations is to urge church members and followers to vote their conscience after becoming educated about the candidates and prayerfully matching their views with God's Word.

16

Should Age Groups Be Separated?

By Wayne Jacobsen

Wayne Jacobsen has spent 10 years in pastoral ministry serving two separate congregations, one as senior pastor and the other as associate pastor. He is pastor of The Savior's Community in Visalia, California. As a free-lance writer, he has been published in several Christian magazines.

Every church I've attended divided people into ages and interest groups. The moment a family stepped out of its car at the church facility, the church programs partitioned them off in separate parts of the facility. Even in many home fellowship programs today the children are graciously excluded. One could attend most churches and never have the chance to pray with a 5-year-old, much less get to know one!

My discovery of the importance of intergenerational relationships came quite by accident. When I first came to this congregation, it was made up of five families. At that size we were not big enough to fragment by age group or any other factor. We became an extended family. We loved and cared for each other regardless of age differences.

During this time I saw the positive effects such an arrangement had on children and adults alike. The lives of our children opened up in the atmosphere of love and acceptance from adults. Their personal growth was enhanced because they felt as if they, too, were part of the body. For adults, our Christian experience became more vital as we learned from their simplicity and childlikeness.

This lifestyle taught us a lot about ministry. It is most effectively extended through personal relationships, not church programs. More was being done for our children out of their friendships with adults than we could ever hope to accomplish in a Bible class.

From child care to visitation, we learned the joys and sacrifices of personal ministry. As we learned it in the church, we also became more effective in reaching beyond it because we were free from our peer groups. I'm as comfortable now with seniors and 5-year-olds as I am with other young married couples, and that freedom significantly increases ministry opportunity.

For the first time in my pastoral ministry I knew I was serving not just parents, but whole families. I enjoyed conversations and activities with 6-year-olds, finding their needs every bit as important as those of their moms and dads. My effectiveness in helping parents with child-rearing increased significantly because of my touch with their children.

Our five families didn't get to stay very long. Others began to come to fellowship. Unconsciously we responded to growth by dividing into age and interest groups. Graded classes were added to our Sunday morning line-up. Informal relationships broke down. it wasn't as easy to seek out children after service with so many adults around.

But that time of church life as one extended family had whetted our appetite. We wanted to stop the flow toward fragmentation and continue to break age barriers.

Jesus rebuked His disciples for trying to separate children from the mainstream of His touch. Instead He welcomed children into His lap.

We've sailed against separating age groups because of God's leading.

We've met objections in fostering intergenerational relationships, such as:

"It's harder to get 'in the Spirit' with children around." For those of us who have always attended church with children safely tucked away with babysitters, worshipping with our 7-year-old fidgeting nearby is a task indeed. Yet, where else will that child learn to worship and understand that his relationship is as important to God as ours? And I question any notion of "spirituality" that can only function in a distraction-free environment. How real is that in our daily lives where distractions abound?

"I'm more comfortable with people I have something in common with." That we are! Just try to lead a Bible study that is as relevant to a third grader as it is to the college student. There's no program that guarantees it either. Both the third grader and the college student must be committed enough to the needs of the other to participate in a way that allows both of their lives to be touched.

We are all more comfortable with people our own age or who share our same interests. Relationships naturally fall that way. That, however, is less God's interest than it is the conditioning of a world with no greater vision than to keep people divided by age groups. Whenever we've moved past the superficialities of our daily activities, we've found we are not so different after all. We are all learning the same lessons, serving the same God and battling the same feelings. Really, how different is peer pressure on the playground from wanting to be liked by our co-workers?

"It's not working that smoothly." Intergenerational friendships don't just happen, they demand constant attention by everyone. It's never a perfected ideal. We're constantly working at it with our goal firmly in mind. This challenge is not for those who like things neatly in place and flowing smoothly. Opportunities for frustration abound; but so do the joys.

"It's demanding." That it is, for child and adult alike. Children get bored easily in adult settings; so we've learned to be a little less adult in some situations. Children must be taught how to participate with adults so they can enjoy with us. Children are shy and find it difficult to talk with adults so we've had to go the extra mile to draw them out by being interested in them and the things that are important to them.

All these excuses can be summed up in one expression: "It isn't easy!" Our flesh always draws us to the path of the least resistance, even though we rarely find easier to be better.

In spite of these obstacles we have found people willing to meet the challenge, and never regretting it. Sure there are easier ways, but learning to involve our children is no different from helping a new believer learn to participate in church life.

Building an intergenerational fellowship is a long process for which we need the guidance of the Holy Spirit. There are no shortcuts. But here are some helpful suggestions to begin the process.

First, discover and teach the congregation a biblical basis of community. The trend toward highly programmed churches has diminished understanding of community and of the individual importance of each person's gifts and needs. As the Spirit refreshes the concept of biblical community, showing us our calling to it and the joys that come from it, people will then be prepared to pay the price it requires.

Second, provide a place for these relationships to be experienced naturally. In our fellowship we use weekly house churches of 10-12 people. We form them only on the basis of geographical proximity. That puts a mix of age and interests in each group. This ensures that crossing generational barriers will not just be a matter of theology, but personal relationship. A single may wince about befriending little children, but will find himself doing it naturally if given the opportunity.

Children are involved in our home groups, and relationships with them are encouraged.

This does not mean there aren't appropriate times for children's classes, marriage seminars, singles' fellowships and the like. There are, but the church's lifestyle must be greater than the sum of isolated pockets of peer group relationships.

Third, have corporate times of worship that involve all age groups. We do that weekly in our house churches and once a month in our Sunday service. We vary the style greatly, sometimes having one of our children's ministry team members leading a more childlike worship and at other times a more adult form that we teach the children to follow with us.

Fourth, and this can be done without a change in church program, encourage people to foster relationships outside their peer group. As a pastor, model it for them. When you visit someone's home, spend some time with the children or play some games together with the whole family. Let singles (and their children) be "adopted" by families to the benefit of both.

Finally, let the concept of "intergenerational" be extended across other barriers, too. In our fellowship we take it in its broadened form to reach past any peer group boundary be it social standing, marital status, race, economic station or special interest. I urge people to seek out friendship with anyone they are normally uncomfortable with: poorer, richer, withdrawn, loud, lonely, outgoing, single, married and so forth.

Every time I hear my children talk about adults as their friends, see a single praying for a married couple, overhear a senior sharing insights with a young married person or hear someone tell of how they were loved by someone unexpected, I know why God chose it to be this way.

17

Are Church Boards a Scriptural Form of Government?

By Ansley Orfila

Ansley Orfila has pastored the First Assembly of God in Slidell, Louisiana, since 1968. Previously he served as pastor of the Bethlehem Baptist Church near Mangham, Louisiana, before affiliating with the Assemblies of God. He is a graduate of Louisiana College and received M.Div. and D.Min. degrees from New Orleans Baptist Theological Seminary. Thirty of his articles have been published by various periodicals.

Following three weeks' absence for a vacation and a denominational meeting, my wife and I returned home with a pleasant feeling. After nine years of service to this church, we both felt confident about having been away this long for the first time. But it wasn't long before that pleasant feeling burst like a pin-jabbed balloon.

One of the board members of our church called and informed me the board wanted to meet me the next night. Never before had they called a meeting; as pastor I'd always done that. Meeting that night would keep two of the board members from choir practice. It spelled t-r-o-u-b-l-e.

And trouble it was, as pastors experienced in serving churches with congregational forms of government will readily recognize. One of the board members with some savvy in getting rid of pastors had called the board together in my absence. No one seemed concerned that the manner in which the meeting had been called was contrary to our bylaws.

When I walked into the meeting, the decision was already settled—it was time for me to leave.

The board was not without reason for concern. Our attendance had slumped after a burst of growth from a bus ministry that was now dying. Worse, our church services had settled into a formality that resembled a well-kept cemetery. However, none of the board members had talked to me personally about these problems in the church, and none came when I called for times of special prayer. Years of progress under my leadership seemed forgotten by the board members as they fell in behind the man who told them they needed to fire the pastor.

I first thought I would resign, but I was concerned for the welfare of the church I loved. I had seen other churches that were manipulated from behind the scenes by a handful of persons who decided what pastors must do and when they must go. The end result of such activities was usually disastrous. So I decided to ask for a vote by the congregation (an amendment added to the bylaws soon after I came).

The man who led the opposition against me stood at the church en-

130

trance during services urging members to vote against me, but I won a vote of confidence by a substantial majority.

Later, while I was praying about the church's problems and about leaving, the Holy Spirit said, "You stay, and I'll solve your problems."

Events in the seven years since then have confirmed that I did the right thing by staying. We have completed our third building program with a beautiful sanctuary to house a growing congregation. Most important, the "cemetery" has come alive as the breath of God has blown over dead bones.

But the purpose of this article is not to announce, "I was right." As I have relived those painful days in my mind, I have come to see that many American churches with a congregational type of government are victims of unscriptural methods of conducting the business of the church.

Every kind of church polity has its unique advantages and problems. But one basic problem common to many churches in this country is implied by the term "church board." Of course, to obtain tax-exempt status, there must be a sufficient number of persons who are listed as officers of the nonprofit corporation, but that does not mean that the government requires churches to be governed by a board.

But many churches in America are operated by a board. The board meets monthly to fulfill such responsibilities as administration of finances, establishment of policies and supervision of the pastor. Occasionally, it is their responsibility to initiate the hiring or dismissal of a pastor. In such churches, the pastor administers the church on a day-to-day basis in accordance with the policies and financial provisions of the board.

This system is instituted with the best of intentions—to apply modern organizational structure to the church. It reflects the efficient and democratic American way of getting the job done. But, in fact, the term *board* (including, *board of deacons)* as well as the concept is unscriptural.

I recognize that not everyone agrees with the concept of congregational government. But denominations and congregations who agree need to take a fresh look at the Word of God to find biblical terms to identify leaders in the local church and scriptural methods for management.

Consider the following:

1. *Terminology.* The New Testament church was governed by elders, who were assisted by deacons (Acts 6:1-4; 20:17,28; Phil. 1:1; 1 Tim. 3:1-13; Heb. 13:7,17).

"Deacon" means "servant," so it is obviously unscriptural for a church to be ruled by deacons. "Elder" is used interchangeably with "bishop," which means "overseer" (Acts 20:17,28; Titus 1:5,7). In

the New Testament, each church was ruled by a group of elders—
men of spiritual maturity who were able teachers of the Word (1 Tim.
5:17).

2. *Qualifications.* The elders and deacons have definite scriptural
qualifications (Acts 6:3; 1 Tim. 3:1-13; Titus 1:6-9), unlike the "official board." In fact, churches often use terms such as "trustees"
or "executive board" to enable them to use officers who may be deemed
not fully qualified for the office of deacon. Lowering qualifications
below the New Testament standard while giving authority not given
in the New Testament sets the stage for trouble.

3. *Responsibilities.* The elders and deacons have definite scriptural
responsibilities.

Elders are overseers of the church (Acts 20:17,28); protectors of
the church against harm from within or without (Acts 20:28-30); rulers
of the church (1 Tim. 3:5; 5:17; Heb. 13:7,17); and teachers of God's
Word (1 Tim. 5:17; Titus 1:9). The church was led by a plurality of
elders among whom the pastor, as shepherd, was leader.

"Deacon" is derived from the Greek word *diakonos,* meaning "servant." Acts 6:1-6, which apparently records the origin of the office
of deacons, suggests the nature of their service. They could have significant authority, such as distribution of funds to the needy. However,
it was authority delegated to them in a specific area by the church's
leaders, not authority over all the church.

4. *Structure.* The New Testament allows for both strong leadership
by an individual pastor and the protection of a plurality of leadership.
No man should have an unlimited right to rule no matter what his life,
his doctrines or his decisions may be. On the other hand, a strong church
is built by the vision and leadership of a strong individual.

At the First Assembly of God in Slidell, Louisiana, where I serve,
we have changed from government by a church board to government
by elders and deacons.

All denominations have established patterns for governing themselves
and usually they give specific direction for methods by which the
churches within their ranks should be governed. Obviously ministers
and church members within such organizations are committed to conform to their accepted forms of government. Any changes must be
brought about by means which comply to their respective rules of order.

But there are thousands of churches empowered with the right to
determine their own form of government—some are members of church
bodies which permit considerable latitude in administrative matters,
others are independent churches. If your church is one of these, you
should ask yourself how closely it parallels what the New Testament
says. Then make it your goal to help pattern your church's organizational structure according to Scripture.

18

Should You Adapt Service Schedules to Special Needs?

By E. S. Caldwell

E. S. Caldwell is associate editor of *MINISTRIES: The Magazine For Christian Leaders*. He served the Assemblies of God as promotions coordinator for the Division of Home Missions and publicity director for the radio-TV department. He pastored 23 years in Idaho and Missouri. He is a graduate of Northwest College of the Assemblies of God and also attended Northwest Nazarene College.

T oo many small churches are being run to suit the cows. I'm talking about church schedules that were set in past generations to accommodate milking schedules. Thirty years ago I pastored such a church. It served families on a dozen farms, plus a few non-farm families from the village. The primary factor that determined when the services began was the farm families' schedule for chores, especially milking. Rightly so, other people willingly adjusted to the farm folks' locked-in routine. So Sunday school started a reasonable time after morning milking, and evening service commenced after the farm chores were finished and the workers were cleaned up and dressed for church.

My next charge was in a medium-sized city. Guess what? The church used exactly the same schedule even though not one farmer was in the congregation. Yes, some of the folk had moved from the farm to the city but they didn't own a cow anymore. Yet they were still worshipping by cow time. I made no effort to change it—I, too, was programmed to the convenience of absent bovines. "Isn't this the way we've always done it?"

My friend Duane Buhler didn't see it that way. He was pastoring in the small town of Cambridge, Idaho, when a huge hydroelectric dam was being built in Hell's Canyon, some 30 miles distant. Construction workers were housed at the dam site and their families lived in Cambridge and other surrounding towns.

Duane wanted to reach these people for the Lord. But he was up against their Sunday schedule, which (for a church-minded family) was: go to morning service, eat at a restaurant, shop at a supermarket and skip the evening service because it started at 8 p.m. and ended too late for the worker to drive to his housing at the job and be up before dawn.

So Duane moved the Sunday evening starting time to 5 p.m. (It was still daylight when the people got out. Unheard of in those days!) Several workmen and their families became a regular part of the Sunday evening crowd—more than doubling attendance for that service.

Looking back, Duane's decision seems only logical, but to many fellow pastors in the region in those days, such radical action marked

Duane as a kind of maverick. "Next he'll be taking out the mourners' bench!"

I called Duane yesterday (pastor of Calvary Assembly's Christian Faith Center, Nampa, Idaho) and discovered that he's still tinkering with hallowed time schedules. He recently shifted the choir practice to 8:15 p.m. Why? "For the sake of the working women who wanted to sing in the choir but couldn't get to church for the 7 p.m. practice sessions."

It proved to be a good move. No choir members were lost; several were added. Not only are the director and choir members pleased, the church is now blessed by a bigger, better choir. More important, people who wanted to be involved are no longer denied the opportunity by arbitrary practice schedules.

Ask yourself if your schedule of services and auxiliary activities cuts out people who might participate if a change in a day or time were made. And don't stop by asking only yourself, or your own ruts of habit may prevail. Poll your church people, especially those who miss a lot of services. Ask them if another time would make it possible for them or other members of their families to attend your midweek service, or ladies' group, or youth meeting, or whatever else your church might offer.

Carefully and objectively evaluate the results of your poll. Discuss the potential benefits of adjusted schedules with your leadership. Listen to objections. Don't listen to voices that say, "But we've always done it this way." It may only be the lowing of the cows.

Every small church that wants to grow must courageously face earnest self-analysis, and one of the easiest areas to analyze is your schedule of meetings. No financial outlay is required to make a change here. But members who are comfortable with present time slots must be willing to pay the price of rearranging their habits in behalf of others. It calls for small but annoying sacrifices.

For example, a timid widow would come on Sunday nights but the late dismissal time means she has to return to her home after dark, and it frightens her to enter her house then. Or the parents of school-age youngsters no longer come to the Sunday night service because experience shows they will have an awful time getting the kids to school the next day.

But Homer and Helen have their Sunday television favorites and moving the service time to 6 p.m. would interfere, so they nix any proposed time change. Someone needs to question whether the church's ministry is to be shrunk to fit Homer and Helen or expanded to include a dozen, a score, or even more who are excluded by a starting time that is impractical or even impossible for them.

And what about the midweek service? When the meeting time was first established, it was ideal for most church people. But is it now? How many have you asked lately?

Times are changing, especially work schedules in typical American families. "The most remarkable trend has been the labor force participation of women with preschool children," says Bryant Robey, editor of *American Demographer* magazine. Nearly half of the mothers with preschoolers worked outside the home, and two-thirds of the mothers of children 6 through 17 years of age held jobs. What does that mean for your schedule of church activities? Can you expect a working mother to drive home from her 9-to-5 job, prepare supper, get the kids and herself ready and drive to church in time for the start of your 7 p.m. meeting? She may be a supermom but she's not a miracle-worker.

Working mothers already carry an unfair load of guilt without the church doubting their spirituality because they can't be in church every time the doors are open.

How do you measure spirituality? One way—a faulty measure—is by the quantity of services attended (four services weekly equals a high score; one, a low score). But this equation omits such factors as job and school schedules, and gives an edge to retired, childless people, not to mention pushy types who know that regular attendance is the route to leadership in a church when they cannot gain it anywhere else.

Remember, though, that even good folk resist change—so don't force it. Give any suggested schedule change a little time so the idea can sell itself.

If your research indicates that some meetings need their starting time altered, proceed with caution. Share the results of your poll with as many churchgoers as possible one-on-one. Beware of presenting a change to a vote until you're sure of the outcome.

It may even be wise to consider changing the day of the week some activities are conducted. This is especially true of youth meetings which frequently conflict with school events. Some oldsters expect the young people to forego school events, especially athletic competitions, whenever they fall on a church night. Some young people may opt for church instead of basketball, but the question is: Which is more important, getting a few kids to conform to the spoilsports' ideas or getting increased attendance at the young people's services?

Perhaps greater participation in the women's group could be accomplished by meeting at night instead of in the afternoon. Suggest that the ladies discuss the idea with those who are not attending. But again, proceed with caution, suggest, don't insist. Sometimes "submission" carries a high price tag. So tread lightly.

If yours is a small church, make it your goal to stop the leaks so it will be a full church.

19

Should the Day of Pentecost Be a Special Day?

By Harry Fullilove

The newly appointed director of spiritual outreach of the Fellowship of Charismatic Lutherans in Ministry (FCLM), Harry Fullilove has pastored churches for 26 years. In his new post, Fullilove will travel world-wide with the message of Pentecost.

I attended a convention last year where an evidently gifted Lutheran pastor gave a great sermon, but he dismayed me when he spoke about "the two great festivals of the Church: Christmas and Easter." I wanted to stand up and cry out: "What about the third one—Pentecost?"

However, he is not alone in his oversight. The Christian church as a whole neglects the importance of Pentecost. The clear reason is that it has never truly come to grips with the Holy Spirit—as a Person, a Gift and a Power.

Alan Walker, a popular Methodist writer in Australia, once said: "When there is an eclipse of the doctrine of the Spirit, a period of deism—of a distant, irrelevant, unreal God— develops." The tragedy of much of contemporary church life is this continued unwillingness to allow the Holy Spirit to speak.

One of the problems is that a spirit of fear envelops those who carry the instruments of power in so many denominational churches. They are so deathly afraid of the "excesses" of Charismatic renewal that they lean overboard to be uninvolved with the Holy Spirit. So we have whole conferences and conventions that avoid the greatest phenomenon of our time—the worldwide flow of the Spirit in just about every denomination, especially in the Third World.

I had the privilege of visiting Costa Rica last year and seeing that the Charismatic movement there was so alive that it was dominant in fully 80 percent of all churches, and instrumental in the massive growth of the Protestant churches. Yet those local churches that ignored or opposed the Holy Spirit movement remained dormant and cold. During the past decade the Protestant church there has grown from 3 percent of the population to 20 percent—a clear evidence of the surge of the Spirit. The same is true in Guatemala, Honduras and Nicaragua.

I was impressed by the words of Rev. Charles Boaz, an American Lutheran Church pastor in Baltimore, who writes: "When we lose anything we always try to replace it with something else. When character is gone, we try to replace it with reputation. When courage leaves us, we cover it up with bragging. When faith is weak, we become strong in intellectual rationalization. When fire from heaven is lacking, we compensate by manufacturing our own. As the church loses its power, it trusts the forms.''

Walker points us to ''a distant irrelevant, unreal God''; Boaz sees ''the church (that) loses its power, trusts the forms.'' The connection is so obvious, yet we fail to realize it. Hence Pentecost is safely accepted as ''the birthday of the Church,'' but the Spirit Himself is downplayed.

So Pentecost is a neglected festival in most churches. The irony is, that in some liturgical churches, including Roman Catholic churches, the day of Pentecost receives more attention than it does in churches that profess to be Spirit-filled.

Yet Pentecost, as seen in Acts, chapter 2, falls right in line with the master plan of God. It was the time for the first great apostolic sermon:

''Jesus of Nazareth, a man attested to you by God with mighty works and wonders and signs which God did through Him in your midst, as you yourselves know—this Jesus, delivered up according to the definite plan and foreknowledge of God, you crucified and killed by the hands of the lawless men. But God raised Him up'' (Acts 2:22-24).

The *kerygma* here contains both the events of Christmas (Incarnation) and Easter (Resurrection), with their challenge to personal faith in Christ:

''Repent, and be baptized every one of you in the name of Jesus Christ for the forgiveness of your sins; and you shall receive the gift of the Holy Spirit'' (Acts 2:38).

Here is the key to evangelism and church growth—the mighty gospel that calls for repentance and faith in Jesus as Savior and Lord. And He is alive!

Praise God for the Christmas-Easter proclamation! Yet that is not enough.

The continued growth of the church depended upon the Holy Spirit. The events recorded in Acts 2:1-3 are more than a backdrop for Peter's sermon—they are the evidence that what he is about to say is true. He says:

''These men are not drunk...but this is what was spoken by the prophet Joel: 'And in the last days it shall be, God declares, that I will pour out my Spirit upon all flesh' '' (Acts 2:15-17).

Pentecost was a festival to be remembered—not just because it marked the lively birth of the church, but also because it revealed the supernaturally empowered and motivated men evangelizing with a holy joy and freedom.

Pentecost should really be our *greatest* festival. Why do I say that? Because Christmas and Easter are basically memorial feasts of a past event, whereas Pentecost is an opportunity for God's people to enter into a new experience of God. We cannot reenact the events of that day some 2,000 years ago, but we can allow the Holy Spirit to "fill our cups" and "permeate our temples" with new life and freedom.

I am not advocating some sort of ceremonial recognition of the day of Pentecost; dead ceremony serves only to embalm reality in ritual. But how tragic it is for pastors and congregations that are today participating in the reality of the outpouring of the Spirit to let that significant day pass by totally ignored.

What were those 120 disciples doing that first Pentecost? They were speaking in unknown tongues "the mighty works of God." They were informally, yet in glorious harmony, praising the Lord for His wonderful power and overpowering love. They were telling Him how much they appreciated that He was not "a distant, irrelevant, unreal God," but was truly near, relevant and real. This early church was not interested in continuing forms and traditions. Forms and traditions had crucified their Lord! They were caught up with the glorious newness of the gospel and its power in those who believed.

It would be a refreshing event in our churches at Pentecost if we would put our bulletins and hymnals in the pew racks. That would free us to raise our hands as "people of joy" so that we could praise the Lord for His wonderful exploits. And we could share with each other, individually and collectively, "the mighty works of God." Perhaps that sounds like a regular service in your church, but in many it would be a Pentecost worship service never to be forgotten!

There is a hymn in my denomination's new hymnal that speaks of "the Church of Christ, in every age beset by change, but Spirit-led." I can attest that change has been its history, and even more today. But "Spirit-led"? How is the contemporary church in America being "Spirit-led" in today's world?

The hymnwriter must have felt somewhat the same. He says that this "Church of Christ...must claim and test its heritage and keep on rising from the dead." The only power that can raise our church from the dead is the Holy Spirit. To ask for a spiritual resurrection must be a cry to heaven for the Holy Spirit to fall on us.

I am not calling for "another Pentecost," for there can never be one, but I do believe that Pentecost Day (check your calendar for the date) can be an opportunity for the Holy Spirit to come upon our churches in a new way—if we really want Him to.

Nor am I trying to tell you what your church should do to give recognition to Pentecost Sunday. But I am asking every Spirit-filled pastor to seek the direction of God prayerfully. Ask Him what kind of special activity would be pleasing to Him in the place to which He has appointed you.

If we cry to God, He will come upon us in salvation, peace and power. Then we will be on our way to genuine renewal. Our neighbors will be amazed and perplexed, and certainly no longer indifferent. It may not be long before our churches become as crowded on Pentecost Sunday as they are at Christmas and Easter. Pentecost will no longer be the ''Forgotten Festival.'' May that day come, Lord!

20

How Should a Pastor Receive a Traveling Ministry?

By Judson Cornwall

Judson Cornwall describes himself as a traveling teacher. He has spent over 50 years in the Christian ministry, nearly 30 of those years as a pastor serving in four churches and the remaining 20 years as a traveling minister. He also taught Bible school for four years and authored a number of books.

In the past few years a fresh appreciation has come for the five-fold ministries Christ gave the Church. We also acknowledge that the apostle, prophet, evangelist or teacher is often a traveling person, while the very nature of the ministry of a pastor calls for residency among his people. In a broad sense then, Paul said that Christ gave resident ministers and traveling ministers "for the equipping of the saints for the work of ministry, for the edifying of the body of Christ" (Eph. 4:12, NKJV).

That each of these ministers is gifted with the grace of God is scripturally declared, but that each is distinctively different is obvious to even a casual observer. Someone gifted in alliteration has described the differences in saying that the apostle governs, the prophet guides, the evangelist gathers, the pastor guards and the teacher grounds. So be it. Thank God for the differences, but the very fact of difference means that a local congregation needs exposure to ministries that are diverse from the ministry of the resident pastor. The pastor needs the input of these traveling ministries, but how does he recruit, receive and respond to these traveling men and women?

Acceptance

If the formula Paul gave the church at Rome is followed, there will be no difficulties. "Therefore receive one another, just as Christ also received us, to the glory of God," he wrote (Rom. 15:7). A traveling minister must be accepted as an active member in the body of Christ, fulfilling a calling as valid as pastoring, if that ministry is to be viable to a congregation. Different does not mean inferior or superior; it merely means different. A traveling minister should not be viewed as a novice needing practice, nor as a superstar demanding pampering. The pastor and the traveling minister are co-laborers in the Lord's kingdom. Each must respect the other in all things or they will not work together successfully. Christ's acceptance of them by calling them into ministry must be the basis for mutual acceptance of local and traveling ministries and ministers. They are interdependent, never independent. Neither develops well without the input and ministry of the other, for none is the body of Christ; we are but members of that body.

Advance Contact

The failure to plan ahead often deprives a local congregation of quality traveling ministry, for the very nature of the task of a traveling minister requires considerable lead time in his planning. Scheduling a year in advance is quite common for traveling ministers, and some must plan up to two years in advance. This is especially true for ministry that will be conducted outside a local church, such as conferences, camp meetings, city-wide rallies and so forth. The logistics of these meetings require advance commitment before the local committee can secure the facilities.

There are few traveling ministers sitting by their phones just waiting for a call to minister, even though they receive repeated contacts which indicate many pastors have this impression. (They can't sit and wait and go out and preach at the same time.) Look ahead, plan ahead and schedule ahead of your need. Those who feel this is unspiritual should remind themselves that God is a God of eternity who sees next year more clearly than we see today. Spur-of-the-moment action is no more godly than advance planning, although, obviously, the Spirit is capable of both actions.

In the interest of saving time, many pastors prefer to make the initial inquiry by telephone. This is probably beneficial for both parties. Whatever arrangements are made by phone should always be confirmed in writing; some of us have hopelessly short memories. If the initial contact is made by letter, a listing of several acceptable dates usually shortens the scheduling process.

Arrangements

Once a date has been scheduled, further arrangements need to be made. As the scheduled time approaches, you will want to recontact your chosen minister to request a photograph and some sort of biographical material. At this time, it would be courteous to invite him or her to bring along his or her spouse or family member, but specify what responsibility you accept in this invitation. Are you offering to pay for the ticket, or just the additional motel expense? Traveling ministers spend many lonely weeks away from their homes, so an invitation to bring along a family member is always heartwarming, even when it is not feasible.

It is also wise to find out what type of accommodation is desired and if books, records or tapes will be brought for sale; if so, does the minister want the church to be responsible for the sales? It is only fair to report the number of services you are planning and in which of them your guest will be ministering. If anything special has been scheduled, such as a ministers' breakfast, a staff luncheon or anything that will affect his time schedule, you should make it known at this point in your relationship. Be sure to ask him ahead of time if he is willing to minister at "extra" events such as a staff or pastors' meeting, rather than simply scheduling it and informing him that he is supposed to speak. Help your traveling minister serve your congregation at his best level by giving him ample time to prepare. Surprises often produce shoddy ministry; advance preparation leads to excellence of performance.

Accommodations

Unless the guest minister has requested otherwise, or there are no such accommodations available in the area, a motel or hotel offers the best accommodations for the traveling minister. A time away from people is necessary if one is to be at his best for public ministry. Even Jesus insisted on getting away from the crowd from time to time.

Perhaps nothing is more disconcerting to the traveling minister than to arrive and find that no provision has been made for his lodging. Being driven from motel to motel while the pastor tries to "pull rank" to get him registered is embarrassing to both the pastor and the traveling person. It is difficult for him to feel wanted when it becomes obvious that no preparation has been made for him. Double-check the registration the day before the speaker is scheduled to arrive, and, if reasonably convenient, pre-register the guest so that he can be taken directly to his room. That is a sure indication he is both wanted and welcome.

Pastors who seldom use the facilities of a motel may find it difficult to comprehend how cold, sterile and commercial a motel room can seem. There is nothing homelike about it. A bouquet of flowers, a basket of fruit or a box of candy with a welcoming note attached will be like a sunbeam on a cloudy day. Flowers are often provided for women in traveling ministry but omitted for traveling men on the mistaken assumption that they are not masculine. Still, flowers give any room a homey touch, and although men will seldom purchase flowers for themselves, they appreciate having them in the room. The little touch of femininity that a bouquet can bring into a room is often a balancing factor which helps temper the loneliness that accompanies a traveling ministry.

If it is absolutely necessary to place the minister in someone's home, be certain the home offers a considerable measure of privacy, without undue noise from small children. Placing a traveling person in a home with a troubled marriage or other family problems in the hopes that some counseling may occur is grossly unfair to all parties concerned.

In all circumstances, make ample arrangements for eating. Not all motels have acceptable restaurants, and some of them do not allow the meals to be charged to the room. If such a situation exists, a cash advance is far superior to asking the speaker to advance his own money and keep receipts to be presented to the church treasurer later.

Today's best motels are often far from everything. They are placed for the convenience of travelers, not visitors. Arranging to leave a car for the speaker's use is a courtesy far rarer than you might expect. If a car is not available or was not desired by the speaker, assign a person to act as chauffeur for the speaker, and have an understood schedule for picking him up and delivering him after services. I have actually experienced having to hitchhike to and from my motel to the convention site because this provision was not offered.

A final suggestion in the accommodations is to have a typed agenda of all services, appointments and schedules with home and church numbers that can be called. This should be in the hotel room right next to the flowers or fruit basket. Let the traveling minister begin to adjust himself mentally before the first service.

Association

Once the speaker is in his hotel room, your responsibility to him has not ceased. Don't just "dump" him and merely wait to see him function in the pulpit during the services. Budget in advance some time to be with this person. The richness of his experience can enlarge your own perspective, and the vision with which you work can enlarge his vision. Perhaps you can arrange to share a meal each day with your guest. Sometimes it is wise to have other members of the church staff join you in this time of fellowship. This time slot should be arranged for the mutual convenience of both of you. If you do this, make sure this is a pleasant, relaxed time of *fellowship*—not an opportunity to "pick the brain" of the guest. Don't make him "pay for" his meal (which he then may not get a chance to eat) by answering all the questions you've been saving up for just such an opportunity.

Unless your guest indicates a desire for extended fellowship, don't consume his every waking moment. Allow him or her some time alone. You will penalize the services if you drain all of his energies between the services. All batteries need to be recharged regularly. Don't exhaust a person and then rationalize your guilt by saying, "I'll be praying that God will give you rest at the next place." That's what they told him at the last place.

A gentle but honest questioning, to determine if he has any shopping needs, shows consideration. To be out of toothpaste or shaving cream can be a real irritant in the motels that do not have a gift shop in them. Even the most experienced travelers fail to pack everything that is needed every time they go on the road.

If the traveler has been on the road for several successive conferences, he or she might deeply appreciate a family situation. How about taking him to your home to share a meal with your family, or at least have your family join the two of you at a restaurant. We all need to keep in touch with the family unit. (Again, make this a relaxed time—no counseling or question-and-answer sessions, please.)

One further word concerning your association with your ministerial guest: find out if he or she would like some protection from people after a service. Some like to mingle with the congregation after a service; some enter into personal ministry after preaching. But others have given every ounce of emotional energy they possess while ministering in the pulpit, and they do not desire to have to repreach the sermon on a one-to-one basis, or hear about problems for which they have no answers. A staff member assigned to conduct the speaker quickly to the pastor's office or directly to the motel after the service often becomes a true deliverer to the speaker.

Acknowledgement

Some pastors explain the financial arrangements at the very beginning, but most tend to leave the guest wondering about how he will be rewarded financially. Those who minister to the Church at large are usually expected to finance their own ministries and to "live by faith." This often means accepting a single offering as a love offering for an entire conference. Seldom is a plane ticket, or money for one, sent in advance. It has happened to me only twice in 15 years of traveling ministry. Furthermore, it is not too unusual for the speaker to have to use his personal credit card as security when registering at the motel. The church's only front money has been for advertising. Everything else is financed by the guest speaker, but he is often left guessing his financial fate until he is taken to the airport at the end of the services. A brief explanation of how the finances will be handled can relax tensions in the traveling minister, making him even more valuable in his ministry.

Determining how much to give a guest speaker is a problem for many pastors. One way is simply to take a "love offering" and give whatever comes in, hoping it will be sufficient. If you elect to use the "love offering" system, please be honest in the way it is done. Don't choose the night with the lowest attendance to take that offering. If an offering is declared to be a love offering for the minister, it is deceitful to take part of it for advertising, overhead or anything else. If the offering is to be shared between the church and the guest, say so. Integrity in the handling of offerings is vital to the life-flow of a congregation.

In trying to determine a fair honorarium, some pastors overlook the days of traveling to and from the service and count only the actual days of ministry. Many people also overlook the fact that the traveling person must maintain a home, a family and an office, as well as recover all traveling expenses, entirely from what he receives from his ministry. It is his only source of income.

The local pastor may have difficulty presenting a check that greatly exceeds his personal salary because he overlooks the harsh reality that the traveling person receives none of the usual pastoral benefits. He receives no housing or car allowance, no paid days off, no sick leave, no vacation time and no entertainment allowance or expense account. He has no office, no secretary, no free phone or mailing service. He does not receive a check 52 weeks of the year; he has no hospital or life insurance paid for by a church; and, of course, he has no retirement program. All of these benefits the pastor enjoys must come out of the traveling man's honorarium.

What is a fair measurement for an honorarium? Perhaps Paul gave a standard of measurement to Timothy when he wrote, "Let the elders who rule well be counted worthy of double honor, especially those who labor in the word and doctrine" (1 Tim. 5:17). That the "double honor" of which Paul spoke concerns the honorarium is made clear by other translators. Norle translates this phrase, "considered worthy of a double reward." Williams says, "considered as deserving twice the salary they get," and the *New English Bible* puts it as "reckoned worthy of a double stipend." Perhaps a beginning basis for determining the honorarium might be double the weekly salary of the senior pastor (and don't forget to allow for non-cash benefits). It may well be that the cost of the guest's air fare should be paid above this.

A final suggestion: present the speaker with his check before he leaves town. Promising to mail it to him as soon as the offerings are counted is a withholding of earned wages against which James speaks with prophetic sternness. Financing a great portion of a series of services and having to leave town with only a promise of better things to come leaves one feeling empty. Too often the check is never sent.

Afterglow

Usually the pastor feels he has discharged his obligations when he deposits the speaker at the airport after the meetings are through. But he can share two further kindnesses with this traveling minister. If tapes of the services have been made available to the congregation, send a set of these tapes to the speaker's office or home. He really does not need to crowd them into his luggage, but he would appreciate having them awaiting him when he returns home.

After a week or so, few pastors will write a thank-you letter sharing their observations of the fruit of the ministry. This is very seldom done in the circles in which I travel, but when it is done it is deeply appreciated, for the traveling person rarely sees the fruit of his labors. When the pastor shares a report, it puts fresh courage in the traveler's spirit and helps him forget his weariness.

How do we receive a traveling ministry? With care in our choice, with candor in the contact, with helpfulness in hospitality, with joy in the joining of ministries, with honor in the honorarium and with gratitude for this gift to the Church. Perhaps the pungent words of Jesus would set the tone of our relationship with traveling ministries: " 'Inasmuch as you did it to one of the least of these My brethren, you did it to Me' " (Matt. 25:40, NKJV). Let's receive one another this way.

21

How Can You Revitalize Your Church Library?

By Lorraine Burson

Lorraine E. Burson has been a church librarian for 26 years and for the last 21 years librarian at the Burlingame Baptist Church, Portland, Oregon. Ms. Burson also is a free-lance writer, church librarian consultant and teacher. She has conducted classes, workshops and seminars on church librarianship in churches and for groups.

Have you got any books that will tell me what a wedding was like during Jesus' day?'' queried a breathless fifth-grade teacher who had rushed into the library just five minutes before the Sunday school opening. Library staffers quickly stepped to the reference section of the church library and helped the teacher locate the information in a Bible dictionary, an encyclopedia, and a volume of the Bible lands and customs. The teacher jotted down a few notes and rushed from the room.

An elderly man, facing cataract surgery, approached the church librarian with an anxious statement: "My eyes won't let me spend much time reading anymore, but I sure miss the hours I used to spend studying the Bible. A friend told me to come and see you, but I really don't know what you can do to help!'' The librarian steered him to the tape collection, explaining that the Bible was on tape in both the King James and the New International Versions in the library. There were also, she added, Bible study and teaching tapes by noted scholars and preachers.

The librarian then led the elderly gentleman to a section of books labeled "Large Print." Here were Bibles, Bible studies, devotionals and biographies. The man's expression brightened as he visualized the new world opened up to him in the church library.

A young woman leading a neighborhood Bible club for children in her home wandered into the library one Sunday to browse for new ideas in presenting to them the life of Moses. She was directed to the card catalog in which filmstrips, slides, tapes, recordings, maps, pictures, flannelgraphs and flashcard stories were revealed, all on the life of Moses. The woman searched out the items and drew up a schedule involving a multi-media approach to the series of lessons.

For the introductory exercise she planned to use slides to show the dress, houses and living habits of people in Old Testament times. The next lesson involved a flannelgraph study of Moses' birth, which she used along with the story on tape. Later lessons were to utilize varying media from the library collection. She was delighted with a church library that allowed her to use audiovisuals creatively and effectively.

These three illustrations point out the value of a multi-media program through the libraries in our churches. Books have always been an integral part of libraries. Books are tremendously important! Elizabeth Barrett Browning wrote, "No man can be called friendless when he has God and the companionship of good books."

Sherwood Wirt reveals in his book *Getting Into Print* that God had not been a living presence in his soul, though he was a minister serving a small church, until one summer when he read Norman Grubb's book, *Rees Howells, Intercessor*. The reading of this book shook his whole chain of spiritual values.

J. Allen Petersen wrote in the May 1982 issue of "The Christian Librarian" about a close friend who challenged him, a new minister at the time, to become filled with the Holy Spirit. Chastised by this assumed criticism, he turned to a study of the Holy Spirit by several dedicated Bible teachers, including Finney, Oswald Smith and Andrew Murray. These books became his constant companion, and were credited with changing his life and perspective in the process.

Charles Colson attributed his changed life from a president's "hatchet" man to one of God's chosen leaders and a prison reformer to the reading of a small book, *Mere Christianity* by C.S. Lewis, given to him by a Christian friend.

Audiovisuals' Great Value

Thank God for good books! But in today's electronic technology we are not limited only to books in our search for help, answers or guidance. Although we acknowledge their eminence among media, the library that has *only* books is missing a growing opportunity to provide spiritual encouragement and training through other avenues.

Consider the benefits of using audiovisuals: any subject taught can be given more appeal and be made more accurate; stories and illustrations come alive; Bible lessons are recreated and made real and living; studies are put in a language students comprehend; lesson applications are emphatically driven home and remembered long afterwards because audiovisuals reach and teach through the eye-gate (it is said that students remember only 30 to 40 percent of what they hear, but 80 percent of what they see); history is bridged; Bible customs, homes and families are clearly illustrated; students' emotions and intellect are touched; attitudes are changed; decisions and action are hastened. There is indeed great value in reading, listening *and* viewing Christian materials.

Defined, media are any objects or symbols as seen by the eye, or heard by the ear, and used effectively to make a lesson clear to the beholder. "Multi" means many. Multi-media refers to a host of media types, housed and used together.

The concept of multi-media has been around for many centuries. John Amos Comenius, a great Christian scholar who died in 1671, and who is recognized by many educational historians as the founder of the audiovisual emphasis, wrote, "The sense of hearing should always be conjoined with that of sight, and the tongue should be trained in combination with the hand. The subjects that are taught should not merely be taught orally, and thus appeal to the ear alone, but should be pictorially illustrated...If this is done, it is incredible how much it assists a teacher to impress his instructions on the pupil's mind."

Even before John Amos Comenius' statement, Jesus had used visuals in His teaching: to the fishermen, He spoke of fish and nets; to the farmer He used the illustration of the sower and the seed. In the Old Testament, media were used again and again to convey God's messages to His people—media such as festivals, the tabernacle, a plumbline, sand, coins, birds, a rainbow and many others. There are scriptural passages, furthermore, that imply God's intention for us to use both our eyes and ears in teaching/learning situations. Proverbs 20:12 reads, "Ears that hear and eyes that see—the Lord has made them both" (NIV). Jesus taught His disciples in Matthew 13:16, "But blessed are your eyes because they see, and your ears because they hear" (NIV). Our reborn interest in multi-media is then scripturally proper.

In recent years people have not only rediscovered and magnified the concept, they have become accustomed to using it—in business, in school, and even in homes for fun and pleasure. Today's libraries, in order to compete, began offering a variety of materials to appeal to the interests and habits being developed by their parents.

Church Libraries' Role

Churches, too, face the alternative of advancing to meet the problems of today with today's technical knowledge, or of regressing into the past. It is imperative that they catch up! Today's church libraries *must* rise to meet the educational changes and trends, and include in their collections the multi-media to meet needs. No other library is equipped to circulate the supportive Bible study materials, or Christian living, witnessing, instructional or counseling materials that meet the doctrinal leanings of the church in which it is housed. The public library cannot. The school libraries cannot. But the church library can dispense a wide range of materials to strengthen and broaden the teachings and ministries of the church.

Has your library caught up with today's changes and trends? Does your library include multi-media?

Several years ago leaders in my church, some of them business men and women well used to working with audiovisuals, began approaching the church library with new concepts and needs for administering their church-related responsibilities. For example, an adult Sunday school teacher wished to illustrate Paul's three journeys by using transparencies on an overhead; the chairman of the Christian education board sought a cassette tape series in which to instruct a class of new teachers; the pastor learned of several highly recommended tapes to use in his pre-marital counseling; teachers in the children's departments desired filmstrips, tapes and other media to aid in new creative methods of teaching; and our youth pastor became enthusiastic over presenting a youth program on video. Out of necessity, our library's collection was enlarged to meet the new demands.

The multi-media library is the resource center of our church. It administers tools, resources and services for spiritual growth and entertainment to all church-sponsored programs, activities and organizations. It reaches out to church boards, committees, missionary conferences, marriage clinics, classes and to individuals of all ages, through multi-media. It offers up-to-date college catalogs for potential students. It distributes missionary prayer letters to encourage concern and understanding of our missionaries' needs. It houses puppets to enliven story hours. It maintains a visual Scripture file to enhance the memorizing of God's Word. It dispenses clippings and pamphlets through a vertical file to apprise the readers of current religious happenings.

It is a place where those who work with people, ideas or problems can come and find a variety of information and materials at their fingertips.

Starting Multi-Media Library

Establishing such a program as this should be taken seriously, and several steps should be taken to secure its incorporation into the existing church library. Just what would the uniting of books and other media in the church library entail in terms of space, time, personnel and procedural changes? Several well-planned steps would ensure a smooth transition.

Step 1. Assembling the collection.

Every church has materials for a "visual aids" library. They may be unorganized, with materials in forgotten closets or hanging unnoticed on classroom walls, but the visuals are there. A search of the church would be the first order. This will help determine what is already available and what may need to be purchased. It might be prudent to enlist the support of the pastor or other leadership in obtaining the release of audiovisuals from the various church departments.

Reorganizing media into one central location is good stewardship of the Lord's money. It can prevent duplication and waste.

Step 2. Space.

With the addition of new materials must come also new allotment of space, new cupboards and/or shelving. With a bit of rearranging of existing shelves, some media may be displayed without further building projects. However, small items, such as slides, filmstrips and tapes are best stored in cupboards or drawers built to their specifications. A retired carpenter in our church kindly volunteered his services and built several units for media, including a compact cassette tape cupboard which could store 1,200 tapes.

Bins can easily be constructed for recordings, and units built to hold large, hanging manila folders for flat pictures, maps and charts. Compact boxes could be used initially for flannelgraphs, flashcard stories, transparencies and vertical file collections. Eventually four-drawer, steel filing cabinets could be obtained. A carefully laid-out plan of available floor space and storage units will ensure adequate room for each media added to the collection.

Step 3. The library personnel.

When additional services and materials are included in an already existing program, usually more persons will be needed to provide for them. It would be poor planning to overload library staffers with too many new duties. Recruit the necessary personnel to keep the work current and available to users.

Step 4. System of organization.

The most logical system of organization is the one that allows for the most convenient use of media in your situation. Four possible arrangements are:

1. An alphabetical arrangement by title;
2. A classified system, usually according to Dewey Decimal classification;
3. A numerical method by accession number, which is assigned in the order of receipt in the library;
4. A chronological arrangement according to the books of the Bible.

All media need not be arranged according to the same system in your library. Choose the system that works best for you.

Step 5. Processing for circulation.

Most media should be accessioned (numbered). The possible exceptions are flat pictures, maps, charts, visual songs and Scriptures, and vertical file materials. A separate accession record should be kept on each variety of media.

Where possible, arrange items for filing in manila folders (flannelgraphs, flannel backgrounds, flashcard stories, transparencies, visual Scriptures and vertical file materials). For these items, type a pocket, a booking card, labels and subject cards. Booking cards would be contained in the pocket pasted to the folder of each. For large items, such as flat pictures, maps, charts and visual songs, the identical procedure may be followed, pasting pockets inside their oversized holders. For small items (filmstrips, slides, tapes, etc.) type only the booking card, labels and subject cards. Booking cards for these materials are kept together in a box, filed in the same order as the media.

Circulation preparations for multi-media are generally more involved than circulating books since audiovisuals may be used several times in one day while books are borrowed and kept for several weeks. It is desirable to maintain a scheduling sheet for audiovisuals to facilitate reserving them ahead of the date of their use. This eliminates the problem of more than one group planning to use the same materials at the same time.

Step 6. Promotion.

Promoting audiovisuals is an important consideration when incorporating media into the church library. Promotion, like circulation, is more complicated for audiovisuals than for books. Although books are useful for program planning, their greatest use is for individual interest. Audiovisual materials can certainly serve for individual learning and interest, but their greatest use is for program planning.

Therefore, promotion must be handled with a special audience in mind: the church's leaders and workers. The purpose of your multi-media library's promotion is to arouse their interest and desire to use audiovisuals in the administration of their duties.

Verbal promotion might include announcements in teacher workshops, announcements from the pulpit and in classrooms, annual and interim reports before the church body, personal recommendations from person to person. Printed promotion might include specially designed bookmarks, handbooks detailing the available media, mailouts of special notices, bibliographies, monthly library newspapers, reviews in the Sunday morning bulletin.

Certain activities also guarantee to lend interest and promote audiovisuals: library banquets, skit and slide programs, library open-houses or coffee/book reviewing hours. A successful program of promotion never stops. Constant advertising brings results!

Is a multi-media library worthwhile? YES! Library staffers, working from the inside, have the opportunity to observe results. They see loneliness, depression, marital discord—many unfruitful conditions—helped through counseling tapes. They see improved teaching situations resulting from using a variety of media. They have the chance to observe the spiritual growth of many people through the use of audiovisuals, books and periodicals.

Remember, the role of the church library, beyond circulating books, is to challenge, clarify, inspire, ignite, stir, shape, encourage, entice *and equip* the people of God. Books and multi-media can share in this role.

22

How Should a Civilian Church Minister to the Military?

By Sam Mayo

Sam Mayo has served as senior pastor of the Bellevue Assembly of God Church in Omaha, Nebraska, for the past 11 years as it grew from a membership of about 75 to about 1,200. Omaha is the home of the headquarters for the U.S. Air Force's Strategic Air Command.

An annual average of over 700 members are transferred out of the church, primarily through military transfers.

I have discovered a whole new world of potential in a uniformed community which has often been forgotten, misunderstood and left out of the civilian body of Christ.

This discovery began several years ago when the Lord called me to pastor a church within a few miles of the headquarters of the Strategic Air Command, defense nerve center for the United States. Although my personal experience with military life up to that time had been limited to an occasional friend in uniform and my ROTC college classes, God challenged me to reach the nearby members of the military and their families.

From time to time I meet pastors who seem to envy all the benefits our church enjoys as a result of the influx of military people. Sometimes these ministers need to be reminded that a similar opportunity exists not far from their church doorsteps. All they have to do is motivate their congregations to welcome the military people who will have so much to offer once they come to know the Lord.

The American government has trained and developed leadership for the church to use if it will. While often it is impossible to involve our congregations in intensive and extensive leadership training, the military provides for such training to be mandatory and an ongoing basis for all of its career-oriented personnel. When these disciplined and committed men and women find their spiritual thirstings satisfied in a born-again, Spirit-filled lifestyle, the leadership training provided by the government becomes a natural tool for the Lord to use in building His church.

There also seems to be a greater maturity and self-sufficiency among military families who usually have to begin things over again in a new community, job and church in three years or less. Because of their international travels, the military family usually has a greater burden for missions. They also are able to contribute new ideas and concepts since they often see things from a broader perspective.

Need for Acceptance

However, military families sometimes find it difficult to be accepted into the lifestream of a large percentage of churches. They are often viewed as "just going to be here a short time," so they are not always welcomed into leadership and elected positions within many churches. Their fresh ideas and new approaches, along with their disciplined logic, methods and lifestyles are often a "threat" to civilians who persist in "doing it the way we've always done it." The organization, chain-of-command and respect for authority mentality is an asset and strength to the local body of believers. As a pastor I've experienced personal growth as these military leaders have encouraged me in delegation of responsibility, accountability and chain-of-command principles.

Depending on the chaplains at the local military installation, as in the civilian church, spiritual temperatures rise and fall in the base chapel. The general consensus is that usually the base chapel is somewhat bland and lacking. There are many reasons for this and I certainly don't want to critique the system.

However, the general failure of the military chapel system to provide dynamic praise and worship, spiritual growth and challenging dimensions for its participants has magnified the need among the military for civilian churches to open their arms to the uniformed community. If a local civilian church has exciting things happening spiritually, then it should be ready to absorb the people the Lord desires to send to them by way of the military.

Sports and Education

Probably two of the biggest areas of interest in the lives of military people are sports and education. The church that sees this need and seeks to establish a quality ministry in these areas can expect a real magnetic pull from the military community. These men and women have often seen the best and worst of programs around the world and can really appreciate ministries that accent excellence. Thus we've found that our pre-school/child-care programs, along with our quality Christian education through the 10th grade, have attracted families to us that we would probably never have reached otherwise. These parents are usually the type that don't take any school system for granted but are concerned and involved in their children's educations.

One of the first things military families want to know when looking for a church is what does it have to offer their children and youth. The dozen ball teams we have each spring and summer are a ministry that goes beyond just playing ball. We have our own coaches and usually have our teams playing against each other, complete with uniforms. The fellowship between parents, coaches and families thus opens additional doors for friendship evangelism.

Our youth and young adult program, numbering about 300 every Wednesday night, has been one of the most attractive assets of our church. There is a great vacuum and spiritual hunger among military youth, singles and young adults. The military youth are "looking for a cause'' that demands their very best. With a leadership corps of about 85 people, and a program that demands radical commitment and dedication to Christ, the military youth are finding what they are looking for.

Diverse Nationalities

The call to military families has found a harmonious chord in our emphasis on a relationship with Christ, instead of a denomination.

Non-discriminatory religious exposure in the military often brings a very superficial knowledge of the Scriptures. So the new revelations of Scripture and of a personal God make them some of the most inspiring people in the world to preach to, as they hang on to every word spoken. It is common to reach out to those who have married Americans and have brought their Buddhist faith or other Eastern religion to our shores with them.

The military brings into the community large groups of other nationalities with spiritual needs. We have a Korean congregation which meets in our church with a Korean pastor who had formerly been a medical doctor in Korea.

Military Marriages

During my ten years of ministry to the military community I have found that the pressures of military lifestyles serve somewhat as a ''refiner's fire'' for marriages. Marriages usually do not remain *status quo* but either get stronger or fall apart. The positive influence of a Bible-preaching church usually finds itself saving marriages which would have failed otherwise. There is a great ministry to those who reach out to faltering military marriages.

A weak marriage obviously experiences great strain and needs ministry and strengthening from the church to survive its pressures. Strong marriages become stronger. When families become separated by remote, unaccompanied assignments, remaining family members need even greater ministry.

Some families experience frequent TDY (temporary duty) trips that keep the military man away from his family perhaps as much as every other week for a week at a time. In some instances special schools might separate families for a month or more at a time. In some branches of military life, such as the Navy, regular and frequent assignments cause extended separations. Obviously, whether the separations are for a few days or even up to a year there must be adjustments for the partner left behind. To take on the ''head of the house'' role and then have to move out of that role and let the ''visitor'' in the home take over until he leaves again can become a very frustrating and straining experience on all involved. Ministry obviously becomes a needful lifeline to such families.

Many marriages hold together until that traumatic time of retirement arrives for the spouse after 20 or more years of military service. Then the pressures and adjustments of retirement and a new life cause it to fall apart. While some military personnel never have retirement traumas, many do. That magic moment that has been a long sought-after goal brings many to a place they've never experienced before. Many people enter the military directly from high school and their parents' home. Their decisions, goals and job descriptions have been spelled out to them for 20 years, and now retirement brings them to a whole new world of decisions and directions. Some military people have planned ahead, and retirement offers additional fulfillment as careers are expanded and more goals realized. However, for many, retirement is a "change of life" that affects the emotions, and marriages often can't take the strain. Scriptural ministry and treatment is desperately needed.

Constant Rotation

One of the great assets to ministering to the military is also its greatest liability: its transient nature. We have "transferred out" of our church more than 3,000 people in the last five years. The positive side is that you don't ever have to worry about "trouble-makers." Just love them and leave them alone; they'll transfer out before long! But to lose valuable men and women into whom you've poured yourself, and then watched them grow from spiritual infancy to giants serving the Lord, is difficult. I'm talking about losing deacons, school teachers, bus workers and departmental coordinators, not to mention certified school staffers who meet Nebraska's difficult criteria for our Christian school system! In one year we usually have to replace at least 150 Sunday school teachers!

Most of the workers we get we have to train from scratch, as most of our growth comes from individuals we have discovered from the ranks of the unwanted and undiscipled. We get them saved, send them through a spiritual "bootcamp" of intensive discipleship, and then hear the news that they have received orders to be missionaries to another part of the world at government expense!

How would you like to lose over 700 people from your church every year? Scrambling just to keep up with the previous year's attendance can be a challenge but we continue to have gains. Last year we averaged approximately 100 over the previous year.

We gain strength in the fact that we are not building our kingdom but His kingdom! We're giving top priority to reproducing leaders and trained workers who will be more effective in God's work as a result of having been stationed at this location. Our dependence on the Lord assures us He'll send some strong potential leadership material for replacements. The refreshing flow of "new blood" coming into the church is always invigorating. The spring and summer transfers bring us excitement.

Need for Change

Let me share one last discovery on what happens when transfers don't take place and a military person remains at your church for a long time.

This is certainly not a hard-and-fast rule and there are always exceptions to this observation. But when people have been in the military for an extended period they will often experience a restlessness about the time their normal transfer pattern comes due. This might be anywhere from a year to a three-year cycle.

If the transfer orders do not come through, the military person or family will usually do one of the following things:

1. Change churches,
2. Change living quarters,
3. Change cars,
4. Change furniture, or
5. Change jobs or career fields within the military.

Because of the transfer cycle they have become accustomed to, they often do not recognize this "need for change."

When a pastor recognizes the possibility of these subconscious stirrings, it makes his ministry more effective as he helps them understand their undefined restless urgings to do things they may wish later they had not done.

An Untapped Reservoir

"Missionaries around the world at government expense" is more than a cliche. I really believe revival is beginning to break out in the military as spiritual hunger and thirstings are coming to maturity. Fellowship groups are something to which many in the military can relate because they have found them to be a primary source of spiritual strength while stationed at remote locations. Thus, whether they are part of a thriving, turned-on civilian church or just a part of a small group of closely-knit believers, the groundwork of a great move of God in the military has already begun. Outstanding men and women of God are becoming strong and effective witnesses in every rank and office of the military. High-ranking officers and every rank of enlisted men are inviting their peers to be part of the Christian family.

The military has been an untapped reservoir of power for the Church. Whether they are part of our fellowship for a month, a year or longer, let us welcome them into our fellowship and share in the revival fires God is stirring among them.

23

Is There Something Behind Those Success Stories?

By E. S. Caldwell

E. S. Caldwell is associate editor of *MINISTRIES: The Magazine For Christian Leaders*. He served the Assemblies of God as promotions coordinator for the Division of Home Missions and publicity director for the radio-TV department. He pastored 23 years in Idaho and Missouri. He is a graduate of Northwest College of the Assemblies of God and also attended Northwest Nazarene College.

Most pastors of small congregations are looking for ideas that will promote growth—not a flash-in-the-pan, temporary surge in attendance but a breakthrough to a higher plateau.

Perhaps you have watched another church, not that different from the one you serve, put a plan into action, break all existing records and maintain most of their gains. So you carefully implemented every facet of their plan. But in your case the plan fizzled. Why? Maybe it was because you did not know, as Paul Harvey would put it, "The Rest of the Story."

Take the case of Jim Davis, the pastor of the Assembly of God in Wilder, Idaho, two decades ago. In the course of becoming acquainted with the people in the little town of approximately 600 and with some of those on the surrounding farms, Pastor Davis discovered that many of the inhabitants were not native to the region. In fact, most of these people migrated to the area from the Midwest during the bleak dustbowl days of the '30s.

He also learned that, despite almost 30 years as residents of Idaho, many of these people remained fiercely proud of their home states, whether Arkansas, Kansas, Missouri, Nebraska or Oklahoma.

Why not latch onto that loyalty as a means of attracting people to church? Pastor Davis asked himself. Why not design a Sunday school attendance contest pitting people from each of these five states against the others?

One advantage to promoting an event in a small town is that it doesn't cost a great deal to advertise. An ad in the weekly newspaper, a few hand-lettered posters in the local mercantile, feed store and barber shop, and you are on your way—provided, of course, that what you are advertising hits somebody's "hot button." Davis' plan did just that.

When "Arkansas Day" was set, all the people in the church from that state enthusiastically contacted all their relatives and friends from "back home," and the little church was packed. It was a repeat performance for each of the other four states, and the same was true for the final Sunday push for "All States."

That contest marked a breakthrough for the church. Attendance more than doubled. Families were added that stayed in the church from then on.

Would a variation of that idea work in your church? Perhaps. But there is something else you need to know before you map out your promotion campaign.

John Shaw, the minister who preceded Jim Davis, left that pastorate a broken man. The physician who examined Pastor Shaw told him that his symptoms were identical to those in the World War II soldiers whom he had diagnosed as having "combat fatigue."

Since I pastored a neighboring assembly at the time, I knew both these men. I also knew something about their board and congregation. No doubt about it, John suffered like a soldier—except his wounds were from his own troops!

When Jim Davis came along, things began to happen. Not attendance gains—at first what took place was a series of funerals. And almost without exception, the church members who died had been the church's trouble makers. As I remember it, Jim conducted eleven funerals in the first eight months he served that church—an astounding number for so small a congregation.

Am I suggesting that these deaths had anything to do with the successful contest and attendance gains later on? Did God have to remove these recalcitrants before He could bless the efforts of the rest of the body? Did prayer have something to do with what happened?

First, I must point out that the church had not moved forward for a long time. Second, I will share a story about Jim Davis' home church in Gooding, Idaho, that became almost legendary.

It seems that an old-time, fire-and-brimstone preacher by the name of Thurman was called to pastor the Gooding Assembly many years ago. When he came, he sensed there was something wrong. And in those days before the emergence of expert analysis of church problems, there was only one answer—pray through!

Several church members banded with Pastor Thurman in intense intercessory prayer, day after day, week after week. They did not know what was needed to bring the revival for which their hearts yearned; they did not presume to instruct God how He would bring life to their dead church. All they did was pray.

Whether what happened was or was not God's answer is for you to surmise. But the intercessors and their pastor came to believe that God removed the roadblocks to revival by "calling home" some of their fellow church members.

They thought it was their secret, that no one outside their prayer band had in any way associated their prayers with the recent funerals. But one day as Pastor Thurman was walking in the business district of the city, he was approached by a nervous little man.

"Rev. Thurman," the man said in an earnest, worried voice, "you don't know me but I live out on a farm in a little house with my wife and her mother. Her mother's in her 80s. She's had a full life but now her mind is starting to go and she is very hard to live with. I wonder, Rev. Thurman, could you pray one of your prayers for my mother-in-law?"

I don't know how the preacher answered the man. And I don't know if there is any connection between what happened in Jim Davis' home church and the one he came to pastor. But I do know there is usually something more behind the success of any contest or promotion a church may sponsor than what is seen on the surface.

Keep looking until you discover *The Rest of the Story*.

24

What Responsibility Does a Ministry Have to the Public?

By James Guinn

James Guinn is a certified public accountant with the firm Guinn, Smith & Company in Irving, Texas, a firm that has provided C.P.A. services to over 250 religious organizations, helping more than 100 non-profit corporations receive tax-exempt status from the Internal Revenue Service.

Guinn earned a bachelor of business administration degree from Midwestern State University in Wichita Falls, Texas, and worked for Arthur Andersen & Company, one of the largest international public accounting firms.

Many questions have come to my attention which indicate that the general public is not knowledgeable of the manner in which tax-exempt (nonprofit) organizations operate and to whom they are responsible.

It seems to be the general consensus, augmented by the attacks of radio, television and newspaper reporters, that there are no controls over nonprofit organizations. Perhaps an understanding of how nonprofit organizations come into being will help dispel this common misconception.

The founders of an organization must incorporate the organization in the state in which operations are based. Accordingly, they must meet the state's requirements for tax-exempt organizations. State requirements include having a duly elected board of directors, and having articles of incorporation and bylaws, which are the rules by which a nonprofit governs itself. In some states nonprofits must file an annual report with the state disclosing gross revenue received by the organization and how the money was disbursed.

The "watch dog" over nonprofit organizations is the Internal Revenue Service. An organization approved for tax exemption by a state is not automatically approved by the IRS. To obtain exempt status as a religious organization under Section 501(c)(3) of the Internal Revenue Code, an organization must have a specific religious purpose. Examples include churches, religious orders, church auxiliaries, missions, evangelists, religious publishers and religious book stores.

Once the specific religious activity of an organization is determined, the organization must file for approval with the IRS on Form 1023. This form, Application for Recognition of Exemption, must be filed within the first 15 months (except for churches) from the date of incorporation.

The IRS must receive and approve a copy of the articles and bylaws of the organization and detailed information regarding their activities and operations. The IRS requires information about the organization's governing body, including the names, addresses and duties of the officers, directors and trustees. The specialized knowledge, training and expertise, or pertinent qualifications of these individuals to manage an exempt organization must be stated.

As part of the application for exemption, the organization must furnish financial statements for the current year and each of the preceding three years. If the organization has not been in existence that long, they must prepare a budget for the next two years.

While the application is pending with the IRS, the agent assigned to the determination can ask any question he wishes about the organization's actual or proposed operations as long as those questions do not pertain to the religious beliefs espoused by the organization. Current IRS policy requires the founders of the organization to sign a statement that all royalties, copyrights and similar rights or intangible assets procured by the organization, or developed at the organization's expense, will belong to the organization. The founders must submit a signed statement that salaries paid to its officers and/or employees will be comparable to salaries paid for similar positions in the secular world.

When the IRS is satisfied that the organization has met all the requirements for exemption, as discussed above, they will grant exempt status. However, the requirement for reporting to the IRS does not end with filing an application for exemption.

Except for churches, all tax-exempt organizations must file an annual report enumerating the compensation and expense allowances received by officers, directors and trustees. The report must also disclose the amount of revenue received by the organization for the reporting period and information about how the organization distributed the donations it received for that period of time.

There is an absolute prohibition against use of a nonprofit organization's corporate assets for the personal benefit of an officer, director, trustee, contributor or a key employee. There are questions on the information return, Form 990, which must be filed annually, with regard to these areas.

A significant portion of my work is comprised of nonprofit organizations, and since I have spent many hours meeting their tax and audit needs, I will answer some of the questions frequently asked.

Q: Can the founder or head of a tax-exempt organization make all the major decisions without the authorization of the board of directors?

A: The head of the organization is only one of the board members. Major decisions must be agreed upon by a majority of the board members and must be in accordance with the IRS rules and regulations. Of course, day-to-day operations cannot be supervised totally by a board; however, major decisions such as property purchases and church expansion must be ratified by the board.

Q: Who sets salaries for the officers of the nonprofit organizations?

A: Officers' salaries must be approved by the directors of the organization. However, salaries and other benefits (such as insurance,

171

automobile and housing) must meet IRS guidelines, which are much more strict for a nonprofit than for a secular organization. If the IRS deems the salary, plus benefits for the officers of a nonprofit organization, unreasonable in relation to the duties performed, it can revoke the exempt status of the organization.

Q: How are funds accounted for that are donated to a nonprofit organization?

A: This is a difficult question to answer, and I can only respond with regard to our firm's clients. The organizations I work with keep records to conform with IRS regulations and guidelines established by Statement of Position 78-10, issued by the Accounting Standards Division of the American Institute of Certified Public Accountants.

Q: Are nonprofits totally tax-free?

A: No, this is a common misconception. Although the laws vary from state to state, in most states nonprofit organizations pay property tax on much of their property. In most states, they pay sales or use tax for items purchased to be used as premiums and for other use by the organization.

Q: Can a nonprofit organization be inherited?

A: The answer to this question is no, a nonprofit organization cannot be inherited by anyone. A nonprofit organization, as referred to in this article, is operated by a duly elected board of directors. The nonprofit organization is, in effect, a public charity operated by the directors who are in a position of trust. Accordingly, if it is determined that the organization is unable to continue its exempt function, all of its assets must be distributed to another Internal Revenue Code Section 501(c)(3) organization.

None of the assets on this dissolution may be distributed to employees, family or founders.

Q: Is it necessary for a nonprofit religious organization to belong to the Evangelical Council for Financial Accountability?

A: The ECFA is an organization which has the reputation for giving the "good housekeeping seal of approval" to religious organizations. However, membership is not required by any law or government regulation. While membership in ECFA may indicate that an organization is following certain good stewardship practices, not belonging to the organization is not necessarily an indication that an organization does not follow proper accounting practices. There could be a variety of reasons for not joining this organization, one of which might be a difference in religious beliefs.

Q: Are salaries paid to officers and directors of religious organizations tax-free?

A: No, the salaries are not tax-free. A possible source of the confusion regarding the taxation of these salaries is the fact that a minister's housing allowance is not subject to federal income tax. Section 107 of the Internal Revenue Code allows a minister to receive a non-taxable housing allowance, but this allowance must be used to provide housing. The rationale behind allowing a minister this non-taxable housing allowance is simple—it benefits the exempt organization. If the minister does not have to pay income tax on the money used to provide his housing, he does not have to receive as much salary from the organization.

Q: Are annual audited financial statements necessary for a nonprofit organization?

A: Audited statements are not a requirement for a nonprofit organization. Since the cost of an audit is high, our firm recommends that most small-to-medium size organizations do not have an audit, unless there is a good financial reason, such as unusually fast growth, or requirement by a bank, major donors or the board of directors.

Q: Can the founders, directors, trustees or employees of exempt organizations have free use of organization automobiles, airplanes, etc., for personal reasons?

A: Any personal use of the organization's assets must be valued at fair market value and added to the taxable income of the individual(s) using the asset.

As you can see there is a great deal of outside regulation of an exempt organization which must be adhered to if an organization's exempt status is to be maintained.

Section III

Solving Personal Problems

25

How Can a Clergy Marriage Have Better Harmony?

By Kent Axtell

Kent Axtell is the founder of Born-Again Marriages, headquartered in Council Bluffs, Iowa. He is the author of the book *Boredom and Back*. He conducts seminars on healing marriage relationships.

Jan and Bill were completely blown out of the ministry. Not because of adultery, not because of lack of money or success, but because of the build-up of pressure. Explosions result from pressure, and pastorates can produce tremendous pressure! Jan exploded first. Whether she wanted it or not, she had become part of nearly every activity in the church. Her level of required involvement became more than she could bear. Although a sharp, capable woman, self-pity had turned her into a wife withdrawn from her husband. She was weary and bitter, and she said she would never again be put into that kind of bondage. It was her turn to be fulfilled. Jan told her husband that he could pastor if he wanted to, but she wanted nothing to do with it; she was going to pursue a career of her own.

Bill was disillusioned, too. He was angry at God and discouraged about his future. The marriage had deteriorated to the point of little more than strife and confusion. The children were badly shaken. Rumblings of divorce made him realize that if he didn't stand up spiritually, and do so soon, there would be nothing left.

He prayed in desperation about the situation. Their marriage had to be healed if their ministry was to be saved. He resigned his church. It was the action of a broken man's hope against hope that things could be salvaged.

Many couples in ministry can relate in one degree or another to Jan and Bill's crisis. One of the greatest needs among leadership in the body of Christ is adequate wisdom to fulfill ministerial responsibilities without allowing damage to the marriage. The typical pattern seems to be that as a ministry grows and succeeds, it requires more and more time and attention, so the leader's marriage receives less and less attention.

Bill and Jan's story has a happy ending. At the time I met them they had returned to the Lord's work, their marriage was in good condition, and their previous problems were solved. And all this in less than two years!

Mutual Agreement

How did they recover? The shortest answer is to say they discovered ideal role models. They moved to a city in Texas and began attending a large church where the pastor and his wife touched people in a very personal way, but without sacrificing all of their time. Jan and Bill discovered that their new pastor/wife team kept themselves free to do only what they mutually agreed was God's direction for them.

The way a couple uses *time* is very much a part of their marriage's success or failure. The use or abuse of time sets up a marriage for either help or harm, improvement or deterioration.

Satan knows how time can serve his purposes. Many of the divorces he has scheduled for three or five years from now couldn't be triggered today because the victims are not yet sufficiently worn down. But unless patterns are corrected, time is on the destroyer's side.

Jan and Bill learned some prayer techniques that had a lot to do with the way they utilized time and made mutual decisions.

The Lord directed them to establish a new church. It was a mutual venture, prayerfully structured. On the first Sunday only one family attended: their own. Soon others joined with them. Jan launched a Bible study at God's direction. Women from a wide area began attending in large numbers. Jan attributes her success to following the Lord's leading in using a "neutral" meeting place instead of the church building.

The church is growing rapidly. Their frustration has evaporated. Their marriage is actually being strengthened while Bill and Jan are carrying out their ministries. They have learned a secret that prevents their relationship with each other from being destroyed. Instead, it continues to blossom.

The Power of Agreement

The secret that works for Jan and Bill and in my own relationship with my wife will work for you. It has worked for countless couples across the country.

Simply stated, the secret is the power of agreement that God offers a couple when they pray together both in English and in the Spirit (that is, in tongues).

This one spiritual principle will give a couple a lever on frustration and turmoil as nothing else can.

In God's sight, a married couple is one—not two, but one. Her ability may be in one direction, his in another, but they are one. The entity that God brings into existence when two people marry is the miracle of "one flesh."

Most people, especially ministerial couples, will agree with the biblical idea that two are supposed to be one. But very few of our Christian friends know how to walk in agreement as a couple.

They have a variety of thoughts about the idea of a couple actually agreeing on a consistent basis. These thoughts range from jokes about if they waited until agreement came, they'd never make a decision, to the thought that surely in some instances the man as head of the home would have to lay down the law and the wife would back what he decided.

The latter seems logical, but what we have seen over and over is that when a decision is made that way, and later roadblocks appear and the demonic heat comes, the wife will be tempted to question, "Was this really God's will in the first place?" Or, if the thing goes sour, to say, "I told you so."

The question I had to ask myself was: if I am head of my home and I can see that power is in agreement, then how do I implement it? The answer was simple. As head of my home, I declared that my wife, Dru, and I would not move on something unless we both agreed from our hearts that it was right. We agreed to agree! No coercion allowed, only heart-felt agreement.

But what if time runs out? Frankly, the deal that can't wait is usually the one that's better left alone. Don't forget, God knows we're on a timetable. When a couple comes before Him with pure hearts, agreed that finding His will is their motive, not to prove one another wrong, the Lord will give guidance.

Our commitment to agreement has worked marvelously. Our premise is that Dru doesn't have the job of convincing me nor me her, but Jesus has the job of speaking the same thing to both of us. If He doesn't do that, the project wasn't for Him in the first place.

This seemingly insignificant incident illustrates what I mean. One time I thought for sure we were to go to our own church service on a particular evening and Dru was equally convinced that we should go to an evangelist's meeting. There was no strife, we just didn't agree. We talked about it a little and nothing seemed to change. So with time to make a decision quickly approaching, I said, "Are you willing to do what I want to do?" She said, "Yes." I said, "Well, I'm willing to do what you want to do." We then prayed and asked God to direct us. It makes me smile just thinking about how simple God made it. In less than five minutes He spoke to me and said, "It's Dru's decision." Boy, was the evangelist good that night!

Some might say that that type of thing doesn't matter much to God, but I would disagree. It was through what happened that evening that the anointing for healing began to be manifested openly in our ministry. As for me and my house, we want what God wants!

Jesus as Umpire

Several scripturally valid ingredients are needed for things to work. For instance, Matthew 23:12 says that if you exalt yourself (your opinion), you will be abased, but if you humble yourself, you will be exalted.

When you and your mate are discussing something and your opinions vary, one or both of you is going to change in order to have agreement. I think it is especially good for the minister who is in the limelight to have the frequent opportunity to humble himself to the question, "Do we really agree? Is this God's leading or just a good idea?"

I can think of several instances when I had an idea I thought was terrific until I shared it with Dru. Without her saying a thing I could feel how empty it was. Then there were other times when I was sure of the wisdom in something and the more I told her the better I liked it, but for some reason she didn't share my enthusiasm. What do you do then?

Dru and I learned a long time ago that we couldn't talk long enough to agree. Colossians 3:15, Amplified, says, "And let the peace (soul harmony which comes) from the Christ rule (act as umpire continually) in your hearts—deciding and settling with finality all questions that arise in your minds." That is exactly what we did. After discussing Dru's answer and my answer, we would then pray together—call Jesus in as umpire—and get His answer. At times it was what Dru had thought and at other times what I had thought and still more times it was a combination.

On items where one of us was quite opinionated, it might not be the first time we prayed that God got the answer through, but in the next day or two when our emotions were not so keyed up, He would softly say, "You know, Dru's right about that," or He might say to my wife that I was right. The thing to remember is that you don't really want your way, you want God's way.

On some items agreement has come as a signal of the timing when something was right. We've learned not to throw an idea away just because agreement is slow in coming. I can tell you this, once you agree to agree, you will grow into the knowledge of how this concept works.

Avoiding Mistakes

There are pitfalls to be avoided.

Often I will have invested quite a lot of time thinking and praying about a situation and perhaps talking to others prior to sharing it with Dru. If she's a little busy, it's easy for her to say, "Well, you know more about this than I do. Why don't you decide?" On routine things that's perhaps acceptable, but on important decisions I've learned that what I'm after is not her knowledge about the decision so much as her spirit's reaction. We refer to this as an inner witness.

We've found that it's far easier to make a mistake through logic than through the inner witness. A few minutes of Dru and me praying together will produce greater accuracy than numerous opinions.

The next pitfall is in making decisions too quickly just because you both agree. Don't bypass praying. Agreement between the two of you isn't much good if God hasn't voted.

Another pitfall is in giving only mental assent to praying together in the Spirit. Praying in English can too easily be an indication of our own ideas or just a skimming of the surface of God's direction in the matter. When Paul said in 1 Corinthians 14:15, "I will pray in the Spirit and I will pray with the understanding also," he was saying that the one was to enhance the other.

Many couples are embarrassed to pray in tongues together. Don't miss the value of this counsel by saying, "My partner and I pray in tongues; it's just that we don't do it together." While praying individually should be a part of every couple's prayer life, it doesn't produce the level of results we're after because it's still a function of the two individuals. What I'm describing is a function of the two as one flesh—a direct resistance to the divide-and-conquer strategy of the enemy.

I don't care if it's been a *dictatorship* for 20 years (and men aren't the only dictators), it can become an *agreement-ship*. Just don't try to make the change in the natural. Do it by praying in the Spirit, in tongues, consistently bringing specific areas before the Lord together and watch Him melt those old deadlocked, stalemated, opinionated areas into fresh and accurate insights.

Matthew 18:19, Amplified, says, "Again I tell you, if two of you on earth agree (harmonize together, together make a symphony) about something and everything—whatever they shall ask, it will come to pass and be done for them by my Father in heaven." On those areas that have never worked out quite right, find out if you really agree or if one of you has just gone along with the idea.

No matter how good an idea this may seem, it will not come to pass unless you make it. Every good and bad thing within 50 miles will give you an excuse to put it off. What Dru and I have found most effective is to make an appointment to pray together. We usually take the phone off the hook and try to have a good block of time.

We often pray 45 minutes or an hour just getting geared down and through the pressing items. That is when it becomes fun because we slip into the creativity of things to come.

It is not a drudgery. I would encourage you to start with at least one hour at a sitting, no less than three times a week and build up from there. I will promise you this—just the time it saves you in eliminating errors and increasing effectiveness will be more than worth it. The harmonizing of the two of you will be a huge byproduct.

My wife often expresses how confident it makes her feel knowing I will not run roughshod over her ideas. I feel the same way. When you know you are on the same team and not in competition with one another, the pressure is off. It is terrific being able to share your ideas without being certain they are right but knowing together you can pray and find out. Sweet harmony.

No More Lumps

One couple told us they had swept things under the rug for 25 years until they found out how to handle these areas through agreement in prayer. On certain topics they just learned to steer clear of one another in their former habits. Did it affect their personal relationship? Of course. Did it affect their family? Of course. Today that couple reports that the lumps have been removed from under the rug and they know they can come to agreement about anything that comes along.

26

How Do You Care for Your Own Family?

By Paul Thigpen

Paul Thigpen is a free-lance writer and editor of *Dads Only* newsletter, a monthly parenting resource for Christian fathers. He earned a B.A. in religious studies from Yale and lives with his wife, Leisa, and daughter, Lydia, in Savannah, Georgia.

Bob Pierce said: "I've made an agreement with God that I'll take care of His little lambs overseas if He'll take care of mine at home." Dr. Pierce was the founder of World Vision, whose compassionate response to the needs of millions took him all over the world.

The sentiment may sound noble, but the results of that "agreement" were tragic. According to the loving but painful testimony of his own daughter, this extraordinary evangelist neglected and hurt his family deeply for the sake of "the ministry." Eventually his marriage was destroyed, his children were alienated and one of his daughters committed suicide.

Sadly enough, the story has been repeated many times over throughout the Church. Pastors, evangelists and teachers— especially those who travel extensively—find themselves torn between the demands of home and ministry, illustrating the apostle Paul's observation so long ago: "An unmarried man is concerned about the Lord's affairs—how he can please the Lord. But a married man is concerned about the affairs of this world— how he can please his wife—and his interests are divided" (1 Cor. 7:32-34, NIV).

The conflict of family and career is admittedly not unique to the clergy. But the particular vocational demands of a pastor, evangelist or other minister tend to intensify several specific challenges which all parents face. A closer look at these problem areas, and how some ministers have coped with them, can offer a number of practical guidelines for building a closer relationship with our families.

Establishing the Priority

Before we can take any meaningful steps toward strengthening our family life, we must settle one all-important issue: Which has first priority, family or ministry? Jack Hayford, pastor of Church on the Way in Van Nuys, California, has labeled the problem the "evangelical syndrome": the misconception that a man can serve God to the fullest only if he is willing to put ministry before family.

It is true Jesus said that whoever "does not hate...his wife and children...cannot be my disciple" (Luke 14:26, NIV). Our love for

God must be even greater than our love for our family. But love for God and love for ministry are not the same thing. If we love God, we will obey Him, and He commands all fathers—including ministers—to love our wives as Christ loved the Church, and to rear our children in a way that will not embitter or discourage them (Eph. 5:25; Col. 3:21). At the same time, broken relationships at home will undermine the effectiveness of all our ministry. If we place career before family, we risk losing both.

With this truth in mind, we must first of all make it clear to the church or organization we serve that our home is our first priority of ministry. Dr. B. Clayton Bell, pastor of Highland Park Presbyterian Church in Dallas, comments, "I've told more than one pulpit committee that I refuse to sacrifice my family on the altar of the church." In this way he has reached an understanding about priorities with his church members at the very outset.

Traveling teachers and evangelists may find that such a priority means sometimes refusing invitations to speak, or even cancelling arrangements already made. Well-known pastor and speaker Charles Swindoll of First Evangelical Free Church in Fullerton, California, admits: "I have to limit my travel and involvements to make time for my children. Just recently my wife and I had to cancel going to an event we had looked forward to for a month and a half. But a situation in our family needed attention, and that was a priority for us."

Dr. Bill Bright, founder and president of Campus Crusade for Christ, International, has spent much of the last few decades traveling around the world. He remembers how making his children a priority once meant keeping his promise to them to play in the snow, rather than visiting with a famous football coach who showed up unexpectedly.

"I was torn," says Dr. Bright, "because I so much wanted to spend time with him: Suddenly I realized that this was a chance for [my sons] to see how important they are to me—no one can jump in and take their time. So I said a few words to the coach and excused myself, trusting he understood my explanation. Even if he didn't, I had to give the boys that assurance that my word to them was true."

Undoubtedly, standing firmly with family commitments has cost these men dearly at times, and we may also have to pay the price of being passed over by a pulpit committee, or losing a chance to speak. But the long-term reward—a healthy family—will more than repay the loss.

The Time Crunch

Once we've made our priorities clear to our congregations and associates, we have a number of opportunities to demonstrate them to our family members as well. For busy ministers, finding time for family is perhaps the most prominent and persistent challenge of balancing home and ministry. To win the battle, we must first deal with the myth of "quality time."

Sadly enough, some parents rationalize spending little or no time at all with their children by calling any contact with them "quality time." But quantity quite often is the essential condition for quality. Relationships simply can't be nourished on a minute a day; it takes time to nourish the trust, openness, familiarity and shared concerns that make quality communication and intimate fellowship possible.

Once we realize that investing a quantity of time in our children is necessary, we can begin finding ways to multiply the scant "loaves and fishes" of moments in our schedule. Consider some of these suggestions:

● Know your limits. Learn to say no and to delegate ministry responsibilities when you can see work encroaching on family time.

● Identify the devourers of family time. Television is usually the worst culprit, so consider planning alternative activities which will give your family members time facing one another instead of the tube.

● Remember that some activities, though legitimate, are not practical for this season in your life. Others may have time to play golf on Saturdays, but a dad who's frequently away from home needs to devote those hours to his children instead. Someday, when they're grown, you'll have time for those things.

Redeem the time by doing routine activities together. Take a child along on errands. Let kids help you do chores, and help them with theirs. Such shared tasks build common experiences and allow naturally for spontaneous conversation.

● Capitalize on the flexibility of your schedule. Though you may sometimes wish yours was an eight-to-five job, you can take advantage of the odd free hours and the movability of some work responsibilities. Take a child out to an early breakfast, then drop him or her off at school. Spend a few afternoon hours with the kids playing ball after school (while most dads are at work). Show up unexpectedly at your child's classroom door for the lunch hour to "kidnap" him or her for a picnic. Arrange to attend a school play in which your child is performing.

● Look for special moments when fellowship means the most to your child. One dad who does this well is Gordon MacDonald, pastor of Grace Chapel in Lexington, Massachusetts, and a well-traveled speaker. He often visits with his daughter at bedtime to chat and give her a back rub for five or ten minutes. Some of their best conversations are during this time together.

● Schedule family life so that all members have regular time together. Perhaps everyone needs to make family breakfasts a priority, or Sunday afternoon walks. Everyone, especially active teens, will have to make some sacrifices here.

● Make the most of mealtimes. They are perhaps the most natural opportunity for family togetherness. Instead of allowing your table to become a fast food counter, insist on at least one meal a day with everyone present to relax and talk about the day. Unplug the phone; turn off the radio, TV and stereo; and let friends know that mealtime is private family time. Prepare a meal together occasionally to extend the time of fellowship.

● Make appointments with your children as you would with anyone else. Write them in your appointment book and keep them. Schedule regular times together that your children can count on. Leighton Ford, for example—an evangelist who has traveled extensively with Billy Graham—for many years used the strategy of writing into his schedule every year certain days when he would do things individually with each child.

Above all, remember that true "quality time" means you must be present to a child not just physically, but mentally and emotionally as well. Children know when they have your attention, and when you're preoccupied. Don't talk about church business over dinner. If your office is at home, keep it physically separated from the rest of your life there—if possible, in a room where you can shut the door behind you when you leave.

Billy Graham once told Bob Pierce (advice which he unfortunately didn't take): "Don't live so close to your office. Make your home some place apart and away, so that when you're home, you're really home. Otherwise, you'll never have a real home life."

Traveling Ministries

Being on the road away from home is another common problem among evangelists and teachers, or pastors whose ministries have broadened beyond their local church. Here are some practical ways to bridge the miles between you and your family:

● Help your children understand why you travel. Tell them about the places you go, the people you meet, the things you do. Let them know where you'll be each time you leave. A teacher of missionary children once observed that children who have a good idea of what their parents do have fewer problems adjusting to boarding school.

● Leave surprises for your family to discover while you are gone. Make a cassette tape to be played each night at dinner, with special words for each family member. Record bedtime stories for younger children. Put love notes or small gifts in places where they are sure to be found: in lunch boxes, coat pockets, the refrigerator. All these let them know they are on your mind.

● Call home frequently while you are gone. Josh McDowell, a popular campus speaker who spends much of his time on the road, makes it a policy to talk to his family by phone every day, without fail. If the cost is prohibitive, keep calls brief and make them when rates are lowest. But remember that in your child's mind, nothing can take the place of hearing your voice.

● On extended trips, send children lots of mail. Besides postcards and letters, try small souvenirs, programs from games or concerts you attend, or paper place mats with games from restaurants where you eat. If you're meeting with someone who is famous, your child might appreciate an autograph.

● Let children know you are available for important matters, even when you are on the road. Make sure the kids know they can call you if they need you, and that you would come home in an emergency.

Bill Bright told his children years ago: "Wherever I am in the world, if you have a need, I will catch the next plane home if you wish. No matter with whom I am meeting, even if it is the President of the United States, if you want to talk to me, you don't have to wait." They tested him to see if he meant it, and he did. But they didn't abuse the privilege; instead it gave them an important sense of security that dad was available.

● Plan your "reentry" time carefully. Homecomings can provide some of your family's most meaningful moments. If you have been gone a week or more, little children may need to get slowly reacquainted. Try arranging for a fun family activity right after you arrive. Unopened mail and phone calls to be returned can wait; give your full attention to the family first.

● Take a child along with you on an occasional trip. Dr. Anthony Campolo, chairman of the sociology department at Eastern College in St. Davids, Pennsylvania, is a frequent speaker at Christian conferences around the world. He once took his son with him on a speaking tour of New Zealand! Dr. Campolo writes: "How could I justify spending money like that?...Because I looked at the outlay as an investment in the same way that an education is an investment, rather than as an expenditure." Though you may be traveling only to a nearby city, the time alone with your child is invaluable, and the experience is likely to be remembered a long time.

The Heart of Our Ministry

"Home," Charles Swindoll has wisely said, "is where life makes up its mind." Whatever difference we may make in the world through our career, it will rarely be as deep or comprehensive or enduring as the difference we can make in the lives of those who share our home. Family and ministry are not opposed to each other; rather, our roles as husband and father are the heart of our ministry. In our families we have an unparalleled opportunity to change the world—by laboring faithfully with those young ones who need us most, to shape them into whole dynamic disciples of our Lord.

27

How Do You Cope With Stress?

By Wayne Jacobsen

Wayne Jacobsen has spent 10 years in pastoral ministry serving two separate congregations, one as senior pastor and the other as associate pastor. He presently is pastor of The Savior's Community in Visalia, California. As a free-lance writer, he has been published in several Christian magazines.

The physician looked up from studying my chart. "Have you been under a lot of pressure lately?" he asked. This was the first indication of the verdict I was waiting to hear. For the last 30 minutes he had poked and probed only opening his mouth to ask what hurt.

Shooting pains in my chest had forced me on this breezy June day into a rare doctor visit. And since my doctor was out of town, I was seeing a referral. "Just a little," I answered sarcastically. Pressure! Is there life without it in ministry?

"Well, I don't know what you do, but I recommend you start looking for another job." After my stunned pause he explained. My problem was stress—nothing physically wrong yet—but something surely would be if my present course continued. "You're too young for that," he pleaded.

His words stung more deeply than the chest pains I'd weathered for two days. "What sort of work are you in?"

"I pastor a church here in town." I had never felt more ashamed—for my life; for the gospel. Not that I was surprised. My flesh thrives on pressure. I have often joked about being Type A—aggressive, active, achieving. I believed we were the real movers in society. An ache or a pain now and then was just part of the price.

Now I was past mere aches and pains. My body forced me to face the facts: I was doing what I sincerely felt was the Lord's choosing but at 29 was listening to a doctor tell me to find another profession. To my dismay I discovered that my Type A personality also spelled agitation and anxiety.

As I drove home I thought of many ministry professionals in a variety of churches and ministry organizations. I knew they battled stress-related illnesses—ulcers, heart problems, hypertension, burnout. I mulled over a statistic someone had given me a few years ago that ministry professionals rank second in the incidents of stress-related illnesses among all occupations.

When I got home and shared the diagnosis with my wife, she nodded in that way of hers that told me she was saddened but not shocked. After a restless night—stressed about my stress—I went for a long morning walk beside a creek near our home. "Father, I don't understand. You called me to pastor, but I can't go on if it's going to tear my body apart."

During our encounter by the creek, God reaffirmed my calling to ministry. Stress was not reason enough to walk away; but neither could it stay. It must be conquered. The pressures of ministry were not responsible for my stress; but how I handled them was. And that mishandling was ultimately caused by my mistrust of the God I was trying to serve. "Father, forgive me and please do whatever You have to in me so that I can serve You even in great pressure and do so in peace!"

That morning of prayer and the responses that followed it ushered in a year of transformation that has revolutionized my life and ministry. I've found great peace and joy in ministry and the symptoms that had become a daily reality in ministry are gone. Even others notice the change. Parting from a brief meeting with two friends I hadn't seen for two years, their last words were, "You have changed since we last saw you. You used to be so restless. We've never seen you so at peace with yourself and your ministry."

My journey took me through four stages: rejecting stress as an occupational hazard, repenting of its root causes, building a new intimacy with the Lord and daily disarming any seedlings of stress.

Part of the Job?

"It is the calling of a pastor to live on the edge of an ulcer." Those words were spoken to a friend of mine by his Midwestern pastor and sadly enough reflect the mentality of too many ministers. I used to wear my chest pains, sleepless nights and jam-packed schedule as merit badges of my selfless sacrifice to God and my indispensable value to His kingdom. But not any more. The lie collapsed that June morning two and a half years ago.

That's not to say that stress is nonexistent for the ministry professional. Never was a job created with more conflicting expectations. To minister well one must be honest, to minister in existing structures one must be well-liked. Rarely do these walk hand in hand. A pastor is expected to be an exciting teacher, able administrator, compassionate counselor, friend to all and available at a moment's notice. If he's not all of these he hears about it.

The diverse concerns of congregation, staff, community, peers and denominational leaders all press in different directions. Often success is measured by statistics over which one has little control or responsibility. Where he is successful statistically the potential for stress only grows. Decisions, demands and expectations increase and preserving success is often more stressful than gaining it.

Ministry abounds with situations where one may have responsibility but no authority to act. Institutional pressures and power-plays are infamous. As one minister recently put it, "The name of the game is survival of the institution and that only comes by compromise." Does that sound like the vocation of a man called to lead people into the glorious life of God's kingdom?

To these major concerns we must not overlook day-to-day decisions, particularly in a job that defies set hours, concrete goals and automatic results. A recent study on stress concluded, "Daily hassles are more closely linked to and may have greater effect on our moods and our health than the major misfortunes of life" ("Little Hassles Can Be Hazardous to Your Health," by Richard S. Lazarus in *Psychology Today,* July 1981).

It's no wonder that ministers fight feelings of inadequacy, guilt, loneliness and pride; all of which produce stress. Pressure is so inevitable that it would seem only fair to count stress as fellowshipping in His suffering.

After all, Paul spoke constantly about the sufferings the ministry created for him—shipwrecks, stonings, deprivation of food, dangers in his travels, rejection by people and even from the "daily pressure" of his concern for all the churches. But look closely. He wasn't speaking of inner tension, stress symptoms, workaholism or mental exhaustion. In fact, when Paul spoke of his mental and physical state he always spoke of peace, "contentment in every situation" and sufficient provision. His conflicts always came from without. Mine were coming from within.

Stress is not sharing in His suffering. It is a self-inflicted disease. *Time* magazine called it a national epidemic. "Two-thirds of all office visits to family doctors are prompted by stress-related symptoms." Stress is a byproduct of 20th century living. "It is a sorry sign of the times that the three best-selling drugs in this country are an ulcer medication (Tagamet), a hypertension drug (Inderal) and a tranquilizer (Valium)."

My congregation didn't need another victim, but an example of freedom. If I couldn't conquer stress, the doctor was right. I needed another vocation.

So I rejected stress as a way of life consistent with Christian ministry. Without that commitment I would never have faced the difficult decisions essential to deal with it. Toleration is always easier than transformation.

Symptoms become battle calls: churning in my stomach; disgust when the phone rings; a racing mind; difficulty in getting to sleep; overtiredness; apathy; sore jaws from clinched teeth; backaches, headaches or neckaches; indigestion; recurring sicknesses; emotional burnout. We can overcome stress before it exacts its price in the major complications of ulcers, heart trouble, exhaustion or hypertension.

Repentance

With this fresh desire for freedom I looked for my way of escape. What needed to change? Certainly I needed more time off. People's expectations would have to be confronted and changed. Others would have to shoulder the burdens I was carrying alone. My list ran on and on.

My list didn't last very long once I began to pray over it and share it with others. I was asking everyone else and everything else to change. How wrong I was! The answer to my stress could not be found in rearranging circumstances and structures. And thank God it couldn't, or I'd never find freedom from stress. The circumstances of a ministry professional will always be full of pressure and conflicts. Healing was not to be found in changing circumstances, but in changing how I responded to them.

That's how I came to repentance. I saw my stress as a sin against the peace, freedom and joy God provides in Christ. Every symptom was not a physical problem to be prayed for but a call to repentance. Each pointed to a place where I was not trusting or following my Lord.

I poured out my heart to Him in repentance and found Him full of compassion. Though my stress wasn't part of my fellowshipping in His sufferings, I knew He was fellowshipping in mine.

My repenting began with generalities —"Forgive me for giving in to stress. Help me find freedom." It didn't stay there long, however. Every time I read the Word it exposed ungodly thoughts and motives. My high-tension lifestyle squirmed under such revelations; but repentance began to root them out and set me free.

Rest

My craving for busyness and long hours (after all, shouldn't we give our best for the kingdom of God if others do it for the world?) was disarmed by God's call to rest. "For anyone who enters God's rest also rests from his own work, just as God did from his" (Heb. 4:10, NIV). I saw that my labor stemmed more from my insecurity about how others perceived me than from my zeal for His kingdom.

My restless mind had long excused itself on the premise that the kingdom of God brings conflict—the sword that divides. If you're going to be involved in conflict with people and issues, you will forfeit peace of mind. Tranquility is only for those who run from conflict. But I didn't find any biblical exception to the promise, "You will keep in perfect peace him whose mind is steadfast, because he trusts in You" (Is. 26:3).

My sleepless nights and tense days weren't all my doing. After all I was bearing the burdens of others caught in desperate need. Who could care more for another than to give up sleep and peace of mind for their needs? "In repentance and rest is your salvation, in quietness

195

and trust is your strength'' (Is. 30:15). Caught again! There is a difference between bearing burdens with people before God and taking responsibility for their needs and responses. Only God can do the latter, and I wasn't giving Him the opportunity.

My excuses crumbled. Toward the end I even grasped for the view that tension is a positive motivator, calling me to action where others were lazy. Couldn't anxiety, correctly channeled, make one do great things for God? ''Do not fret—it leads only to evil'' (Ps. 37:8). Stress cannot motivate me to do what is right. How often my anxiety about another person has compelled me to a conversation that only made matters worse!

A tension-filled life is not the result of diligence, conflict, compassion or zeal. It is the result of a mind controlled by anything other than God's Spirit. ''The mind controlled by the Spirit is life and peace'' (Rom. 8:6, NIV).

Don't get me wrong. I wanted nothing more than to serve God and be obedient to Him, but other motives ran beneath the surface of my actions that polluted my prime objective and created anxiety. I want God to use me successfully and there's a part of me that wants others to think me successful. The two can easily blur together. No greater danger exists in ministry than when one pursues his own aims convinced that they are God's.

God's Word pointed me in another direction—a lifestyle of peace in the midst of conflict, rest in adversity, diligence without self-effort, success based only on obedience to God.

The peace of Christ can only ''rule our hearts'' when we completely abandon our personal desires in order to obey His will. Thus my repentance eventually led to a new pledge of allegiance. As long as I sought to fulfill my desires for affirmation and success by pleasing others or myself, stress would remain my ever-present tormentor.

Paul reminds us that this conviction must rest at the heart of spiritual service. ''If I were still trying to please men, I would not be a servant of Christ'' (Gal. 6:10, NIV). If I would trustingly follow His mind in whatever circumstances I found myself, stress would be disarmed.

How do we do that, though, when His desires seem less real than the press of immediate circumstances? Oswald Chambers, author of *My Utmost for His Highest,* answers: ''The great solution is the simple one—'Come unto Me.' Whenever anything begins to disintegrate your life with Jesus Christ, turn to Him at once and ask Him to establish rest. Never allow anything to remain which is making the dis-peace. Take every element of disintegration as something to wrestle against, not to suffer.''

Intimacy
Intimacy! I wasn't walking close enough to know His will or, if know-

ing it, close enough to follow when the consequences of doing so were painful. Those failures were the breeding ground of my stress. Freedom came as I gave diligence to developing a more intimate relationship with Jesus, releasing His leadership and grace into all situations.

This is not to say I wasn't at the time already having daily devotions and prayer—but that demands on my life had outgrown the depth of my personal relationship with the Father. That intimacy needed to deepen by giving Him more time and more concentrated attention.

For me intimacy with the Lord is summed up in these three simple truths:

First, Jesus has a will about everything in my life. He alone can balance all the priorities of family, ministry and personal growth. I don't have to live out my ministry with my faltering guesses of what is best for me to be doing at any given time. All I need to do is please Him.

In the past two years that simple truth alone has set me at rest in the midst of many anxious moments. How often it has come to mind when demands were great and the week was short. And it helps me in counseling sessions when I worry whether I can truly offer help. I literally feel the stress drain out of my body when I remember my calling.

Second, He wants me to know that will. The first truth is only a false hope if we can't know what His desires are. Living our lives by guidelines and priority lists simply doesn't work. Some weeks I need 12 hours on my Sunday morning sermon, on others it comes together in only two or three. I can minister effectively only if I know daily what the Lord calls me to do. Knowledge of His mind and will is available to me if I seek Him and feed on His life regularly through prayer and devotional Bible reading. I find that as I center all my thoughts on Him, submit my plans to His will and listen to Him, His wisdom replaces pressure as my constant companion.

I don't mean He hands me a list every morning. But throughout the day I have inner convictions of where I need to be, what I need to be doing and how long I ought to be doing it. Occasionally they flow with my routines and plans. More often they don't. But when I follow His leading the results amaze me.

One Thursday afternoon as I nestled down in my study to finish my Sunday morning message I received an emergency call. A couple was in the middle of a marriage-threatening conflict and wanted help now. I told them I'd see what I could arrange and call them back in five minutes.

I looked at my half-completed sermon notes spread across my desk. Friday and Saturday were booked solid with meetings and appointments. I could feel the anxiety rise as I tried to figure out what to do.

Then I caught myself, leaned back in my chair and simply prayed, "Lord, where do You need me, here at my desk or at their house?" Deep inside I felt I should go and give up my study time. The next morning I was informed both of my Saturday meetings had been canceled. There would be time enough for my sermon!

Other times I've felt as directed to stay at my desk and have found the situation beautifully handled by others in the congregation.

Third, God gives enough grace every day to follow that will. Often God's will means I have to give up things I want to do, and sometimes following His will creates conflicts I'd rather not face. But when I'm seeking to please Him I find peace, strength, time and energy sufficient for the task. Even major conflicts lose their sting when I'm walking close to Him. But when I get out of that closeness to Him, the smallest things trigger anxiety and worry.

A new pattern of discipline has evolved out of this commitment to intimacy. The first 45 minutes of every day are given to devotional reading and prayer—sorry, no study allowed here for upcoming sermons or articles. One day a week I fast and especially give that day to discerning what His priorities and assignments are for me—personally first, then as regards my congregational ministry. I also have a weekly "staff meeting" with the Lord set aside just to pray.

I find many insights rising out of these times that shape my whole week. They also disarm my frustrations with time constraints and measurements of success. If I'm pleasing Him, that's all I need to know.

Support

There's another key here to my freedom I cannot omit. Our church has been committed to wholesome intimacy in relationships between believers. We have sought to build supportive and caring relationships for every member of the body. How important these were in my transitional time! Both my "house church" and our elders listened to me and contributed to my insights. They received my confessions with forgiveness. They helped me affirm God's direction—particularly in those instances where my obedience might cause problems. And they supported me when it did.

What I've gained through this transformation is only an approach to stress, not the ridding of it. The war goes on.

When I drift away from intimacy with the Lord, all my anxieties and desires to please people come rushing in like a flood. Those times are humbling because I realize that I've not changed so that stress no longer affects me, rather I am secure from stress only when I'm walking close to Him.

I know now what to do when my stomach begins to gnaw or my jaw tightens, or I feel like throwing out the phone. The first place I look is not at the crisis but whom I'm pleasing.

Each symptom is now a warning light on the dashboard of my life. It calls me back to the throne for "repairs." Where am I failing to listen to Him? Where am I failing to trust His work in me? Where am I failing to follow His will? I always find answers at the throne, if not alone then with my co-pastor, an elder or my "house church." The problem can be identified, isolated and eliminated.

For two years I have found freedom from the stress that used to drive me and the physical symptoms that plagued me. When I begin to feel the chill of its icy tentacles, I deal with it. In quietness and rest I go before Him. That is at once both the most effective moment of my life and also the hardest. It's so easy to skip or abbreviate, especially in the midst of tension or busyness.

Not long ago I lay awake in the middle of the night as a result of pain from an injury suffered in recreation earlier in the evening. As I used some of my old techniques to get back to sleep when sleep doesn't come easily, I suddenly realized how long it had been since I had needed those techniques that once had been quite regular for me. I stretched out on the bed and gave thanks to God for the freedom from stress I now enjoyed.

I've noticed too how easy it is to pray, study or counsel without a thousand anxieties battling for my attention. "You will keep in perfect peace him whose mind is steadfast, because he trusts in You" is now more than an abstract, unbelievable hope. It's a reality!

28

How Do You Make Stress Work For You?

By Paul L. Walker

Paul L. Walker has served as pastor of the Mount Paran Church of God in Atlanta, Georgia, for the past 24 years. He serves as a member of the Church of God Executive Council and clinical member of the American Association of Marriage and Family Counselors. Walker holds a number of degrees from several universities. He also is a member of the panel of advisors of *MINISTRIES* magazine.

W hat is the most frightening experience you have ever had? A sudden accident? A devastating sickness? A near tragedy? The ravages of combat in war? The terrifying experience of being lost or left alone?

Most of us have had a frightening experience in a storm, for storms are very much a part of our lives. Every year some 10 hurricanes sweep across coastal areas and leave a wake of destruction and devastation. Sometimes we call them cyclones or typhoons; but, regardless of the terminology, hurricanes mean winds up to 150 miles per hour. These winds have caused approximately 1,500 deaths and $20 billion in property damage over the past 20 years.

Between 500 and 600 tornadoes rip across the countryside every year. While there are no instruments capable of measuring their wind velocity, indirect measurement shows wind over 250 miles per hour, with a force that can drive a broom straw through a two-by-four piece of lumber.

We all know about meteorological storms, but what about the emotional storm of stress? Like the disciples in Matthew 8 we have all experienced what they must have felt when suddenly, "without warning, a furious storm came up on the lake, so that the waves swept over the boat. But Jesus was sleeping. The disciples went and woke him, saying, 'Lord, save us! We're going to drown!' " (Matt. 8:24,25, NIV).

We have to get the setting and take a look at the Sea of Galilee to understand this story. It is just a small lake, eight miles wide and 14 miles long. The problem arises where the Jordan Valley makes a cleft in the very rim of the earth, creating a depth of approximately 680 feet below sea level. It is bordered on the east side by the Golan Heights, comprised of limestone rock standing 2000 feet above the sea and merging into the Gilead Mountains. It is bordered on the west side by valleys, hills, crevasses and rocks. The result is a natural funnel which draws winds from the west side through the cracks and crevasses into powerful air swirls which hit the sea with a glancing blow, bounce off the Golan Heights, and return to the sea, causing a whiplash motion and creating high, variable turbulence with tall, devastating waves.

The Sea of Galilee, thus, is a geological deception. On the one hand, it is very calm, serene, tranquil and gracious. On the other hand, it can be lashed into a storm of earthquake proportions, with winds coming from every direction and waves so high that the boats are hidden from view.

This is what happens in many respects in our own lives. Winds come from every direction. Waves get so high we get lost from view, and just like the disciples, we panic. We cry out to God, "Don't You care about us? The waves are in the boat! The ship is about to be swamped! We are going to drown, and You are asleep!"

The pressure of life hits us. We get worried, and the end result is a state of stress. But what really happens when we get this state of stress?

Stress is fear, and fear does strange things to us. It immobilizes us, makes us uptight and causes extreme anxiety. Our muscles become tense. Our breathing gets deeper and faster. Our heartbeat rates increase rapidly, blood vessels constrict, blood pressure rises and perspiration increases. The pituitary glands and adrenal glands begin to pump hormones into our bodies, and our systems become alarm reactors. As a result we sometimes get a giddy feeling to the extent that we feel detached from the situation and wonder if what's going on is really happening to us.

Stress is a sense of prolonged worry to the point of distraction. It is a state of the mind and a condition of the emotions. We feel helpless and hapless, incapable and inadequate. We feel harassed, tormented and plagued. It is an incessant kind of frustration that causes us to become despondent, depressed and inactive. We don't know what decisions to make. We are not sure what alternatives to choose. We just don't have the right answers, and we really are not sure of the right questions.

Yet here we are in the 20th century, living in the most affluent society ever devised. Why are we so worried? What is it that keeps us uptight? What causes this sense of stress?

We worry about our national situation: our politics, the economy, our morality, the crime rate, rising inflation and our future as a nation. Can democracy survive? Can the Republic really last? Will the Constitution really see us through? Do we have the leadership we need, or has the American dream turned into a nightmare?

Most of the time it gets more personal. The waves get in the boat and we battle an individual storm. When we don't have a job, it's an individual storm. When we can't pay our bills, when we are heavily in debt, when we are on the verge of a divorce and when we feel as if we have lost touch with our children, it's a storm.

The end result: we feel as if we are in a deep, dark pit where light cannot penetrate. We become restless, nervous and filled with dread. We dread to think of the future. We dread sickness, old age, dependency and death. We dread facing a job we don't really like. We dread coming home at night because of a tension-filled house and the hostility of unresolved conflicts. It all eats away at us and we call it stress.

Then when it looks like the end, Christ steps up and in one statement—"Peace, be still!"—the whole scene changes. The wind dies down. It becomes completely calm and He says to His disciples, "...Why are you so afraid? Have you still no faith?" (Mark 4:40, NIV).

We know suddenly that in Christ we can have power over stress. The apostle Paul tells us in no uncertain terms, "Don't worry over anything whatever..." (Phil. 4:6, Phillips). Then he goes on to chart the course by saying: "Tell God every detail of your needs in earnest and thankful prayer, and the peace of God, which transcends human understanding, will keep constant guard over your hearts and minds as they rest in Christ Jesus. Here is a last piece of advice. If you believe in goodness and if you value the approval of God, fix your minds on the things which are holy and right and pure and beautiful and good" (Phil. 4: 6-8, Phillips).

The following is a plan to release power over stress:

Pray in Detail

"...Tell God every detail of your needs in earnest and thankful prayer..." (Phil. 4:6, Phillips). This is the beginning point—learn to pray in a way that will bring results. Tell God the details of your needs in an attitude of thankfulness.

God has promised to answer. In the Old Testament, the prophet Isaiah tells us, "Then, if you call, the Lord will answer; if you cry to him, he will say, 'Here I am.' If you cease to pervert justice, to point the accusing finger and lay false charges" (Is. 58:9, NEB).

In the New Testament, Christ promises us that if we ask, it will be given; if we seek, we will find; if we knock, it will be opened. "For everyone who asks receives; he who seeks finds; and to him who knocks, the door will be opened" (Luke 11:10, NIV).

Will it work here in the 20th century? To answer the question here is a letter received from a businessman in Atlanta:

Dear Pastor:

A miracle has taken place in my life. The pain and suffering I brought on myself could not have been completely changed if this were not so.

My addiction had become so great, I was not able to function in speech or normal physical movements. My body shook constantly, and my mind was so twisted I could not make a simple decision. My marriage had fallen apart, and I had lost contact with my children.

For years I had prayed for God's help to overcome my weakness, and for years I felt He had not answered my prayers. Now I know He did answer them. I know He had to let me go through the horrors and nightmares I have had so that I could understand and appreciate what it means to enjoy the love and peace of mind that can only be found by accepting God as my Savior.

I finally realized I had failed completely in trying to control my life. I asked God to take my life because I knew then neither I nor any human being could help me but that God could and would if I would let Him. The teachings I learned in Christ and the friendships I made gave me the faith that my life would be changed if I let God have control.

The first few days were not easy, but I saw I could make it one day at a time. Each morning I ask God for strength and help and at night I thank Him for His protection and guidance.

Life today is great, and I am at peace with myself. My family and friends love me, and I even love myself. When I get upset I remember to let go and let God take over.

Faith in God will bring miracles.

Your friend,
Russell

This is the way to have power over stress. "...Tell God every detail of your needs in earnest and thankful prayer..." (Phil. 4:6, Phillips).

Practice God's Peace

Following the affirmation of prayer, Paul gives us the second phase of the plan by stating: "...the peace of God, which transcends human understanding, will keep constant guard over your hearts and minds as they rest in Christ Jesus" (Phil. 4:7, Phillips).

Of all the statements in the Bible, this is perhaps the most profound. The peace of God stands as a guard over our hearts and minds. We can actually rest in Christ Jesus without worry, fear or stress.

This is the legacy Christ has left us. Christ states, "Peace I leave with you, my peace I give unto you: not as the world giveth, give I unto you. Let not your heart be troubled, neither let it be afraid" (John 14:27, KJV). In John 16:33 He makes us this promise, "These things I have spoken unto you, that in me ye might have peace. In the world ye shall have tribulation: but be of good cheer; I have overcome the world" (KJV).

The question is, "How do we get to that? How do we learn to practice peace?" The answer is found in releasing the potential power we each have to appropriate the very glory of God into our own lives, regardless of the circumstances. Second Corinthians 3:18 tells us that "...(we) reflect like mirrors the glory of the Lord..." (Phillips). This really means that we reflect the character of God, the magnificence of God, the righteousness of God, the excellence of God, the grace and dignity of God. Isaiah states that:

"He gives vigour to the weary, new strength to the exhausted. Young men may grow weary and faint, even in their prime they may stumble and fall; but those who look to the Lord will win new strength, they will grow wings like eagles; they will run and not be weary, they will march on and never grow faint'' (Is. 40:29-31, NEB).

With this resource of God's peace we can understand that good stress is healthy. In fact Dr. Paul J. Rosch, who began his stress research three decades ago, has made the statement, ''People who thrive on stress might die without it.'' In corroboration he points out the following:

''Look at symphony conductors. They undergo physical exertion, deadlines, traveling, dealing with prima donnas in the orchestra. But, on the other hand, they have pride of accomplishment, the approbation of their peers, the plaudits of the audience.

''Look at the life and health records of conductors and you'll see it's outstanding. They live forever. Look at them...The real secret to a long and healthy life is to enjoy what you're doing and be good at it. It's not to avoid stress.'' (Adapted from Susan Seliger, *New Woman* magazine, November 1982, p. 46).

Even Dr. Roy Menninger, president of the Menninger Foundation in Topeka, Kansas, believes the view that stress is bad has gone too far. Dr. Sidney Lecker is more emphatic. He asserts: ''Stress is essential for meeting challenges. If you didn't have it, you'd be dead.''

In this context research consensus seems to be if we feel in control of our lives we can channel the stressful energy that accompanies our drive to achieve and make ourselves healthier than those who avoid conflict and competition all together.

Further, the latest research points out that the ability to control stress is within our own power. It is the attitude that we have about ourselves and our environment that most influences whether we will be hurt by stress.

The point is that each of us has the potentiality of the spirit of an eagle. We can have this sense of freedom. In God's peace we can have power over stress at every turn.

I was preparing a sermon one time on this Isaiah text and asked my wife, Carmelita, what she knew about eagles. She answered, ''Not much, but I'll do some research for you.'' I thought she would come up with the usual facts about wingspan, habits and flying ability, but instead she said, ''I have found out eight things about an eagle: He soars high. He flies fast. He sees far. He lives long. He hides well. He has extreme confidence. He has clean habits and he looks after his family.''

This is the spirit of practicing peace and the power that overcomes worry. God wants each one of us to soar high, fly fast, see far, live long, hide well, exert extreme confidence, practice clean habits and look after our families. With His Spirit motivating this process, we can generate power to defeat the debilitating effects of stress.

Program Your Thinking

Finally, Paul brings the entire plan into focus with the statement, "...Fix your minds on the things which are holy and right and pure and beautiful and good" (Phil. 4:8, Phillips).

The apostle knew we would be confronting a brainwashed world. He was aware of a coming pressure-cooker age, designed to stretch us to the breaking point, until we would lose our sense of objectivity, our sense of absolutes, our sense of divine identity and our sense of spiritual values. That is why he calls for a positive mind set in this text and a renewed mind in Romans 12:2.

The brain is the most complex mechanism ever created. In one way it is like a telephone switchboard that connects incoming and outgoing calls. In another way it is like a computer that makes decisions about which circuits to link and which calls to connect. However, the crowning achievement of the brain is the capacity to think, perceive and experience. Further, the way in which these three processes combine determines what we call learning. In turn, what we learn and how we evaluate this new information shapes our behavior and the kind of lifestyle we pursue.

In a very real sense, we are what we think. Proverbs 23:7 says that as we think in our hearts, so we are. Paul says that we need to be transformed by the renewing of our minds (Rom. 12:2).

To be transformed is to change form completely, as illustrated in the transfiguration of Christ (Matt. 17:2) or the transition of a caterpillar to a butterfly. It is to undergo a spiritual metamorphosis. To be renewed is to experience a thinking renovation with a subsequent change in character toward the excellency of Christ. It is to program our brains with the power of Christ to the point where we can truly fix our minds on "...the things which are holy and right and pure and beautiful and good" (Phil. 4:8, Phillips).

The trick here is to trust the Lord to help us convert bad stress to good. In this regard it is apparent from the research that bad stress can inflict real bodily harm. Rosch makes the point that if bad stress is occasional, the body's immune system can bounce back. If it is prolonged, the immune system is thrown out of whack. Further, repeated and unremitting episodes of bad stress mean repeated release of adrenaline. If the problem prompts no physical exertion to use up the adrenaline—and most stresses in modern life are of a mental rather than a physical nature—then excess adrenaline will remain in the system and can play a part in the build-up of cholesterol in your arteries to the point that it will eventually lead to heart disease.

Susan Seliger gives a definitive overview of the process of converting bad stress to good:

"Before an event expected to be stressful, visualize what may take place. Such a rehearsal will make an actual event seem familiar, helping you to relax and handle the situation with confidence.

"During a tense situation, such as taking a test or meeting a tight deadline, talk nicely to yourself; don't harp on poor preparation or performance. Instead, you should make your innver voice offer praise and reassurance.

"Afterward, luxuriate in the relief of the burden's being lifted. Even if things didn't go so well, avoid puritanical self-criticism. This refreshing interlude can help strengthen your system to better resist the wear and tear of future distress." (Adapted from *New Woman* magazine, November 1982, p. 48).

It is one thing to talk about stress, and it is another thing to take the stress test to determine our individual response. For instance, try this stress test to determine how you stack up by answering yes or no to the following statements:

1. I always eat or walk too rapidly.
2. I always rush people to hurry up and say what they are going to say.
3. I am always thinking of my problems even when I am talking to someone else.
4. I always take work on a vacation.
5. I always feel guilty when I sit down to rest.
6. I am always packing more and more activities into less and less time.
7. I am easily irritated by little things.
8. I often lash out at the people whom I love the most and who love me the most.
9. I sense a loss of self-esteem and intimacy with others.
10. I often feel a sense of loss of spiritual presence in any relationship with God.

Consider also the following seven telltale signs of bad stress as taken from the article, "Stress can be good for you" (*New York* magazine, August 2, 1982):

1. Cold hands, especially if one is colder than the other.
2. Indigestion, diarrhea, too-frequent urination.
3. Being susceptible to every cold or virus that goes around (which could mean that the physical strains of distress are weakening your immune system).
4. Muscle spasms or a soreness and tightness in the jaw, back or neck, shoulders or lower back.
5. Shortness of breath.
6. Headaches, tiredness, sleeping too much or too little.
7. Becoming suddenly accident prone.

The point is that when we recognize any of these signals, we should stop what we are doing—if only for two or three minutes—take several deep breaths and try to relax. In this state of relaxation it is then important for us to pray in detail, practice peace and program your thinking.

From the biblical standpoint we are told to be transformed in our minds into the very image and mindset of Christ.

Perhaps this entire process is best illustrated by the testimony of an early church Christian martyr who found power over stress while imprisoned in a deep, dark dungeon:

"In a dark hole I have found cheerfulness; in a place of bitterness and death I have found rest. While others weep I have found laughter; where others fear I have found strength. Who would believe that in a state of misery I have had great pleasure; that in a lonely corner I have glorious company, and in the hardest bonds perfect repose. All these things Jesus has granted me. He is with me, comforts me and fills me with joy. He drives bitterness from me and fills me with strength and consolation."

This is the process: Pray in detail, practice the peace of God, program your thinking. It will work! The Bible is true! "Don't worry over anything whatever..." (Phil. 4:6, Phillips).

29

How Can You Develop a Writing Career?

By Anne Elver

A homemaker and free-lance writer, Anne Elver has taught classes for writers, spoken at writers' conferences and led seminars on pastors as writers. A pastor's wife, Mrs. Elver has won a number of writing awards.

Would you like to extend your ministry to people outside your congregation without neglecting your church? Do you wish to use sermon research and studies further? Would you like an audience where everyone absorbs your words willingly? Could your church use some public relations work? Would you like for your words to acquire more durability and punch?

If you answered "yes" to any of these questions, read on. There is a way for you to accomplish everything mentioned above. The secret is extending your ministry with the written word.

There are additional advantages for the pastor who writes. Clyde Lee Herring, a pastor in Tulsa, Oklahoma, has supplemented his ministry with writing for 20 years. His work includes four books, several hundred magazine articles, Bible studies and an ongoing piece for a monthly youth publication.

Why does Herring do this? He says, "I believe writing and preaching are complementary. In fact I write a full manuscript of my sermon before preaching it. It is *the* main preparation. Though I do not use the manuscript or notes of any kind during the delivery, I find that writing the sermon makes it far superior to simply delivering it freestyle.

"I write also because it causes me to reflect and think on a wider variety of subjects than otherwise. Of course, the research that goes into writing is of great benefit throughout my ministerial duties. It has honed my skills in public speaking. It has made my writing for our own church paper far superior to what it would have been otherwise.

"I write because it extends the influence of my ministry. For example, one quarterly I've written for has a circulation of 400,000. There's no way I could speak to that many people weekly for 13 weeks."

My husband and I consider ourselves a complementary ministry team. He pastors and I write. Frequently, we mutually research topics for our separate ministries. Our ideas are complementary, and benefit from double research and exposure. Harry preaches on a topic we've jointly studied and approximately 80 people benefit; I write about the topic, extending our ministry greatly. I've heard from people in various places, writing to say something I authored met their needs.

K. Maynard Head authors a syndicated newspaper column and knows the value of this. He says, "The newspaper column...can be one of the most effective methods to lead people to Christ." The average pastor has limited contacts with unbelievers through a church ministry; this isn't true when he writes in secular publications.

I have noted this outreach to unbelievers from a newspaper column. Once I authored a column, "Moms and Tots." My column wasn't specifically Christian, but I planted the Christian message inside helpful hints for young mothers. One day a distraught mother called, wanting to see me. We met in her home, and I shared the gospel with this young woman as we talked. She was unchurched, and had no contact with me apart from my column.

How do church members feel about a pastor who writes? This is where the public relations potential comes in. Herring says "My church members share a pride in the extension of my ministry...everywhere my name is printed, it is in connection with the congregation." Occasionally, someone in our church sees an article I've written. I've always sensed love and support from them when this happens. Sometimes I write articles about church events for local papers. Our people enjoy reading about happenings they're part of; I feel this promotes good will toward our ministry and toward the church in the community.

How do a pastor's words acquire durability and punch when written? Look at his audience. Every congregation contains people who are distracted during sermon delivery. For example, a young mother might worry about her child in the nursery. Some teens endure the sermon, rebellious and resentful of family standards dictating church attendance. A pastor's accent may distract a listener. Members may have hard feelings between themselves. Some attend church in poor health. All of these factors affect the impact of the spoken word.

A reader is not bound by these factors. Your average listener retains 10 percent of what he hears; this multiplies when the words are read. A reader absorbs words more thoroughly. There is never an accent barrier between an author and reader. The message in written form doesn't fight rebellion, feelings or distraction in a reader as it must in some listeners. Written words have a greater life-changing punch for these reasons.

How do a pastor's words gain durability when they're written? *In His Steps,* for example, is still as thought-provoking today as it always was. Many church fathers left a rich legacy of written words inspiring today's Christians.

Contrast this to the spoken word. Seldom does an individual remember a sermon or have access to it a year later. A magazine article, book or tract might be saved, read several times and stored somewhere. Years later, somebody might read it and receive ministry, long after the author's death. The durability of the written word isn't measurable but it is real.

The above advantages of extending your ministry with writing multiply when you consider that pastors are uniquely qualified to write, and have credibility with publishers. Two editors from Bridge Publishing, Inc., Lloyd B. Hildebrand and Drew R. Thomas, surveyed trends in best-selling Christian books for six months and found pastors' names appearing repeatedly on best-selling books.

Why is this? Pastors are sensitive to people's needs, and meet them by addressing specific needs through preaching. The written word carries the same satisfying potential that preaching does. Pastors with effective pulpit ministries who write meet needs outside their local churches, and people need their message.

My husband and I especially appreciate the extension of a pulpit ministry via the written word. Twelve years ago, neither of us had a joyful, yielded relationship with the Lord. Someone gave us a book meeting our need. It was *It Can Happen to Anybody* by Russell Bixler. The dear pastor authoring the book exposed his feelings, failings and spiritual search so that we both identified with him. We went on to seek the best God had for us after reading the book, and the Lord began working in our lives more deeply than before. Several years later, my husband left a secure career and comfortable life to attend school and after that entered the ministry. Our ministry today was inspired from the pastor who ministered to us in writing.

Pentecostal and Charismatic pastors gain another advantage from writing. Many readers don't understand the Charismatic experience, and would welcome information from an author with first-hand knowledge. A Charismatic pastor who writes may bridge the gap people frequently keep between themselves and anything faintly resembling Pentecostalism.

Brenda is a friend I met at a writers' conference. She subscribed to several magazines which were steady outlets for my writing, remembered some articles I'd authored and complimented them. We visited several times during the conference, discussing many things. My Charismatic involvement came up during one conversation. Brenda reacted with surprise and curiosity.

We discussed her questions about my experience. Before we parted she said, "You're the first Charismatic I've really talked to. It's obvious I've been mistaken about that subject. You're as sensible as anybody, your writing isn't heretical, and you aren't weird. Thanks for sharing freely. I was a bit nosey. Let's keep in touch." We hugged and went our separate ways. I feel she accepted me (Charismatic leanings and all) because my writing prepared the way.

So you're convinced you'd like to enrich your ministry through writing. Will you have time to write, in addition to your pastoral duties?

Let's see where writing pastors get time. Herring says, "Writing time is made, not born. It's hard to find time to write. The sin of procrastination is a constant struggle. One must give up something to do something else. I give up some TV or book reading time to write. How do I do it? I apply the seat of my britches to the seat of the chair...and write." Herring writes at home, recognizing his church ministry as top priority. Should a conflict develop between writing and pastoral duties, his writing temporarily takes second place.

Charles Lee Stanley, senior pastor of one of the largest churches in the United States, supplements his ministry by writing. How? He says, "The key is discipline. I find that if I write early in the morning when I am fresh and quiet, before I am caught up in my daily schedule, I have the most freedom in expressing the message God has given me." Two of Stanley's children are studying journalism and they help him.

Carlton Myers, pastor of a church in Virginia, writes also. He says, "Writing is a part of my ministry; and, as it does not take time from my church responsibilities, it is a proper use of my time." Myers feels he owes his church six days a week, barring weddings, funerals or other unforeseen events. He writes on Sundays.

Every pastor's schedule is different but the pastor who wants to write can find time. Perhaps some vacation time could be used this way. If a tight schedule is a hardship to getting the written message out, a pastor might consider working with another writer, getting his message publishable. Many Christian free-lance writers welcome this kind of work. Another possibility is hiring help for editing, typing and the like. Many journalism and business students do this work reasonably. However a pastor gains publication, the key is discipline. Writing takes effort but busy schedules are manageable.

Once a time for writing is found, where do you begin, and what do you write about? The best way to begin writing is to write what you know about. Stanley's book grew out of a question from a counseling session. Since between 70 and 80 percent of Christian best-sellers are teaching books, Bible study and sermon series ideas are possibilities for publication in the form of books, tracts, articles and curriculum items.

The pastor in search of subjects to share can do some self-examination and find topics easily. What's your background? Have you had any memorable experiences? What's the Lord doing in your own life? My husband preached his introductory sermon to our present congregation, telling about the struggle he overcame with materialism in his former occupation. With his permission, I wrote a personal experience article from the sermon, and a Christian publication has it scheduled to appear soon. Many of my published works originate this way.

Sometimes people in your congregation share publishable experiences and testimonies. You might suggest writing these. A pastor doing this serves his congregation in a deeper way. A man in one of our past congregations had an interesting experience witnessing to a seatmate on an airplane. I wrote this story, cooperating with our member, and the resulting article, "The Seatmate," saw publication. When the article came out, Bill mentioned how pleased he was to see his story in print and glad the story could bless others through publication.

How does the pastor with a written message get it published? Most pastors already have some tools of the trade handy—a typewriter or word processor, paper and reference books. In addition, you need up-to-date copies of writers' market books, and subscriptions to various writers' magazines. In addition to printed material for writers, there are conferences. These are listed in the writers' publications. Many denominations sponsor writers' conferences, and you can get on their mailing lists for notification. You'll find advertisements for conferences in publications put out by their sponsoring organizations. Conferences and writers' publications yield practical help for the business end of being a writer, as well as inspiration.

If you feel your writing skills themselves need improvement, there are helpful courses in colleges, YMCA and YWCA's, churches, writers' groups and other organizations. Ask around for information on ongoing local assistance. There are correspondence courses if local training isn't available. Pastor Myers honed his writing skills this way. There are also excellent books on writing, so visit your local bookstore and browse through these, purchasing those that meet your needs.

We live in a literate society. The writing pastor reaches more people than otherwise. Writing stretches a pastor's growth, forcing him to think deeply and widely. Most pastors write anyway for church bulletins, sermons and newsletters. Why not extend this ministry? People need your message.

30

How Do You Recognize a Missionary Call?

By C. W. Howard III

C. W. Howard III is assistant director of Career Planning and Placement, Old Dominion University, Norfolk, Virginia, and was recently elected president of the Mental Health Association of Tidewater. He has pastored two churches, assisted in organizing another church, served interim pastorships in 13 churches and spent 25 years as a professor of psychology. Howard also has conducted leadership groups.

What compels a young woman such as Marilyn Laszlo of Wycliffe Bible Translators to leave her family and friends in America and move to a small aboriginal tribe where she does not understand the language? A place where she does not eat the same food or share the same culture, and almost dies from malaria and other diseases?

What motivates any person to go to the uttermost parts of the earth, or even to a nearby city, and live apart from family, friends and familiar surroundings?

"The notion that every Christian is a missionary, popular as it might be, misconstrues the fundamental nature of the missionary call," says C. Peter Wagner in *On the Crest of the Wave.* "To clarify this matter, the most important consideration is understanding the relationship between the missionary call and the biblical doctrine of spiritual gifts."

Wagner uses Paul, in contrast to Peter, to illustrate: "Paul's spiritual gift enabled him to minister in another culture. The best statement of what this missionary gift does is in 1 Corinthians 9:22 where Paul says, 'I have become all things to all men, that I might by all means save some.' Not everyone can do it. Peter, for example, couldn't. That's why Paul says clearly, 'The gospel for the uncircumcised (Gentiles) had been committed to me, as the gospel of the circumcised (Jews) was to Peter' (Gal. 2:7). If we adopt the hypothesis of the missionary gift, all these pieces fall into place.

"Just having the missionary gift doesn't guarantee that a person will be a good missionary, but it increases the probability considerably. It helps the person learn the new language and culture. It reduces (but never eliminates) the effects of culture shock."

Wagner defines the gift: "The missionary gift is the special ability that God gives to certain members of the body of Christ to minister whatever other spiritual gifts they have in a second culture. It is the specific gift of cross-cultural ministry."

The aim of all missionary endeavors should be a clear and persistent witness in the missionary's words and actions to "Christian truth and life, and the building up of living Christian communities, trustfully leaving to God what He will do with the work of His servants," says

Hendrik Kraemer in *The Christian Message in a Non-Christian World.*

With this aim in mind, a missionary is free from anxious thinking and acting and will have a total spiritual outlook of lifting up his eyes to the Lord for his help.

The only valid purpose of missions is to call people to confront God's acts of revelation and His salvation for man as the Bible presents them, and to establish a community of believers who will serve Jesus Christ, Kraemer concludes.

All other motives, such as transmitting Christian ideals into a village, people or civilization, or even instilling the blessings an enlightened spirit can give into an emerging world culture, should be secondary. The same motives that impelled the first apostles are the only valid, tenable motives and should therefore be primary.

The missionary needs an untiring and genuine interest in the ideas, sentiments, institutions—in short, in the total life of the people among whom he works, for the sake of Christ and the people.

If a man feels someone is interested in him out of intellectual curiosity or merely to see him converted, and not because he is a person, then there cannot arise a meaningful relationship, that indispensable basis for all spiritual contact between two people. Without this acceptance and relationship, the door to that person and to his world remains locked.

God's love is remote and abstract. The missionary demonstrates God's love by showing a genuine interest in the total life of the people to whom he goes.

What the people learn of Christ depends largely on what they see of Him in a missionary. Unfortunately, they often see arrogance or even ignorance in a missionary who does not accept or appreciate them in their environment or place in history.

God's love motivates the missionary to reach out to a person in need and communicate God's solutions to his needs. Even when rejected and humiliated, a missionary must continue to have and show a servant's love, or at least be growing toward having that kind of love.

Pride and prejudice are other self-serving motives which have, along with ignorance, contaminated the missionary's message.

Bring Glory to God

Our motivation for missionary work and evangelism has often been misdirected. Going out to seek a lost soul and bringing him into a saving knowledge of Christ seems like a worthy goal. But the missionary's primary goal should be to glorify God.

As Juan Carlos Ortiz, pastor of a large congregation in Buenos Aires, wrote in *A Call to Discipleship,* "We are not going to save souls because of the souls. We are going to extend the kingdom of God because God says so and He is the Lord. Our motivations must be cleaned up."

219

Reliance on the Spirit

In his book *Christian Mission in the Modern World*, John R. W. Stott says Christians must never try to bludgeon people into God's kingdom but must humbly rely on the Holy Spirit's power to convict and woo. Therefore, the missionary needs the kind of motivation that is truly guided by the Holy Spirit.

Johannes Blauw writes of this dependence on the Holy Spirit in *The Missionary Nature of the Church*. He says the primary motivation for preaching the gospel comes not from the outside, based on the "need of the world." Nor does it come from within, as in the "religious impulse." Instead it comes from above, as a "divine coercion, as a matter of life and death, not for the world, but for the church itself."

As the apostle Paul declared, "Woe is unto me, if I preach not the gospel!...And this I do for the gospel's sake, that I might be partaker thereof with you" (1 Cor. 9:16,23).

How does a missionary seek the Holy Spirit's guidance in motivation? Norman Grubb in *Touching the Invisible* describes the basic principles the Worldwide Evangelization Crusade has used in its administrative and field work.

Much of the group's praying, although sincere, lacked confidence. So often they were not sure if their requests were according to God's will. They prefaced most requests with a phrase such as, "If it is Thy will." Often they rose from their knees as unsure of the answer as before they asked. If they had been asked whether a particular prayer would be granted, they could only have responded, "We hope so."

They began to study the prayer lives of the men of the Bible. They found that these men first discovered whether their prayer was God's will; then having received assurance on this point, they prayed, received by faith, persisted, declared things to come, with all the authority of God Himself.

The WEC staff saw this again and again in the Bible. "Elijah suddenly appears on the scene and announces, 'As the Lord God of Israel liveth, there shall not be dew nor rain these years, but according to my word.' " James called this "effectual praying."

Another example the staff found in Scripture was that of Hezekiah, a "man of sincere, but unavailing prayer, and Isaiah, a man of effectual prayer." In a crisis Hezekiah cried out to God and sent a message to Isaiah, seeming to despair of the Lord's hearing his prayer. But Isaiah answered, "Thus saith the Lord, 'Be not afraid....' "

Guided Praying

The WEC staff became more and more impressed that "effectual praying must be guided praying." They realized "the first essential was not to pray, but to know what to pray for," and that special and clear provision had been made for this knowledge in the Scriptures.

According to the apostle Paul in Romans 8:26,27, the Spirit is given expressly to guide our praying, for "true prayers are God's prayers prayed through us—they issue from God's mind, are taught us of His Spirit, are prayed in His faith, and are thus assured of answer."

Thus, Grubb notes, the WEC's meetings took on new form, and those present kneeled to pray only after they had received directions from God. They met in groups not just to read the Bible or discuss a doctrine, but to seek practical answers to problems which confronted them.

They would outline and discuss a certain matter, inviting opinions and criticisms. Gradually they would become convinced that a certain outcome would glorify God—"a certain sum of money by a certain date; a move of the Spirit at a certain place; the granting of an official permit; a reconciliation."

They would examine the Scriptures for examples on which to base their faith, looking at such men as David, Daniel, Moses and Paul. "Were these men sure of their guidance?" they would ask. "Did they believe and declare it? Did it come to pass? Can we fairly compare our situation to theirs?"

If so, then and only then, the group members would pray, believe, receive, declare their faith and persist with all authority of the Master's words, "Whosoever shall say unto this mountain, Be thou removed—and shall not doubt in his heart, but shall believe that those things which he saith shall come to pass; he shall have whatsoever he saith" (Mark 11:23).

In a similar manner, the missionary must learn to depend on God and seek His will through immersing himself in prayer and God's Word. Then God's purposes, and not his own needs, will motivate him. A missionary can easily justify his actions when he fulfills his own motives. But when he seeks the Holy Spirit's guidance in finding God's will, in order to bring glory to Him, then God will reap the fruit of his missionary efforts.

As Wagner says, "If God gives you a missionary gift, He also calls you to use it for His glory. If He calls you to be a missionary, He will give you the gift you need for the job."

What motivates a young woman to leave America and live with a small aboriginal tribe? What compels any missionary to go to the uttermost parts of the earth? It is that "divine coercion from above." That's why he or she reaches out to others, demonstrates God's love and seeks to bring Him glory.

31

How Should You Cope With Criticism?

By C. M. Ward

C. M. Ward, chancellor and former president of Bethany Bible College in Santa Cruz, California, is one of America's foremost evangelists and radio/television speakers. A former pastor, Bible college instructor and editor, he also was radio evangelist for "Revivaltime," the international radio voice of the Assemblies of God. He has written 23 hardback volumes of radio sermons, authored over 250 booklets and has recorded the entire Bible on cassette and 8-track tapes.

The price of leadership is criticism. No one pays much attention to last-place finishers. President Harry Truman said, "If you can't stand the heat, stay out of the kitchen." You will be harassed. Count on it!

Certain criticism can be justified and one can learn and improve by it. I can either distress or please the public. I have been guided for years by a line which says, "A chip on the shoulder indicates wood higher up."

Second Corinthians includes the apostle Paul's defense of himself. It is a classic for all public figures. Paul's adversaries demeaned, plagued and abused him. They heaped scorn on his physical presence. They indicated that he was a bluffer without real apostolic authority—one who wrote muscular letters without forcibly and visibly interpreting them. "When I therefore was thus minded, did I use lightness? or things that I purpose, do I purpose according to the flesh, that with me there should be yea, yea, and nay, nay? But as God is true, our word toward you was not yea and nay" (2 Cor. 1:17,18).

No preacher is any more popular than the last good sermon he or she has preached. Let God bless you and the aisles are blocked with handshakes, congratulations, autograph hunters, offers of entertainment, invitations, adoration. But strike out, have a difficult time, and you could drive a jeep through the same aisles. Public life is precarious. One moment you are a hero, another moment you are a heel. Some of the same fickle people in the crowd that cried, "Hosanna," a few hours later clamored, "Crucify."

Occasionally there are bits of heckling and bantering. I have had committee members say to me, "There are better preachers than yourself." I reply, "Yes, but where can you get so much for so little?"

You cannot afford to become edgy. Under God, the authority is in your hands. You must use that authority judiciously. Under God, the preacher behind the pulpit is the home-plate umpire. Bill Klem, the legendary umpire in the National League, called a pitch much to the distress of the hitter. The player threw his bat in the air in disgust. Mr. Klem did not remove his mask or raise his voice. He said, "Sir, if that bat comes down you are out of the game."

Strength is in maintaining calmness. "Who, when he was reviled, reviled not again; when he suffered, he threatened not; but committed himself to him that judgeth righteously" (1 Pet. 2:23). Never lend dignity to meanness or littleness.

The public must retain freedom of expression, this side of libel. People pay the bills. They make possible whatever benefits I enjoy. Safety is not in throttling or in censorship. Safety is in truth.

There will always be the cheap-shots types, like Shimei who foulmouthed David. Let time be the arbiter! The gullies are lined with false prophets.

Never, never take it out on the audience! Get it out of your system with a punching bag in a gymnasium or with a set of golf clubs. Never "wrestle against flesh and blood"!

"A soft answer turneth away wrath: but grievous words stir up anger" (Prov. 15:10). George Bernard Shaw, the Irish playwright, had his critics. After one opening, a critic voiced his displeasure. He said, "It's rotten! It's rotten!" To which Shaw replied, "I agree with you perfectly, but what are we two against so many!"

Your wife is in your corner. Listen to her! Her loyalty is unquestioned, yet in a helpful way she can assist you by pointing out faults or inaccuracies. Dr. Robert C. Schuller says he depends upon his wife to monitor him. If he speaks loudly, she will plug her ears with her fingers. If he cannot be heard she will cup her ears with her hands. He says, in all justice, there are times when she holds her nose.

Elijah succumbed to opposition. Jezebel was a firecracker. Her opposition sapped the preacher's strength. "It is enough; now, O Lord, take away my life; for I am not better than my fathers" (1 Kings 19:4). Elijah was shaken. The task behind the pulpit is never easy. You must keep your face into the wind. From that point Elijah's days were numbered. His successor, Elisha, was chosen. The repetitive battles had fatigued Elijah. He would be removed with great honor from the action.

Watch weariness! Satan will take advantage. You can say things when weary that otherwise would not be said. One careless phrase can destroy a ministry. You bite your lip after it is said, but it is too late. Remember, the San Francisco earthquake only lasted seconds, but it destroyed a city.

It must become a part of me—SPEAK, NEVER STRIKE. "No striker" (1 Tim. 3:3). There is a good rule in professional hockey for head officials, the referees. Hockey is a very physical sport. It is football at 40 miles an hour. As a result, the games incite disagreements between the players. When these moments occur, the linesmen intervene and do their best to separate the combatants and restore order. During the melee the referee stands aside. He can cooly judge the right and wrong and assesses the appropriate penalties. If he allowed himself to be involved in the brawl he could never judge dispassionately. "Not a brawler" (1 Tim. 3:3).

Isaiah, who knew the many changes of public opinion, said, "In quietness and confidence shall be your strength."

The late Herman Hickman, great football coach at Tennessee, Army and Yale, said, "When you are being run out of town, get to the head of the line and look as though you were leading the parade."

32

What About Self-Employment Tax?

By James Guinn

James Guinn is a certified public accountant with the firm Guinn, Smith & Company in Irving, Texas, a firm that has provided C.P.A. services to over 250 religious organizations, helping more than 100 non-profit corporations receive tax-exempt status from the Internal Revenue Service.

Guinn earned a bachelor of business administration degree from Midwestern State University in Wichita Falls, Texas, and worked for Arthur Andersen & Company, one of the largest international public accounting firms.

Because of well-meaning but misinformed fellow ministers and tax practitioners, many ministers have been ill-advised with regard to their self-employment taxes. Some ministers believe they have opted out of the Social Security program when, in fact, they have not.

Prior to 1968, services performed by a minister were exempt from Social Security, unless he requested Social Security coverage by filing Form 2031. The ministers who filed Form 2031 made an irrevocable election, and can never again be exempt from Social Security.

Beginning in 1968, a minister is automatically included under Social Security unless he files Form 4361, Application for Exemption from Self-Employment Tax, which is accepted and approved by the Internal Revenue Service. Therefore, ministers who did not opt into the Social Security program prior to 1968 and who did not file Form 4361 on a timely basis after 1968 should be paying the self-employment tax.

A minister who realizes he has been in error and should have been paying self-employment taxes should immediately file amended tax returns for the years on which the statute of limitations has not run out (three years from date of filing the return) and pay the self-employment tax. Of course, the Internal Revenue Service will assess substantial interest and penalties.

Hopefully the Internal Revenue Service will accept the amended returns and take no further action.

Exemption Requirements

A minister requesting exemption from Social Security coverage must meet one of the following two tests:

● A religious principles test, which refers to the institutional principles and discipline of the particular religious denomination to which he belongs; or

● A conscientious opposition test, which refers to the opposition of the individual clergyman because of religious considerations (rather than opposition based upon the general conscience of the clergyman).

Under either alternative, the clergyman's opposition must be based on religious grounds [Internal Revenue Regulations 1.1402(e) - (a)(2)].

When applying either test, the minister is stating that because he meets one of the tests, he is opposed to the acceptance (with respect to services performed as a minister) of any private or public insurance which makes payments in the event of death, disability, old age, or retirement; makes payments toward the cost of, or provides services for medical care (including benefits of any insurance system established by the Social Security system).

In test (1), Internal Revenue Code 1402(h) provides exemption based on the sect's, group's or denomination's recognized religious concepts and theology that are opposed to the Social Security program. Test (1) primarily applies to Christian Science practitioners and members of religious sects who have taken a vow of poverty, such as Roman Catholic priests and nuns.

For most evangelical ministers the exemption would arise from applying test (2), the opposition of the individual clergyman because of religious conscience, not general conscience.

A minister wishing to obtain exemption must file Form 4361 in triplicate during the first two years he has performed services as a minister and has $400 of net earnings from self-employment, a part of which was from the ministry.

The ploy of becoming reordained is not valid. This was tested in tax court in 1978 and it was determined that reordination did not start a new period of eligibility with regard to the two-year time frame. Accordingly, only during the first two years after the first ordination can the election be made.

Form 4361 is signed under penalties of perjury so it is very important that careful consideration be given to filing for exemption. Also, keep in mind this election is irrevocable.

Keep in mind that just because the service has approved Form 4361, your exemption can still be questioned upon audit of your tax returns. The service may take somewhat of a "back-door" approach to invalidating the Form 4361.

For example, if the exempt minister is a member of a religious denomination which does not forbid its ministers to participate in the Social Security program, then the individual minister's election could be suspect, that is, if he is a member of a denomination that allows participation in Social Security, how could he oppose it on religious grounds?

Another Internal Revenue Service approach may be in the area of retirement and insurance plans. If a minister has filed the form stating he is opposed to accepting insurance and retirement benefits on religious grounds as discussed above and then participates in any public or private plans, the service could take the position that the election is invalid.

The Internal Revenue's position is stated in the following Revenue

Rulings:

Rev. Rule 68-188. An individual may not qualify for the exemption from self-employment tax under section 1402(h) of the Self-Employment Contributions Act if he is a member of a religious group by reason of whose tenets or teachings he is conscientiously opposed to receiving the benefits of public, but not of private, insurance of the type described in section 1402(h)(1) of the Act.

Rev. Rule 77-88. A member of a religious group opposed to acceptance of benefits of any private or public insurance who purchases a retirement annuity from an insurance company is not eligible for exemption from self-employment tax under section 1402(g) of the Code.

Keep in mind that Revenue Rulings are IRS interpretations of the law, not the law. However, should IRS assert its self-employment tax during the audit of a minister's tax return, litigation would probably be required to settle the issue.

If Form 4361 is completed properly, the IRS will probably approve the exemption as they do not initially check the information provided and because the minister has signed the form under penalties of perjury. However, the Internal Revenue Service cautions the minister on the form that it (the form) is not proof of the right to an exemption from Social Security Tax. What is proof is the religious belief of the minister and/or of his denomination's belief and other pertinent facts which IRS could check out under audit conditions.

If the IRS were able to invalidate the Form 4361 election, the service would be within its legal rights to assess delinquent taxes plus interest and penalties for past years.

The minister who is a member of a religious denomination whose tenets of belief oppose participation in Social Security and who participates in no insurance or retirement plan has the greatest likelihood of sustaining his election.

If after careful consideration a minister believes he meets one of the religious opposition tests and chooses to file Form 4361, it is recommended that he attach either a statement out of his denomination's creed that states their opposition to Social Security for religious reasons or a statement for himself supported by Bible references showing individual religious opposition on theological grounds.

This is not foolproof, however. If IRS approves the exemption with the statement attached, you have gone on record and they are at least aware of the grounds on which you base your opposition.

Many ministers have not elected out of Social Security coverage for various reasons; however, the primary reason seems to be the fear of having the election invalidated. In any event all is not lost for those participating in the Social Security programs as there are some death and disability benefits. The ratio of benefit to payments made would vary from person to person based on years in the Social Security system and other factors so no attempt is made here to evaluate the Social Security program.

The major complaints are the instability of the program, the belief that the same dollars invested wisely by the minister would reap far greater returns, and limited retirement benefits.

Numerous tax cases support the fact that economical reasons and personal non-religious opposition are invalid for purposes of filing Form 4361.

It is suggested that all the above factors be considered before application for exemption from self-employment (Social Security) tax be made.

33

What Is the Call of God?

By Elmer L. Towns

Elmer L. Towns is dean of the School of Religion, Liberty University, Lynchburg, Virginia. He has taught in Christian colleges for 27 years and authored 46 books relating to church growth, theology and the Sunday school. Towns has received degrees from three theological seminaries and two universities.

The ministry is more than an occupation or a job, it is a call from God. The salary is lower than most other positions of equal responsibility. The demands are great, the hours are long, the burdens are almost unbearable. Ministers are gossiped about and lied about. They are criticized to their faces, and carnal church members connive behind their backs. The pastorate is one of the most demanding positions, and no one man could remain as pastor without the inner assurance that the Almighty God has called him to that office.

What makes a minister give up sleep to prepare sermons and pray for power on his message? The call of God. What motivates a minister to spend all day knocking on doors instead of getting a better-paying job when he knows his family doesn't have as many nice things as the neighbors or he doesn't have the freedom to be with his family as much as some others? What possesses a man's heart to lay brick on a church, to paint old pews, to run a mimeograph, to get on the radio and preach the gospel? The call of God.

A man at the assembly line hears something no others perceive: it is God's call. He begins to march to a different drumbeat: it is God's command to go and build a church, even when his friends think he is crazy. A man attempts to do what seems impossible. He speaks in public when his grammar is shoddy; he knocks on doors, knowing he cannot sell. He attempts to teach the Bible when he has little formal education. He tries to build huge auditoriums, not knowing construction or architecture. He manages a large corporation, though ignorant of financing or advertising. Why does a man dream the unthinkable and attempt the impossible? He feels God has called him and all he can do is obey. This minister knows that with God's calling is God's enablement and that if God has called him, he can serve the Lord.

The ministry is not something a man chooses. A young man does not look through the want ads and, not finding a position, turn to the pastorate. The New Testament church begins with a God-called man who is willing to make any sacrifice, pay any price, forsake all and build a church in the name and after the pattern of Jesus Christ who said, "I will build my church" (Matt. 16:18).

234

The Biblical View of Call

Even though the term *call* or *calling* has a technical use in today's church, it is used in three ways in Scripture: first, the call to salvation; second, the call to sanctification; and third, the call to full-time Christian service.

1. *The Call to Salvation.* In Scripture the word *call* is designated as the invitation of Jesus Christ for a person to become saved. Jesus said, "Come unto me, all ye that labour and are heavy laden, and I will give you rest" (Matt. 11:28). In essence, He was calling people to salvation. Later Paul designates this call, "Among whom are ye also the called of Jesus Christ" (Rom. 1:6). He also tells us, "All things work together for good to them that love God, to them who are the called according to His purpose" (Rom. 8:28). We know this refers to salvation.

2. *The Call to Sanctification.* God not only calls men to salvation, but He also calls them to grow to completion or maturity in Jesus Christ. This is a call to sanctification. Paul reminds the Corinthians, "God is faithful, by whom ye were called into the fellowship of His Son Jesus Christ our Lord" (1 Cor. 1:9). He had already indicated that the Corinthians knew Christ as Savior, but he was inviting them to grow deeper in fellowship with Jesus Christ.

The high call for every Christian is to be as sanctified as possible in fellowship with Jesus Christ.

3. *The Call to Full-time Christian Service.* The greatest honor that can come to any person is to be set aside by the Holy Spirit to serve Jesus Christ with all of his life. These people are identified as those who are in the professional ministry. Today they are pastors, assistant pastors, evangelists, missionaries, Bible teachers in colleges, and others who serve in full-time ministry; by which they are supported financially full-time. In the Old Testament, the high priests were full-time servants. "No man taketh this honor unto himself, but he that is called of God, as was Aaron" (Heb. 5:4). This verse gives us insight into full-time Christian service. In the Old Testament a priest had to be born into the tribe of Levi, but not every Levite became a priest. Only those who were called of God were set aside for actual service in the temple.

Barnabas and Paul were called of God to full-time Christian service. Remember even at Paul's conversion it was indicated that he would be a unique servant and messenger to the gentiles (Acts 9:15-16). However, after 14 years of learning and apprenticeship—by serving Jesus Christ in the churches at Damascus, Tarsus and Antioch—Paul was ready to be separated into full-time Christian service. We read the account, "As they ministered to the Lord, and fasted, the Holy Ghost said, Separate me Barnabas and Saul for the work whereunto

I have called them'' (Acts 13:2). Note that these two men who were called into full-time Christian service were actively involved in serving Jesus Christ. The call did not come to two unconcerned high school boys who were sitting on the last pew in the church. These were active church leaders who were called into full-time service.

A second part of the call is that they were to be separated, indicating they were no longer considered laymen. A third part of the call to full-time services was accompanied with self-examination and searching the mind of the Lord. Barnabas and Saul were fasting and praying to the Lord when they were called. A last part of the call is that it came from the Holy Spirit. No man can issue the call to himself. He can desire the office of a bishop (1 Tim. 3:7), but the call of God comes from the Holy Spirit.

Illustrating the Call

When Jesus Christ walked along the shore of Galilee, He called Peter and Andrew to follow Him. This illustrates the call of God. They had to give up their nets (occupation) and follow Jesus Christ full-time. Even in this illustration we see the place of a Christian college or a seminary. The call to full-time Christian service includes the call to prepare. They were called to follow Jesus Christ, but for three years they were sitting at His feet, learning how to be disciples.

When Paul wrote to the Romans, he identified himself as ''Paul, a servant of Jesus Christ, called to be an apostle'' (Rom. 1:1). In a similar manner, every minister of Jesus Christ should be able to identify himself as one who is called to serve Jesus Christ.

Deeply convicted during a Sunday evening church service, Tom Berry went home unsaved. Alone with his Bible at home later, he knelt and prayed, ''Lord, if You will save me, You can have all of me.'' He knew if he were to be saved, Christ would have to do the saving. Later in Canton, Texas, while milking a cow, he felt in his heart that God was calling him to preach. He went in the house and announced his decision to his mother, who was shocked; young Tom had been a jokester in school. But God sometimes uses other men to help confirm a call to the ministry. Tom Berry spent a Saturday night at the Texas State Fair in Dallas carousing around. When he got home, he was burdened and he felt God telling him, ''I've called you to preach and here you are messing around with sin.'' About 2:30 a.m. he made a complete surrender. Later, on the parking lot of the church, his pastor asked, ''Tom, what are you going to do with your life?'' Three weeks later Tom was in college preparing for the ministry.

Saved as a teenager, John Powell, pastor of Reimer Road Baptist Church, Wadsworth, Ohio, was out of the will of God for a number of years. After his rededication as a young husband and father, he began to teach in the Sunday school. A year later, he felt God was calling

236

him into the ministry. One Sunday when a missionary speaker did not show up, his pastor spoke on "Being a Missionary at Home." At the invitation, Powell wanted to go forward but was afraid. Finally, he went forward in surrender to the ministry, and found that God had been speaking to his wife in another section of the church—she too had come forward. Powell told the pastor, "I think God is calling me into the ministry." The pastor boldly announced, "John has surrendered for the ministry."

Bruce Cummons, pastor of Massillon Baptist Temple, was a diligent young man serving God in the Akron Baptist Temple after his return from military service. One evening he was so burdened that he went walking by Lake Erie, stretching himself out on the grass to pray. The burden would not leave. Finally, he said in desperation, "Lord, I'll do anything. I'll preach the gospel if you want me to." Immediately the burden lifted, and Bruce knew that God had called him to preach the gospel. Until that time he was not aware that God was speaking to him about the ministry. Young Samuel in the tabernacle heard the audible voice of God in the night. God had to call three times before Eli recognized it was God and told the young boy to say, "Speak...for thy servant heareth" (1 Sam. 3:10). It was not until Samuel responded correctly that he knew God was calling him.

Sometimes God calls through another person. As the elderly prophet Elijah stood before God on Mt. Sinai, God called him to go and anoint his successor, Elisha. We have the record in 1 Kings 19:19-21 of Elijah throwing his mantle across young Elisha's shoulders as he plowed. God uses his servants to extend a call to young men. Ed Nelson, pastor of the South Sheridan Baptist Church, had led singing for a revival by Dr. Bob Jones, Jr. It was during the days of World War II and most of the young men were in the service. He confessed he was not a good song leader but did the best he could; there was no one else available. An elderly lady came to the platform and looked up at young Ed as he bent over to speak to her. "Ed, I believe God is calling you to the ministry." He slapped his knee and exclaimed, "That's the funniest thing I have ever heard!" Several in the auditorium heard his loud response but the lady got him to promise to pray about it. Eight days later, he was plowing sugar beets before the sun came up on a Monday morning; the burden of God was driving him to desperation. Ed Nelson got off the tractor and knelt in the wet sod, surrendering for the ministry. God had used a saintly grandmother to reach his heart.

Some 132 young men have gone into full-time Christian service from Trinity Baptist Church, Jacksonville, Florida, as of 1975. The powerful preaching of Bob Gray won many of these young boys, and they were eventually called to full-time service.

If a church is effectively preaching the gospel and teaching the Word of God, then young men will be called into full-time Christian service. If a church doesn't have young people going into the Lord's service, then something is wrong with its ministry.

A Definition of the Call

When I attend an ordination service I always ask the candidate the following question, "What is the call of God, and how do you know that you have it?" I feel that if a candidate cannot identify the call of God and convince the council that he has been called to full-time Christian service, then we should not ordain him no matter what, and no one should have "hands laid on him" if there is not absolute assurance that he has been called into full-time Christian service.

Once a young man answered the question by indicating the command in Scripture was the call of God. He noted since Jesus had commanded to go and preach the gospel to everyone, he should do so. This answer was not enough. Surely the call of God is based on the command of Scripture. But the command of God is given to everyone. Every Christian should preach the gospel to all people. That is the basis for the call. But the call to full-time Christian service is more than the command of Scripture. It is a unique experience that only those who have been set aside by Jesus Christ have received. The command of Scripture is to everyone. The call of God is more particular. It is only to the recipients.

Then the candidate gave a second basis for the call of God. He said the call of God was the need of people to hear the gospel. He went on to indicate that there were thousands of needy people in the city who needed to get saved. Once again the candidate had to be corrected. The need is an obligation upon every Christian, but the need alone is not the call. Every Christian meets needy people every day of his life, but this does not constitute a call to full-time Christian service. The call is based upon the need of people to hear the gospel, but the call of God to full-time Christian service is a unique experience that goes beyond the obligation of every Christian.

Therefore the call to full-time Christian service can be described in three ways: first, burden; second, desire; and third, by fruit.

1. *The call of God begins with a burden.* Several of the Old Testament prophets indicated that their message was the burden of the Lord (Mal. 1:1; Hab. 1:1). A burden is an obligation or a compulsion. A young man who is called into full-time Christian service has a burden or a compulsion to serve Jesus Christ. The need of lost people adds to the burden he gets from Scripture, but the burden is a unique and inner awareness that he must serve Jesus Christ with all of his life.

The call to full-time Christian service has no alternative. God does not say to a young person, "I will call you to serve Me full-time if you cannot get a better job." The call to full-time Christian service

238

carries the weight of "ought" or "must." When a young person is called into full-time Christian service, he must obey. There is no alternative.

2. *The call to full-time Christian service involves desire.* A man knows he is called of God when his greatest desire is to serve Jesus Christ with every part of his life. This involves his will; it is surrendered and he wants to spend all of his time serving Jesus Christ. Usually the call to full-time Christian service comes to those who are actively involved in some kind of ministry—working in bus ministry, teaching Sunday school, serving as a deacon. They want to serve God with all of their heart and their time.

Jeremiah experienced the burning desire to preach the Word of God. Someone told him he could not preach. He responded, "But His Word was in my heart as a burning fire shut up in my bones, and I was very weary with forebearing, and I could not stay (keep quiet)" (Jer. 20:9).

For many years I have dealt with young men who are studying for full-time Christian service. The ones that delight me the most are those young men who just have to preach when they enter their freshman year. They are willing to preach in children's church, in the rescue mission or in the nursing homes. When a man has the fire burning in his heart, he will sometimes go out into the woods and preach to an empty hillside. This is more than practice; it is preparation for a lifetime of delivering the Word of God.

3. *The call of God is evidenced by fruit.* When God has put his hand upon a young man and separated him to full-time Christian service, there will be corresponding fruit. Therefore, before a council ordains a young man into the full-time ministry, there should be some evidence that God has used his preaching and teaching of the Word of God. Jesus noted, "Ye have not chosen me, but I have chosen you and ordained you that ye should go and bring forth fruit, and that your fruit should remain" (John 15:16). The word *ordain* means to lay hands upon, and Jesus was indicating that He had chosen people to put His hands upon them to bring forth fruit.

The symbolic laying on of hands at an ordination service indicates that God has put His Spirit on the ministry of a young man. When he has preached, people have gotten saved. When he has taught the Word of God, people have become better followers of Jesus Christ.

Characteristics of the Call

Some people are called immediately when they are converted. They know when they pray for conversion, God also wants them to be a minister of the gospel. Recently in ministerial classes at Liberty Baptist Schools, I asked for a show of hands on this subject. In the classes, only about 10 percent of the students lifted a hand to indicate they were called into full-time Christian service at the same time they were saved.

That suggests that most young people were called into full-time Christian service at some time after conversion.

Some people receive a sudden and clear call to the ministry. They have been serving Jesus Christ, but in one experience, such as during a youth camp, or in a sermon, God impressed upon them to be a full-time Christian servant. Their call became a life-changing event. And from that moment on, they were no longer the same.

On the other hand, the call of God has come gradually to many others, much as the light of a new day gradually lights up the sky. They begin to feel a burden for the ministry as they serve the Lord. Each time they preached or taught, their desire grew to preach or teach again. Their call to full-time Christian ministry was gradual.

I asked the students at Liberty how they were called into full-time Christian service. Approximately 10 percent say they were called suddenly, while 90 percent indicate the call came gradually.

Views of the Call

W. T. Purkiser, in speaking for the position of the Church of the Nazarene, states concerning a *call*: "It is a definite call; it is a personal call; it is a call to service which can be rendered according to the ability of the called; it is a real challenge; and to refuse it is to go against God's will."

T. Harwood Pattison suggests that a call to the service of God is always a call from Him, that a young man who has this call has entered the first step in the Christian ministry. "The true man enters the ministry not for the sake of what he can get out of it, but for the sake of what it can get out of him." Pattison then lists how the call comes and how it can be recognized.

How it comes:

1. Suddenly and unexpectedly with some unquestionable sign.

2. Gradually like the dawn of a new day. "Without any question the call to preach comes to many a young man with his conversion."

How it can be recognized:

● When it is plainly the work of the Holy Spirit. "Separate me Barnabas and Saul for the work whereunto I have called them."

● Plain by the providential leading of God. "Because a man has failed elsewhere is no reason why he should conclude that he will succeed in the ministry."

● Rigid self-examination. Challenge the purity of the motives.

● Must be influenced by the judgment of Christian friends and the will of the church to which he belongs.

● Ability to preach and the willingness of people to listen.

A. H. Strong concludes, "The candidate (called) himself is to be first persuaded. 'For though I preach the gospel, I have no thing to glory of; for necessity is laid upon me; yea, woe is unto me, if I preach not the gospel' (1 Cor. 9:16). 'And I thank Christ Jesus, our Lord, who hath enabled me, in that He counted me faithful, putting me into the ministry' (1 Tim. 1:12). But, secondly, the church must be persuaded also, before he can have authority to minister among them (1 Tim. 3:2-7; Titus 1:6-9).

W. B. Riley, gives three tests:

1. Compulsion should take the form of conviction.

2. Competence is a prominent evidence: "apt to teach" (2 Tim. 2:24).

3. Church's observation of fit characteristics.

Though his book was written in 1874, William S. Plumer offers keen timeless insights. He states:

● All are not called. All are bound to glorify God and serve their generation.

● God alone can call anyone.

● The greater part of mankind is not called. No wicked man is called.

● The Scriptures do in many ways require that every minister in God's house shall be called to his office by the Lord. (Num. 18:7; Deut. 18:20; Isa. 6:8; 11:2,3; Ezek. 13:3; Matt. 4:18-20; Acts 13:2; Rom. 1:1; 1 Cor. 1:1; Tit. 1:6; Heb. 5:4.)

● The judgment of the fathers of the Church in past ages fully coincides with these teachings of Scripture. Vinet says, "We must be called of God...whether external or internal; the call ought to be divine."

● It is a great and undeserved honor to be put into the sacred office.

● Yet, great as the honor is, it does not puff up a good man.

● Some bad men have entered the ministry.

● What is the call? If a "call" is real, it will gain strength by time and test.

Even though there is confusion in some circles about the call of God to full-time Christian service, there is little doubt in the mind of one who has been called. It is an inner assurance that God's hand is upon his life for a special purpose. The confusion usually comes from those who are not called. Perhaps a few questions would be helpful to guide those who are struggling with the call of God.

Has the person been genuinely converted?

Is the person growing in his Christian life?

Are his motives pure?

Does he possess the physical and mental ability to serve Jesus Christ? (If a candidate has disabilities that would hinder his service, we can seriously question if God has called him into full-time Christian service. However, God has called people with disadvantages, therefore it is their duty to demonstrate and prove the call of God.)

Does the candidate have a love for people and the Church of Jesus

Christ?

How has the candidate evidenced his burden to preach and teach the Word God?

How have people in his church and Christian friends responded to his call? (When people around the candidate do not feel he has been called to Christian service, he should demonstrate that he has been called of God.)

What success of fruit has the candidate had in Christian service? (Everyone has to begin somewhere and perhaps the candidate has not had any outward success. This does not mean he has not been called, but he should demonstrate within a reasonable length of time his call of God by the fruit in his ministry.)

What preparation does the candidate have for full-time Christian service, and is he willing to attend a Bible institute, a Christian college or a seminary to get the best possible preparation for life? (A candidate does not have to have training from a Christian college, but he must have a desire to be the best-trained servant possible.) When it is evident that a candidate is bypassing further training for some reason such as laziness, fear or other known reason, he should be counseled regarding his problem. Those who are called should have the best training possible and not close future doors because of lack of training.

Conclusion

The call of God into full-time ministry is not the call to salvation, although it includes that. The call into full-time ministry is not the Great Commission to go into all the world, although it includes that. The call of God into full-time ministry is not the knowledge that all men are lost and need salvation, although it includes that.

The call of God into full-time ministry is exactly that. It is God calling a person to win souls, build churches, teach the Bible and serve Jesus Christ. A man knows he is called because of the burden God gives him to reach the lost. He knows God has given him a desire to preach. He has the inner assurance that he is to serve God. Just as he knows that fire is hot and up is up, so he knows God has called him to preach the gospel and build a church. He responds as did Isaiah, "Here am I, send me."

34

What Should You Do to Prepare for Retirement?

By Michael Mudry

Michael Mudry is senior vice president of Hay/Huggins Inc., Philadelphia, Pennsylvania, and a partner in charge of the firm's practice in denominational benefit plans. He has over 30 years of experience in the pension field with clients, including many of the mainline denominational churches. Mudry has written numerous articles and papers on such topics as "Asset Valuation Methods," "Charitable Gift Annuities" and "ERISA," which were published in periodicals. Before joining Hay/Huggins, Mudry was an actuary in the individual and group departments of Traveler's Insurance Company.

One of the realities hardest to pound into a minister's mind is the actuarial fact that one day he will arrive at retirement age. Then what? Without a retirement plan, a clergyman and his wife may come to face the foreboding prospect of a meager existence in their declining years. But if adequate provision has been made, the prospect of those final years glows bright with the promise of a well-deserved rest, free from financial anxieties.

Most denominations offer pension plans. The boards of these plans strive to attract participation by all their ministers and churches. But most fall short (one board boasts one billion dollars in assets, yet only about 50 percent of that denomination's ministers are participating in that retirement program).

And then there are the men and women who serve non-denominational churches. For them to have retirement plans, they must act on their own initiative to set aside funds during their years of active ministry.

When ministers retire, their standards of living during retirement compared to those just prior to retirement will depend to a large extent on the degree to which they (and their employers) have set aside funds for that purpose during their years of active service. Unfortunately, it is too easy to focus during active service on immediate financial needs and to defer the financial commitment necessary to accumulate adequate funds for retirement purposes. The consequences of such deferral are frequently that a minister no longer has enough time remaining to accumulate sufficient funds to make adequate retirement provision. Therefore, it is essential that, early in their careers, ministers obtain sound financial guidance which recognizes not only their immediate financial needs, but also their retirement responsibilities to themselves and their spouses.

Retirement Income Goals

What is a goal toward which ministers should direct their retirement financial planning? Based on various studies made over the years and recognizing the typical level of ministerial salaries, it is estimated that an initial annual gross retirement income of about 65 to 70 percent of the annual gross income just prior to retirement would provide a single minister with a standard of living reasonably commensurate with that which existed just prior to retirement, while 70 to 75 percent is more appropriate for a married minister. These percentages take into account a number of factors that reduce outgo during retirement as compared to pre-retirement years, such as double exemptions for tax purposes, elimination of Social Security taxes, the tax-free portion of Social Security benefits and a decreased need for savings.

Furthermore, the gross pre-retirement income used in developing these percentages should take into account the value of parsonage or housing allowance so as to be more comparable to industry, where the gross income received by an individual must provide for housing. Thus, higher percentages would be needed if the retirement income goal were to be measured against the pre-retirement income excluding the value of housing.

Obviously, it is not possible for any generalization to be universally applicable. Thus, the percentage needed could vary under differing circumstances, depending on such matters as salary level, health, type of housing, etc. However, the 65 to 70 percent for single ministers and 70 to 75 percent for married ministers can be considered as rough guides.

Three-Legged Stool

How are these goals to be attained? While there are a number of investment vehicles available for setting aside funds for retirement years, many pension planners classify them as being in three categories—much like a three-legged stool which requires that all three legs be sturdy enough to support the total post-retirement needs of an individual and spouse. The three legs are Social Security, private pension plans of employers and personal savings of the individual.

The degree to which each of these categories of retirement income is applicable would not be the same for all ministers, but would depend on individual circumstances. For example, in some denominations, Social Security plus the benefit provided from employer contributions to the pension plan of the denomination serve to meet the goals by themselves, with little or no need for additional income from personal savings. Nevertheless, it is generally considered that, in order for retirement income to be adequate, it be provided from all three categories of advance financing.

Social Security

Since most ministers are covered under Social Security, it is normally the first item of retirement income that is taken into account in pension planning. Even though ministers are not usually legally considered self-employed, the pay Social Security taxes under the Self-Employment Contributions Act (SECA) as if they were self-employed.

Accordingly, the responsibility for the payment of the entire tax falls on the ministers. As the result of Social Security amendments which became effective January 1, 1984, contributions required under SECA have been raised considerably—putting an increased financial burden on ministers.

Many churches assist their ministers by reimbursing them for at least one-half their contributions, in order to place them in a position somewhat comparable to that of the typical employee who pays only one-half the Social Security tax, with the employer paying the other half. This is complicated somewhat in church circles because it was possible in the past for lay employees to be exempt from Social Security. However, effective January 1, 1984, lay employees must be covered by Social Security, so the employer must pay the employer portion of the applicable tax related to the wages of such employees. This creates an added cost for some churches, which might affect their willingness also to reimburse the minister for one-half of his or her SECA taxes.

The Social Security pension payable to a single minister who retires at age 65 tends to be about 25 to 40 percent of salary at retirement, with the higher percentages applicable at the lower salary levels. For married ministers, the Social Security pension (including the spouse's pension) usually ranges between 35 and 60 percent of the minister's salary at retirement, again depending on salary level, and also on the age of the spouse at the time the spouse benefit commences.

Of course, in order to receive a Social Security benefit, a minister must elect to participate in the program. Some ministers do not, since they have the right to exempt themselves from Social Security taxes. Those ministers who do exempt themselves must rely on the other two legs of the retirement income stool. It appears that ministers are increasingly choosing exemption, so a review of the exemption requirements seems appropriate here.

The act allows a minister to be exempt from Social Security only if he or she is opposed, either conscientiously or due to religious principles, to the acceptance of any public insurance covering death, disability, old age, retirement or medical benefits. However, regulations make it clear that the conscientious opposition must be based on the minister's religious beliefs rather than simply his or her general conscience; and opposition due to religious principles must reflect the explicit discipline of the minister's denomination. Thus, the exemption can really be based only on religious considerations.

Since very few denominations take a stand opposing Social Security, it is likely that some ministers filing for exemption are not doing so for truly legal reasons, but for other reasons, such as economic considerations, that are not valid. A minister who is considering filing for an exemption should examine his or her reasons thoroughly and not attempt for invalid reasons to evade the law that applies to the rest of the population.

Private Pension Plans

The second leg that provides the basis of retirement security is provided by contributions by employers to private pension plans. Although the word "employers" may be questionable in certain circumstances, I shall employ that term for the purposes of simplicity.

It is frequently argued that, when an employer contributes to a private pension plan on behalf of a minister, the contributions are really being made by the minister. This position reflects the premise that there is a total compensation package which the employer is willing to finance, so that the minister must accept a smaller cash salary if a portion of the total is to be paid by the employer into a pension plan. Since the total amount of the package could have been paid in cash, the pension contribution really represents the minister's contribution rather than an employer contribution really represents the minister's contribution.

Arguments can be made for and against this position. The degree of validity of any argument would be affected by the extent to which the denomination enforces a requirement for the employer to make pension contributions on behalf of a minister as part of the minister's call. I shall refer to a contribution made by an employer as being an employer contribution, regardless of any questions as to its real source.

What investment vehicles for pension purposes are available for employer contributions? One of the first possibilities which should be considered is the pension plan operated by the denomination (if in fact such a plan exists). Many denominations have pension boards whose responsibilities include the establishment of a plan under which retirement benefits are payable. These plans may or may not require contributions by the minister in addition to those paid by the employer, although usually the employer is allowed to pay the contributions of the minister required. The plans may also pay death, disability and other benefits, or such benefits may be provided through the pension boards under separate plans.

The pension plans are operated under Section 401(a), 403(a) or 403(b) of the Internal Revenue Code in order to obtain the tax advantages available thereunder.

The plans are designated either as defined benefit plans or defined contribution plans. Under the former, the amount of benefit is determined by a formula contained in the plan (such as an annual pension of 1¼ percent of the total salaries on which contributions have been paid to the plan over the years). Under a defined contribution plan, though, the contributions are accumulated in much the same manner as in a savings account, with the balance at retirement being converted into a lifetime pension.

The members of the boards which operate these denominational pension plans are usually elected by the assemblies, meetings, conferences, etc., of the denomination and normally include ministers and lay members of the denomination. The board members are selected carefully so as to provide expertise in various aspects of the operations of the plans, including legal, financial and actuarial. The board members receive no pay for their service as members, but serve solely in the interests of plan participants.

Because of the voluntary service of board members, the absence of commissions and taxes, and the economies of group operations, the denominational plans offer the potential for better results than if the contributions were paid into an individual plan established for the minister. Therefore, every minister (and employer of a minister) should, as a first step, contact the pension board of the denomination before beginning to make contributions for pension purposes elsewhere.

In addition to required contributions to the plan, the pension boards also frequently accept additional contributions on behalf of an employee. Such additional contributions are generally made on a tax-deferred basis under Section 403(b) of the Internal Revenue Code. This section of the code is also referred to as being for tax-deferred annuities, tax-sheltered annuities or retirement income accounts. Contributions under Section 403(b) may either be made directly by the employer or indirectly through a salary reduction agreement under which the minister agrees to have his or her salary reduced and the employer agrees to transmit it to the pension board for 403(b) purposes. Where the contribution is by salary reductions, it amounts to tax-sheltered personal savings. Annuities under Section 403(b) can also be purchased from insurance companies if the denomination does not accept 403(b) contributions or if there is a preference for a funding medium other than the denominational pension board.

It would be possible for the employer to establish its own pension plan, but normally the small number of covered plan participants make this an expensive alternative if a denominational plan is available. If a denominational plan is not available, though, the establishment of a separate plan becomes comparatively more viable. Such a plan would have to meet governmental standards in order for the income on the funds being accumulated to be tax-exempt and for the contributions not to be taxable to the minister at the time they become vested. A separate plan can be self-administered (usually with a bank as trustee) or handled through an insurance company. Furthermore, a number of organizations such as banks offer master plans which tend to have lower administrative costs than if a separately designed plan were instituted.

An employer may also contribute to a simplified employee plan (usually referred to as a SEP). A SEP is basically an employer-funded individual retirement arrangement (IRA). The limit on annual contributions to a SEP is the lesser of $15,000 or 15 percent of the minister's compensation. SEPs must be established on a non-discriminatory basis, so if the employer has more than one minister or also has lay employees, they must all be covered after age 25 and three years of service.

It is also possible for employer contributions to be paid for retirement purposes into a so-called cash or deferred arrangement operated under Section 401(k) of the code. Since such a plan is technically a profit-sharing plan, it might appear on the surface to be unavailable for use by a not-for-profit organization. However, General Counsel Memorandum 38283 indicates that, in order to promote incentives for efficiency of operations, even not-for-profit organizations are permitted to establish profit-sharing-plans. Nevertheless, because of the availability of 403(b) annuities and for other reasons, the 401(k) vehicle has generally not been used for ministers.

The size of the pension provided by employer contributions varies greatly, depending on a number of factors such as the type of funding vehicle, length of participation, contribution level, etc. Some denominational pension plans provide pensions that amount to about 50 percent of the minister's pay at retirement after 40 years of participation. In such cases, ministers who have participated in both the denominational pension plan and Social Security would normally receive, at least initially, a sufficient total pension to meet the general goals discussed earlier for maintenance of the pre-retirement standard of living. Of course, other denominational pension plans provide smaller amounts of pension. The degree to which these pensions plus Social Security meet the retirement goals would naturally depend on the individual situation.

Personal Savings

A number of vehicles are available into which a minister can place personal savings for retirement purposes. As previously mentioned, the minister may participate in a denominational or other pension plan that requires member contributions, which represents a form of personal savings. Also, as previously mentioned, the minister may enter into a salary reduction agreement under Section 403(b) of the Internal Revenue Code, under which the employer withholds funds and transmits them to a denominational pension board or to an insurance company. This really amounts to personal savings despite the required involvement of the employer in the savings process.

A well-known vehicle for personal savings toward retirement is the individual retirement arrangement (which is more frequently referred to as an individual retirement account or IRA). Everyone has been made aware through the media and through advertising by banks, invest-ment brokers, mutual funds and insurance companies of the signifi-cant details about IRAs and their tax-saving benefits, so it is not necessary to say much here about them. However, since ministers do have the availability of both IRAs and 403(b) arrangements, it might be worthwhile for a minister to consider which is preferable. IRAs have the advantage of allowing the minister to defer the contribution for a given tax year until the date for filing his or her tax return (usually April 15 of the following year), whereas under 403(b) the payment must be made by the end of the year to be excludable from taxable income that year. Furthermore, by not involving the employer, a con-tribution by a minister to an IRA enables the minister to keep his or her financial affairs more private.

On the other hand, the IRA has the disadvantage that a 10 percent tax penalty is imposed if any amount is withdrawn from the IRA before the minister attains age 59½, except as the result of death or perma-nent disability, while no significant penalty need be imposed upon withdrawals from 403(b) accounts. However, each 403(b) arrangement sets its own rules as to whether or not early withdrawals are permitted and as to the restrictions or penalties imposed if a withdrawal is allowed. If the right to make withdrawals from 403(b) accounts is granted, some restriction or penalties (usually minor) must be made applicable in order to avoid taxation on amounts that would otherwise be deemed to be constructively received by the minister.

The maximum amounts that a minister can contribute under an IRA now would normally be $2,000, $2,250 or $4,000, depending on marital status and, if married, whether the spouse also receives any compensation. In contrast, although the calculation process is com-plicated, it is usual under 403(b) that a minister can contribute up to one-sixth of his or her gross compensation. IRAs and 403(b) accounts are not interrelated, so that a minister can contribute under either without reducing the amounts that might otherwise be contributed under the other.

Comments should be made about Keogh plans which can be estab-lished by self-employed individuals. Even though a minister is treated as if self-employed for purposes of Social Security, regulations relating to Keogh plans make clear that ministers would normally be considered as common-law employees for purposes of such plans, and not as self-employed, so would not be eligible to establish Keogh plans. Accord-ingly, a minister should consider initiating a Keogh plan only if satisfac-tory evidence exists that he or she is truly self-employed and not a common-law employee.

The various types of vehicles described so far provide some degree of tax deferral in connection with contributions made. It is always possible, of course, to set aside money on an after-tax basis for use during retirement years. These funds can be accumulated in many ways, such as in stocks, bonds, real estate, precious metals, jewelry, life insurance cash values, or insured annuity contracts, and can be converted during retirement into additional amounts available for meeting retirement needs (although with liquidity problems in certain cases).

Usually, amounts available for retirement purposes from personal savings (and to varying degrees from employer contributions) can be considered as lump-sum equivalents of shares of stock, a personal residence, IRA account balances and the like so that decisions are necessary in order to convert them into funds available for retirement needs. Different decisions may be made in different circumstances, or by different people in the same circumstances. For example, if Social Security and the employer-financed pension are adequate together to maintain the minister's pre-retirement standard of living, the items into which personal savings have been converted (be they stocks, a home, paintings,) could be utilized in a number of ways, such as:

● Accumulated, together with future earnings or appreciation thereon, and included in the minister's estate or used for a future "rainy day."

● The earnings used to increase the standard of living (for example, for travel delayed during the minister's service), but capital invaded.

● The earnings and capital both used to increase the standard of living, thus reducing or eliminating any estate.

A minister who has the above choices would usually be considered fortunate. Probably a more likely scenario is that, for various reasons, the combination of Social Security and the employer-financed pension would not be adequate to maintain the pre-retirement standard of living. In such an event, the decisions needed in connection with personal savings would be the degree to which income on such savings (or income and principal) would be needed to cover retirement expenses not being met.

Decisions concerning the use of personal savings during retirement can be difficult. Amounts that may have seemed adequate at the time of retirement to cover future needs might easily become inadequate if catastrophic medical expenses are incurred, costs of living escalate greatly due to inflation or the annuitant lives to an advanced age. Some of these potential problems can be mitigated. For example, it would be advisable to use some of a retired individual's personal savings to purchase adequate medical insurance to protect against the financial impact of costly medical needs. The threat of inflation is partly offset by automatic increases in Social Security benefits. Furthermore, some denominational pension plans also provide varying degrees of protection against inflation by increasing benefits periodically from favorable investment experience that frequently accompanies inflation.

As for longevity, annuities payable for life can help eliminate the fears of outliving resources. Thus, Social Security and pensions which are payable for life are better suited to meet the contingency of long life, since they cannot be outlived. But monies accumulated under either employer plans or personal savings in the form of investments have the inherent risk of fluctuating in value and being expended while the retiree or spouse is still alive.

Nothing can take the place of planning for retirement. There are a number of available investment vehicles for this purpose, but they are of no value if not used sufficiently in advance to accomplish their purposes. Obtain sound financial advice! Contact your denominational pension board if one exists! Such boards very often have knowledgeable staff members who can provide valuable advice. Above all, don't delay setting aside retirement funds, because you may run out of enough time to accumulate an adequate pension level or retirement fund.

Solving Communications Problems

35

How Can a Preacher Achieve Total Communication?

By C. M. Ward

C. M. Ward, chancellor and former president of Bethany Bible College in Santa Cruz, California, is one of America's foremost evangelists and radio/television speakers. A former pastor, Bible college instructor and editor, he also was radio evangelist for "Revivaltime," the international radio voice of the Assemblies of God. He has written 23 hardback volumes of radio sermons, authored over 250 booklets and has recorded the entire Bible on cassette and 8-track tapes.

Great personalities of platform and stage have learned to use total speech. The voice is capable of tone and timing, or pitch and pace. It can reverberate or be reduced to a whisper. William Jennings Bryan had such control that he could be heard without difficulty in the right field bleachers, from home-plate without the aid of public address system or sounding board.

It is a delight to an audience to hear good grammar, choice composition and each word distinctly. Here is a little tip I learned from years of broadcasting. Begin as you would drive a car—in one of the slower gears. Then move forward toward the speed and rhythm—a *cruising speed*—where you and the audience feel comfortable. If you attempt to start otherwise, you may "flood the motor," stumble and compound error.

The voice is a marvelous instrument. It must be used as an expensive pipe organ. The diaphragm must be used as the bellows, so there is always a steady flow of breathing. The notes are shaped by the mouth and lips. There is a considerable range of *tones*. It can be seductive, commanding, questioning, appealing, abrasive, scornful. The voice must be the main agent to interpret and carry the message to the audience.

Jesus spoke to great crowds. He used natural carriers. He used the mountainside water to amplify his voice. The audience reaction was that He "spoke as one having authority." He spoke in short sentences, brief paragraphs and with the verb toward the front of the sentence.

You are "the umpire behind home-plate" when you stand at the pulpit. What you say must be heard and understood.

The speaker has *much other language* at his command. There is, for instance, the language of the eye. Peter had this *command*. All leaders do. "And Peter, fastening his eyes upon him...said, Look on us" (Acts 3:4). You are on second base when you learn to look in the eye of all segments of your audience (including the gallery). Eye control is so important.

The best I knew was George Jeffrys, who liked to be called Principal George Jeffrys of the Elim-Foursquare, Great Britain. He could *hold* thousands in London's Royal Albert Hall by his powerful eye language. The eyes may speak pathos. They may laugh, twinkle, suggest mischief, question. The language is superb.

The eye has the power of *guidance*. An audience will follow direction from the speaker's eyes. The intensity acts as do the headlights of an automobile. They deliver feeling and *conviction*.

There is the language of dressing the platform. Aimee Semple McPherson was the best at this. She knew the power of *contrast*. She dressed in a simple, long, white gown. And she preferred to have a row of gentlemen ministers, dressed in navy blue, seated behind her.

Those who remain upon a platform, including musicians, must be trained to rivet attention toward the speaker. The wandering eye, any sign of indifference, can be fatal to the message and hoped for results.

There is the language of appearance. An audience is impressed from shoeshine to haircut. Are the clothes well chosen? Are they coordinated? Shirt, socks are an anathema. Bare flesh is repulsive. A well-chosen tie, not garrish, but sharp, can focus an audience's attention. Casual wear is never in keeping when the high-calling is at work at the pulpit. A crumpled suit, a missing button, an undisciplined shirt-collar can turn off audiences.

A confident stride toward the pulpit, head up and shoulders squared, speaks to an audience. They feel someone is there to take charge. On the other hand, when a speaker slumps over the podium, when he braces himself, first on one foot, then on the other, the speaker transfers to the audience a sense of nervousness.

There is the language of the hand. The hand is the king-member of the body. When the eye fails, the hand can substitute. When the voice fails it can substitute. *Gesture is probably the most difficult of all languages to master.*

Dwight L. Moody was the best. He had no superiors. The hand, or hands, used properly can say a lexicon of things. The hand can say: "Stop," "Give," "Have mercy," "Are you listening?," "Take it away," "How could I have been mistaken?"

The ability to use hands properly separates the veteran from the amateur. The beginner seldom knows what to do with his hands. They are in and out of his pockets. He seemingly cannot find a place to put them. So he conveys the impression of awkwardness to the audience.

Flowers provide powerful supporting roles. Martin Luther preached with a full bloom geranium before him. It had a tendency to soften his stern message of reform—to make it more palatable to the audience. The language of lighting, color, ventilation, properly ushered patrolled aisles, all are auxiliary language to the speaker.

A few speakers finally acquire the language of *pause*. The silent interval can be as important to the speaker as a quarter- or half-rest note to the musician. *It brings attention.* Paul Harvey has made a fortune by using it. Loudness and machine-gun delivery can be hypnotic, but "in quietness and confidence there is strength."

The speaker should ask himself or herself, "Do I want this audience to *receive* the message, or do I simply want to impress the audience?" Language is that crowning gift from the Creator to mankind—the ability to communicate. The preacher's business is to use this gift effectively.

Above all there is the language of anointed speech when the speaker is clothed with the Great Communicator, the Holy Spirit. This is the ultimate in excellence.

In the early 1930s, as a rookie speaker, I came under the ministry of George Chambers, general superintendent of the Pentecostal Assemblies of Canada. He was one of the most meticulous dressers I have ever known. His smile was contagious. His knowledge of the Word was impressive. His weakness was grammar. He could murder the Queen's English. But the moment the anointing, or unction, came upon him, he would speak correctly. A Shakespearean actor would have approved. He could be stenographically reported—and was. It made a remarkable impression upon me. Jesus promised, "He shall guide you into ALL TRUTH."

36

How Do You Give an Effective Evangelistic Invitation?

By Frank Crumpler

Frank Crumpler is director of the specialized evangelism department, Southern Baptist Home Mission Board, Atlanta, Georgia. He has served as pastor of five Southern Baptist churches, served three years as director of evangelism for the Baptist State Convention of Virginia and has 10 years' experience teaching pastoral evangelism seminars. He is the author of two books, *God Is Near* and *The Invincible Cross*.

Nothing can take the place of an effective invitation in a Spirit-directed evangelistic service. The preacher has both the responsibility and privilege of "drawing the net" during the invitation. It is during the climax that every other part of the worship event reaches its focal point.

Thus, the invitation is so important that it should have the highest priority in the service. That importance demands that the invitation be well planned and effectively presented. All parts of the service of Christian worship are important—prayers, congregational singing, reading of Scripture and the preaching of the gospel—but these are not complete without the invitation. The essence of the good news is brought to fruition in the invitation.

There is an art to giving a good invitation. Some preachers get into a "rut," giving the same invitation at the close of every sermon, so the people automatically begin to think about leaving as soon as the invitation hymn is announced. The evangelistic preacher who fails to develop his skill in giving the invitation is losing his greatest opportunity to "harvest" lost souls. Since skill in giving the invitation has to be developed and practiced, a preacher should take every precaution to plan the invitation, making sure he is living up to his highest potential as a harvester of souls.

It is helpful for you to write out in detail the words of your invitation. Doing this, as you planned your sermon, will help you set up what you are going to say. This might seem unnecessary, but it is good discipline and helps you to recall certain sentences and phrases of the invitation as they were written. This will also help you to evaluate the content and review the arrangement of words in the invitation.

Mentally "walking through" the invitation gives emphasis to the instructions or appeal that is made at the close of the worship service. If you spend hours preparing the sermon, you should give more than a few minutes to preparing to give the invitation.

The invitation should be carefully planned with the minister of music, the organist and the pianist. It is most important that each person taking part in directing the choir or congregation, playing the instruments or greeting those who respond to the invitation, is well prepared, alert, attentive and knows exactly what to do and when to do it.

Everyone who hears the claims of Christ is an eternity-bound person. His decision and response could and ultimately will affect his eternal destiny. This should be seriously pondered by the preacher before he preaches. Many lives, to whom we make the offer of Christ, are lonely and broken. Jesus Christ can put broken pieces back together again. Peace, joy, purpose, removal of guilt and forgiveness are available to those who are willing to accept them. The first step to experiencing these benefits can be made during the public invitation.

By giving priority to the invitation, you can be used effectively by God to lead the hearer to a life-changing experience with Christ.

In Spiritual Power

The invitation, given in the power of God's Holy Spirit, carries with it the authority of heaven. Allow God's Spirit to be in complete control of the invitation. Every word should be carefully chosen and spoken with persuasion.

There should be no manipulation or coercion in a Spirit-directed appeal. When the claims of Christ are preached with conviction and compassion, the Spirit will be at work in the hearts of hearers. The preacher cannot be clever and compassionate at the same time. Depend on God's power to move people to action. Be confident that God is at work in the invitation.

Do not threaten the hearer with the possibility that he may not have another opportunity. If you do remind him of this possibility, make sure he knows it comes from a heart of Christian love and concern.

Don't argue your point too long. You might lose your hearer's confidence. Learn to be forceful without being overpowering and obnoxious. You are God's messenger and it must be His invitation. God has declared, "Not by might, nor by power, but by my Spirit, saith the Lord of hosts" (Zech. 4:6). Only by the power of God's Spirit can men be led to make deep and lasting decisions. Keep the invitation in God's hands.

Make It Plain

Always keep the invitation simple. The importance and urgency of the invitation demands that it be made clear. Be sure the hearer knows exactly what kind of response you expect. An appeal to those who have never accepted Christ to come forward should be direct and plain, but never demanding.

Quotations from the Word of God have peculiar power to get attention and drive home divine truths. Use well-chosen Scriptures to make the invitation more forceful and gripping.

Sometimes reinforce the simplicity of the invitation by using quotations from hymns or poetry. Avoid worn-out cliches. Be natural and let your compassion for people come through.

If your appeal is intended to spur more than one type of decision, make each kind of appeal distinct so those who come forward know why they are coming.

Billy Graham is a master at extending the invitation because he begins his invitation when he begins his sermon. He weaves into every point of his message the fact that the hearer will have an opportunity to act on its truth at the close of the message. Any preacher can punctuate his sermon with a reminder that the hearer will be asked to make a life-changing commitment to Christ.

You should devote some time to prayer and preparation for the invitation just as you do to the sermon. It does help, occasionally, to write out the invitation you plan to give. Read and reread it until it becomes a part of your message.

Avoid re-preaching your sermon or using long illustrations in the invitation. If response is slow, don't interrupt. Just have the organist and pianist ready to turn to another hymn when it is appropriate.

By all means inform the music director and instrumentalists what you plan to do if the invitation is prolonged. Alert them to watch for your signal if you want another stanza or a different hymn. Never stop or interrupt an invitation when people are coming forward.

Keep in mind that children, who might also need to make decisions, are present. If a child can understand your invitation, the adults can too. You can't make it too simple. You're preaching for a verdict, so expect the proper response. Make it clear to the people and trust God's Spirit to move them to action.

When you invite people to receive Jesus Christ as Savior and Lord, encourage them to make a specific and open commitment to this invitation. For example, say something like this: "This morning Christ invites you to turn from your sins and accept His offer of forgiveness and salvation. As an indication of your decision, I invite you to slip out from where you are standing and come forward. I will meet you here at the front to pray with you about your decision."

Be Pertinent

A sermon on prayer should be followed by an invitation of commitment to a life of prayer. The same is true of stewardship, Bible study, witnessing, faithfulness or other topics. Keep your invitation pertinent to the sermon. Of course, you will always want to invite the lost to accept Christ, but it is only reasonable that you give a sermon that can be responded to by Christians as well.

A message on the Lordship of Christ deserves an invitation for Christians to enthrone Jesus as Lord of their lives. A sermon on jealousy can be followed with an invitation to those who need to rid their hearts of jealousy. The list could go on and on. Keep the invitation in perfect harmony with the sermon. Make it pertinent to the message.

Remember to distinguish each invitation from the other so people will not be confused. You will discover a new enthusiasm and excitement in your own heart as you invite people to respond to the Holy Spirit's leadership—and usually that enthusiasm will be caught and felt by the congregation.

Be Prayerful

Some effective and well-known preachers prefer not to conclude the sermon with a prayer. They feel this signals to the congregation that the service is over before the invitation begins. This may well be the best practice. An alternative is to pray preceding the sermon for those who need to respond. No matter where it is done in the service, the congregation should be led in prayer for those who have needs and should respond.

Prayer is one of the most essential elements in the invitation—pray for response, preach for response and expect response. The best preparation for the invitation is prayer. Ask Sunday school teachers to lead in prayer for the invitation before their classes leave. Ask the congregation to pray as you preach that the invitation will be a time of divine confrontation between God and those who need to respond.

Pray as you stand waiting to meet those who will come forward. Pray and keep on praying. Lead in prayer again before you ask the congregation to sing the final stanza of the invitation hymn. An invitation saturated with prayer is the most effective one you can give.

C. E. Autrey reminds us in his book, *Basic Evangelism,* that the element of prayer is of greatest importance. He said:

"Let him pray until his greatest desire is to see the lost saved. Lost men are under the wrath of God. They are not aware of their condition. The evangelist knows this and must, by his firm, tender pleas, lead the sinner to realize his guilt before God. Mere perfunctory concern in the evangelist cannot be used of God to bring a sense of dire need in the sinner's heart."

Real transformation of life in an invitation is not the work of human contrivance. It is the work of the Holy Spirit. He alone can convict of spiritual need. Only He can reveal Christ savingly. He is the only one who can perform the miracle we call "new birth." Thus, the entire evangelistic invitation must depend on the Holy Spirit's power. Because this is his work, we should saturate the invitation with fervent prayer.

Be Positive

A positive attitude is a winning attitude. Being positive encourages response, while being negative makes it difficult for people to respond to the invitation. When giving the invitation, do not ask, "Are there some present today who will accept Christ?" Make it positive by saying, "There are several (or many) here today who will accept Christ."

Never say, "Will you come?" Rather say, "While you come...." Avoid words like "if" or "perhaps." It is better to say, "I believe you will come as we sing."

Avoid using humor. Keep your voice low and let your compassion come through. Move toward the people, especially those who are coming forward. By moving a few steps toward them, your body language puts them at ease and encourages other reluctant ones to step out and come forward.

Give each person your attention and have counselors ready to pray with those who need prayer. Do everything you can to take the fear out of responding.

Be Persuasive

Paul said, "Knowing therefore the terror of the Lord, we persuade men" (2 Cor. 5:11). Do not be apologetic. You are appealing to your hearers to do what God desires of them. Be courageous in calling people to make right decisions. Persuasion is never to be regarded as manipulation. Too much persuasion will produce insincere profession of faith, which is worse than no profession at all.

Avoid any movement by the choir or congregation that will hinder the invitation. It might be best for the choir to remain seated until the congregation stands. Use familiar hymns with a positive message that can be sung without hymnals and with little or no direction.

The closer the message gets to the invitation the quieter the service should become. Avoid loud, fast music, and ask the people to remain still and prayerful as others are making decisions. Remember, response is brought about by the Holy Spirit. Your part is to create the best atmosphere for decisions and response. With much tenderness, compassion and optimism, call those who are going to respond to move forward.

We can plant the seeds, water and cultivate them, but God Himself gives the increase for His harvest.

Be Pleasant

You should make a conscious effort to keep the closing moments of the service from becoming somber and morose. A pleasant expression on the faces of choir members and the preacher helps maintain a warm friendly atmosphere.

Keep a pleasant tone in your voice as you say something similar to the following:

"We are going to stand in a moment to sing a familiar hymn. (Organist/pianist moves to the instrument.) As we sing, Christ invites you to respond to His call. Many are here this morning who wish to come forward and accept Jesus as Savior and Lord. We urge you to come. I will meet you here at the front and we will take time to pray with you about your decision. (Instrumentalist begins to play softly.)

"I know there are many who have felt the leadership of God's Spirit to recommit your life to deeper and more serious Christian living. I'm sure you are going to come to indicate your desire for closer fellowship with Christ." (Preacher moves down to floor level and checks to see if his counselors are in place. The congregation begins to sing as the music director leads. Cue the counselors as people come forward.)

Be Patient

Some hearers may be struggling with an important decision. Therefore, it is necessary to allow time for response. Give your hearers enough time to decide and respond. Never rush the invitation. Each service will determine how much time to allow for an effective invitation. Never cramp the invitation by preaching up to the end of the hour. Expanding the last point of the sermon may mean losing the harvest of souls for God. Plan for response and expect it, but more importantly, allow sufficient time for it.

Be prepared for different types of responses. When someone comes to unburden his heart with a problem, ask one of the counselors to come and take that person aside for a quiet talk and prayer. A room near the worship facility should be prepared for this purpose. This will free the preacher to greet others who are coming forward.

Thank the congregation for their prayers, patience and understanding. You might wish to follow this simple invitation.

"We have come to the most important time of the service. Will you bow your heads, please? (Organist/pianist moves to instrument.) Some of you have burdens on your hearts today—a lost loved one, some private problem, some need in your own life. Say, Pastor, pray for me. Indicate this by lifting your hand right now. (Instrumentalist begins to play. Acknowledge those who lift their hands.) Now those of you who lifted your hands—lift your heads. I want you to come and spend a moment in prayer at the front of the altar. Lay your problem before the Lord. Come right now as the choir sings. (The choir begins to sing.)

"Now I want every person here who has not accepted Christ as your personal Savior to raise your heads. (They look up—wait.) Good! We would like to talk with you and pray with and for you before you leave today. (Preacher moves to floor level.) I believe you're going to come forward now to accept Christ as your Savior. I'll meet you here at the front while the choir sings. Stand right now and begin your move forward. Those who have needs to pray about are going to come and kneel here right now—don't hesitate—come right now!" (Choir begins to sing and counselors are cued as people come forward.)

Here is another example of an invitation that might be helpful. The preacher may say:

"Let's bow our heads. (Organist/pianist moves to instrument.) Many

265

of you in the service tonight have heavy hearts. You feel the need for God to strengthen you in the Christian life, you have a problem or you need the power of God to take over in your life. We want to pray for you right now as you admit to God your need by lifting your hand. That's right—lift them up right now. Now, lift your heads and look at me. I want you to come forward and stand in front of the pulpit facing this way for this prayer. (Instrumentalist begins to play.)

"Now, while these are coming—some of you have never made a public profession of faith in Christ. I want to pray for you right now. By lifting your hand, you are saying, pray for me. Lift your hand right now—that's right. God bless you. Now everyone who lifted a hand, I want you to come here to the front—stand for a moment and I want to pray with you. If you will receive Christ as your personal Savior, one of our counselors wants to give you some material to help you in the Christian life. That's right—stand up and come right on." (Instrumentalist and choir begin the song. Cue the counselors to come while others respond.)

Prayer, study and practice are keys to improving your evangelistic invitation. Observe other preachers, study your congregation and learn from your mistakes. God's Holy Spirit will take your efforts and multiply your effectiveness.

Christ has promised to honor the faithful proclamation of His Word. Be a yielded and surrendered instrument in God's hands so that it will be His invitation completely.

As God uses your gifts and abilities to preach and give an evangelistic invitation, His kingdom will be increased, and as your ministry reaps the harvest, it will bring honor and glory to God.

37

How Do You Communicate With a Reluctant Husband?

By Edwin P. Anderson

Edwin P. Anderson is director of Renew Counseling Center (formerly Emerge Counseling Center), Minneapolis, Minnesota. He also has served on the pastoral staffs of a number of churches and as pastor of Grace Community Church, Danvers, Massachusetts. Ordained to the ministry by the Assemblies of God, licensed as a consulting psychologist by the Minnesota Board of Psychology, Anderson is a conference and retreat speaker, a member of the American Association of Pastoral Counselors and a free-lance writer.

Pastors are sometimes inundated with requests to help the ravaged hearts of people trapped in mismanaged marriages and broken homes. Helping a marriage with one stubbornly reluctant partner is a great challenge, especially if that person shows little interest in matters of faith. How you help will enhance or decrease your credibility as a pastor called to minister the healing message of Christ.

Consider the following scenario in a pastor's office:

A Christian wife who is estranged from her husband seeks help to justify her complaints. The husband tolerates, with some hostility, her spiritual activities. He feels that she is neglecting him; but she feels justified in her neglect due to his lack of interest in spiritual matters.

A well-meaning friend suggested that the Smiths consult her pastor. When their appointment came, the husband spoke haltingly, underscoring his comments with obscenities. His wife's apologetic, penitent smile evoked hostile glances from him. Her self-righteous attitude barely concealed a tangle of wretched self-hatred. Her comments meandered aimlessly through defensive thickets designed to protect her from herself and anyone else.

Unimpressed by her show of piousness, her husband gravitated to displays of affectionless candor, rigidly erecting his own defenses. He considered her religious affectations effeminate, not for him.

It appeared, the pastor thought, that the husband exhibited a need to exert his masculinity. His crass behavior had earned for him an ignominious reputation among his wife's acquaintances, and his wife was just as disapproving. By the end of the first counseling session the pastor was sure of one thing: his abilities would be stretched to the limit while attempting to help the Smiths!

The church has long been considered a home for the spiritually destitute and haven for emotional cripples, and pastors take the identity of a wound healer.

There is something about a pastor that speaks reassurance. He holds out hope—sunshine rays in a darkened world. And many pastors are willing to run the risk of being hurt by people who long for emancipation from emotional pain. But well-intentioned caring is not always enough. For better results, pastors need to know what they are doing and why they are doing it.

When the pastor's efforts fail to reveal the problem or provide an answer, the counselees will eventually turn away in disappointment. The problems remain.

Some consultants would say the Smiths failed because they did not listen to and apply what the pastor advised, or they did not respond to an ''answer-man'' approach. Others would insist that the pastor's counseling approach was at fault.

Some would feel that the counseling sessions failed due to the Smiths' lack of respect for the pastor and the Word of God, and that the couple should have been ungrudging respecters of his personal authority. Otherwise they should not have expected effective results.

If this holds true, in most cases control of counseling would be solely in the pastor's hands. But this makes counselees increasingly dependent on the pastor and less capable of taking responsibility for themselves.

The Smiths came with a set of problems that would frustrate anyone. The answer-man approach would have been acceptable to Mrs. Smith but not to her husband. Mrs. Smith's reason for seeking counseling was to put her husband in his place through the use of a recognizable authority. Mr. Smith's motive was appeasement. Neither motivation was adequate for positive change.

The pastor ended up frustrated because his directions were not adhered to. Mrs. Smith lost faith in the pastor, seeing he could do little with her husband, and Mr. Smith continued as before with his belief that no one could possibly help his marriage.

Because he has a place of leadership among God's people, the pastor is seen in a position to judge. Whether or not he judges is not the point. The real issue is what the counselee thinks he does. If he points out failures which are due to a faulty conception of the principles of godly living, he will be viewed as a moral judge. This is a pastoral counseling trap.

We pastors are called to be prophetical, to point out discrepancies in daily living that cause Christians to experience defeat. But when we do, our role as understanding counselors is vexed by counselee defensiveness. Consequently we end up attempting to counsel people whose defenses must first be penetrated before we can deal with the problem that brought them to us in the first place.

A Better Way

There is a better way to deal with this problem. Counselors of all kinds, secular or church, need to understand their primary role as accepting rather than judging, listening rather than exhorting.

This does not mean that pastors have to tolerate sin. No, the pastor's acceptance of the sinful person takes the form of Christ's love when He met the woman at the well. He worked toward restoration, not judgment; at reconciliation, not condemnation; at forgiveness, not retaliation.

What the Smiths need is not a referee or a moral judge. They need a pastoral counselor who will attempt to see both sides of their story with neutral acceptance—without making judgments about who is most "right." This can be difficult since pastors are encouraged to demonstrate their convictions by siding with the forces of good against evil. If a pastor openly concludes that one is more right than the other, he has probably lost an opportunity to minister to the condemned party.

If it is obvious that there have been violations of Scripture, the pastor's best policy is to allow the Scripture to speak for itself. Pointing out a biblical pronouncement against the behavior of either spouse allows the Scripture to speak as intended. And the Holy Spirit is able to apply that message appropriately. The pastor then is only a mouthpiece for the Word, not the Word itself.

When Scripture does not make a pronouncement about a counseling issue it is best for a pastor to refrain from interjecting his personal opinion because he will be seen as taking one side against the other. But no pastor should be neutral when an obvious offense has been committed against the Word. Many people are looking for direction and need to be shown the error of their ways.

A pastor/counselor needs to ask himself a few questions in order to avoid manipulating his counselees:

- Why do these people need me to lead them?
- Why are they too weak to determine for themselves the best choice?
- Are they chronically dependent?
- Does it make me feel good to control people, to have them depend upon me?
- Will they accept my direction because I push it on them or because they respect my judgment?
- Do I feel the need to be in charge? Or must I take charge because I feel it is the responsible thing to do?
- Can I relegate my role to being a catalyst? an observer? an enabler?

Some pastors feel they are not counseling unless they are doing something for their counselees. Feeling their role is to solve problems, they unwittingly remove much of the counselee's personal responsibility. "Fixing" is not going to help a married couple like the Smiths, who seem to care as little about their marriage as an unconcerned alcoholic does about his alcoholism.

No matter how hard you try, you will find that your pastoral counseling efforts will be met with resistance unless your counselee is sufficiently motivated to receive your help. Therefore, an appraisal of the counselee's motivation for coming to you should be determined early in the counseling relationship. Make sure you know why your counselee has come.

A Resource, Not a Problem

Once you determine that Mr. Smith is reluctantly involved in this meeting, enlist his cooperation by identifying him as a resource to help his wife. He will, for the time being, no longer be a counselee but a resource in the counseling process.

And be sure to maintain a relationship with the "identified patient," in this case Mrs. Smith, by using her reasons for coming as the chief motivators for the counseling relationship. You do not have to agree with her complaints, but make it clear that you are doing your best to see her point of view. This will subtly move the counseling pressure off Mr. Smith and onto Mrs. Smith, who appears to be the most motivated for counseling at this time.

As you gain rapport with Mr. Smith during the counseling sessions, you will likely see him begin to change his attitude toward counseling and become more willing to disclose personal issues about himself.

Proceeding this way will enhance the possibility that the one most motivated for counseling will make some of the necessary changes for marital growth and the least motivated will continue as an ongoing observer and a resource in counseling. Eventually the observer, in this case Mr. Smith, will desire a more active role in marriage counseling. If not, you have at the very least acquired a participant-observer to team up with you while making each person aware of the problems in the marriage.

Clarified motivation and unified counseling goals will give the Smiths a chance to help each other and themselves in a constructive, empathetic environment.

By being aware of the stresses placed upon the uncooperative spouse you will more easily understand him and his reluctance to be involved in counseling. The fact you have tried to understand his point of view will benefit further your attempts to engage him, the reluctant partner, in counseling.

38

What Does It Take to Be Bold?

By Peter W. Starr

Peter W. Starr is pastor of the Church of the Cross, a non-denominational fellowship in Scranton, Pennsylvania. He is a graduate of Princeton Theological Seminary and is working on a book on the second coming of Christ.

The only saint which the devil fears, said Wesley, is the one who, understanding the Bible's message to men, both speaks and lives it *zealously*.

A Methodist Charismatic once said to me: "The Spirit-baptism is not for everyone. We should not pour others into our mold." It sounded so innocent and tolerant that I was tempted to let the remark pass, but I now realize that we err in turning God's commands into modern options that attempt to save people from hard decisions.

We should challenge the idea that one way to heaven is as good as another. Not only ought we to declare that there is no other name given under heaven whereby we must be saved, but also that being filled with the Spirit is a divine command (Eph. 5:19).

Jesus was firm: "Whosoever then relaxes one of the least of these commandments and teaches men so, shall be called least in the kingdom of heaven" (Matt. 5:19).

This generation, like many before it, is characterized by its love for a value judgment called pluralism. It maintains that all roads lead to the truth and hence all are equal. Basically, this was the same social platitude that confronted the early church. How did God handle it? He gave His lackluster band of followers a power to testify of Him that even their enemies could neither gainsay nor resist. Being filled with the Spirit enabled God's people to speak boldly in a new way.

Today's pluralism, embraced by all mainline denominations, preaches tolerance for all religious expressions and makes no distinction between truth and error. Two years ago, the United Presbyterian Church advertised courses in yoga at its Western retreat ranches and still encourages its pastoral counselors to teach meditation techniques (borrowed from Eastern religions) to local pastors.

In connection with this kind of trend, Paul wrote, "A little leaven leaveneth the whole lump." Like leaven added to a lump of bread dough, the sin of pluralism spreads quickly through the church of Jesus Christ until it rises into arrogant humanism. As children of the light, we are called not to accommodate ourselves to darkness, but to expose it.

Look at the church in the book of Acts: they would not be intimidated or silenced, and under pain of death, announced that only *one* way to heaven existed! As long as we settle for the soft path, comfortable and gray, instead of the narrow path of persecution that leads to life, we will dishonor Christ and deceive ourselves.

We must get off the fence. Any religious institution that long enjoys a cozy social acceptance eventually becomes Laodicean: prosperous, content and spiritually lazy. Is this not a description of the church in America, by and large? Therefore, our immediate goal should be to turn from the blithe self-concern one finds everywhere ("Praise the Lord, all is well with my soul!") to the sort of vigilance that acquires true spiritual wealth.

I wonder how the Spirit reacts today when so many of the Charismatic/Pentecostal ranks seem content to sit back in home meetings, praise and healing services (which in themselves are good), without feeling impelled to go forth and challenge the godless assumptions of our pluralistic society? Certainly, it is easier to stay put in those meetings, look after our own concerns, and conveniently forget that our Lord's enemy is stealing our victory.

Some people believe that the acquisition of tongues-speaking is enough to make one into a fanatic. For me, it has been a blessed part of my Christian experience. Yet, like my rebirth, it is nothing more than a beginning in my development as an effective Christian. If I exult in tongues as my "union card" in the Pentecostal movement, I am no less backslidden than the third generation pew-warmer who attends church out of habit. It is crucial that we of the Charismatic/Pentecostal experience grasp this as a biblical priority at stake: "Desire the spiritual gifts, especially that you may *prophesy*" (1 Cor. 14:1). For all the good which "tongues" ministers to the individual believer, it is proclaiming the inspired Word of God that serves the common good.

Instead of individual "highs," we ought to seek those highs that come as a result of expressing our gifts in concrete acts of love. Then we may boast with Christ, "The Spirit of the Lord is upon me, because he has anointed me to preach good news to the poor...release to the captives, and recovering of sight to the blind" (Luke 4:18).

As stewards of God's gifts who shall one day give account for our use of them, we must ask: what can we do to repel Satan's attack against the souls of men in our day? The answer lies in the demonstration of the power of God.

Ours has always been a society built upon belief in a single God whose values as revealed in the Scriptures were our values. Such is no longer the case. This ground has been rent by a seismic shift in thinking occasioned by humanistic religion and the god of technology.

How have we answered this break with the past? During the last 40 years, almost every effort by evangelical Christians to reverse this trend has gone to restate our belief in the inerrancy of the Bible. While this is surely commendable, Christianity has still lost ground in the process to its humanistic counterparts. The reason, I believe, lies in our failure to apply the counsel of that inerrant Word, namely, that Christians who are the witnesses of the living God *must* be filled with the Spirit.

Let us use the sword of the Spirit (notice the weapon: Word and Spirit combined) to turn the battle to the gate. Let us be Spirit-empowered! The world is looking for an answer, but it will never be the answer of a cold orthodoxy.

It is hard to imagine today's church as being remembered for its zeal. Our prosperity, yes; our orthodoxy, yes; but our zeal for the kingdom of God?

Today's man and woman need to be energized in obedience to the truth. That is why the energy of God—contained in the Person of the Holy Spirit—is so essential. As He energizes us from within, we are able to overcome purposelessness and lukewarm discipleship.

Will our God remain silent and aloof, allowing us to go along the merry road to destruction? Does He not warn Laodicea, "Those whom I love, I reprove and chasten; so be zealous and *repent*" (Rev. 3:19)? One cannot deal with fence-sitters with the voice of moderation; they must be warned in a style reminiscent of John the Baptist.

Pastors and teachers: repent! You must be the ones to stretch the people beyond themselves; to bid them take up their crosses and follow Christ.

In this way, our hideous lethargy will be cast out and replaced by the boldness which is born of the Spirit of God.

39

What Is a Pastor's Responsibility?

By E. S. Caldwell

E. S. Caldwell is associate editor of *MINISTRIES: The Magazine For Christian Leaders*. He served the Assemblies of God as promotions coordinator for the Division of Home Missions and publicity director for the radio-TV department. He pastored 23 years in Idaho and Missouri. He is a graduate of Northwest College of the Assemblies of God and also attended Northwest Nazarene College.

The superchurches may be grabbing the headlines but the bulk of believers still worship in caring churches where attendance averages fewer than 100. In what size church were you saved? Baptized? Spirit-filled? Called to preach? It was probably in a church with fewer than 100 in attendance, because two-thirds of the 326,000 or so churches in America are that size.

And that pastor who impacted your life as an example of Christlikeness—was he a big-shot preacher in his denomination or was he little known beyond the environs of his parish? It is likely that the latter is the case.

So why should you bemoan the modest number in your flock? You have the potential of building a small church into a strong body.

The "failure syndrome" Satan attempts to foist on pastors of small churches is as big a lie as any he ever fathered. Don't listen to him!

When Jesus told His parable about the seeking shepherd, He could have spoken of a flock of two dozen sheep—or 2,000. After all, He's the Great Shepherd of countless bands of "sheep." But what number did he choose? 100!

I know it would be faulty exegesis to expostulate that Jesus advocates one shepherd to each 100 sheep; i.e., one pastor for 100 persons. But the fact that He spotlighted this ratio cannot be totally ignored. Certainly the idea that one lost sheep demands some shepherd's attention is central to Jesus' teaching.

It is true that pastors of most small congregations labor under the disadvantage of a limited income for both their church and themselves. And daydreaming about the advantages of a larger salary is commonplace. But suppose for a moment that your income had no relationship to church size. What number of persons could you adequately serve as the Lord's shepherd? Underscore that word *adequately*.

I discussed this with a Disciples of Christ pastor who had 1,500 members. He complained that about all he did through the week was attend committee meetings. He stated that the ideal number for one man to pastor was 300; after that, additional staff should be added, and complications tended to set in. Of course, 300 on the roll means 150 in the pews in some churches. So his conclusion was not that different from mine. I once deduced that I could provide sufficient pastoral attention, with a satisfactory number of home visits, for a congregation averaging 150.

Jesus gave a simple, yet all-encompassing command to Peter: "Take care of my sheep" (John 21:16, NIV). And Peter relayed a similar command to every shepherd who would follow him: "Tend the flock of God that is in your charge, not by constraint but willingly, not for shameful gain but eagerly, not as domineering over those in your charge but being examples to the flock" (1 Pet. 5:2,3, RSV).

Not how many sheep but the quality of care is the Lord's paramount concern.

Shepherds sometimes wander off course. Those religious leaders of Ezekiel's day did. Listen to the prophet's indictment: "You do not feed the sheep. The weak you have not strengthened, the sick you have not healed, the crippled you have not bound up, the strayed you have not brought, the lost you have not sought" (Ezek. 34:3,4, RSV).

What is the ideal church size for you to fulfill these assignments? To how many sheep can you provide ample nourishment—a stable diet of spiritual food? Microphones can amplify your voice so many can hear but a feeding process requires more than mere words. Peter pinpoints that words-made-flesh element: "being examples to the flock." The absence of example is why neither video counseling cassettes nor satellite services can make pastors obsolete.

How many weak can you be responsible for strengthening? It takes time, one-on-one, to put a scrawny sheep into a personalized regimen that will make him strong in the Lord and the power of His might.

And how much time can you devote to healing the sick? "Thou anointest my head with oil" of the Old Covenant is to be actualized by the shepherds of the New Covenant for their sheep: "He should call for the elders of the church to pray over him and anoint him with oil in the name of the Lord. And the prayer offered in faith will make the sick person well; the Lord will raise him up" (James 5:14,15, NIV).

Those crippled sheep, hobbling along after being mauled and beaten—how much time can you devote to them? They huddle on your pews so preoccupied with their bruises that they cannot enter into the worship you are leading. The Lord expects His shepherds to bind up the brokenhearted, as He also did.

And what about the straying stragglers? It takes a special kind of determination to get such self-willed sheep back into the fold. One thing about the small size of your flock: you can spot the missing stray early and go after him before the ravening wolves isolate and devour him.

One more responsibility: "the lost." The size of your flock may be small but its numbers will grow if you seek the lost. God called you to be more than a sheep keeper; He called you to seek the lost.

God put you with that flock. Your responsibility and accountability are in place. The Lord put you there to succeed. Jesus said it: "Fear not, little flock; for it is your Father's good pleasure to give you the kingdom" (Luke 12:32).

40

How Do You Gain Loyalty?

By Bob Heil

Bob Heil is director of the Christian Outreach Center, Hillsboro, Missouri. He also serves as international advisor-at-large for Women's Aglow, is a member of the steering committee for the National Leadership Conference and has authored the book, *Lessons From the Furnace.*

Potiphar had many servants who were faithful to do the tasks assigned them. But in Joseph he had something more. He had *loyalty*. So "Potiphar left all that he had in Joseph's hand; and he knew not ought he had, save the bread which he did eat" (Gen. 39:6).

Amasa had never learned loyalty. He had joined Absalom in his rebellion. Now, however, he was pardoned by King David and raised to the position of David's commander-in-chief. He was very grateful, but in the very first task he was asked to perform, his lack of loyalty surfaced again. It almost caused a civil war.

Sheba, a rebel from Benjamin, was beginning to assemble the northern ten tribes to rebel against David. David knew that time was of the essence. So he commanded Amasa to gather as many of the troops of Judah as he could within a day and a half that they might strike Sheba and those with him before they had a chance to mobilize.

Amasa thought he was being loyal, but he decided to take extra time so he could gather many more troops from Judah. When the morning came for him to appear before David, there was no Amasa and there were no troops. David, realizing that the situation was desperate and immediate action was needed, sent his household troops against Sheba. (The record is in 2 Samuel 20:4-6.) Amasa had failed because of this subtle form of disloyalty.

If you as an elder are asked by another to do something, can that person relax as Potiphar, knowing it will be done and done well? Is he free from having to ask again and again?

In a congregation there are usually one or two men on which God has put a mantle to guard the overall direction of the flock. No one else sees the congregation quite from their perspective. All too often, however, other elders are raised up who also want the best for the flock, who want to do things right, but who want to do it their own way. Like Amasa they may cause disaster. They have not learned that loyalty is of more value than their own opinions, even when their opinions are right. If they want to do something their own way, they should talk it out with their leader and get his blessing first.

What Loyalty Looks Like

Loyalty means you want the one you serve to be blessed. The heart-set is as that of Eliezer, the servant of Abraham. The focal point of Eliezer was to please Abraham, not just to get the job done. When he was sent to find a wife for Isaac he prayed, ''O Lord, God of my master Abraham, I pray thee, send me good speed this day, and shew kindness unto my master Abraham'' (Gen. 24:12). His focus was on his master, not his performance.

Loyalty means that the one you serve can trust you. He knows that you will not only do the task that was assigned, but that you are *for* him. He can rest in the knowledge that his wishes and vested interests are safe with you.

Loyalty means you serve the way you have been asked. You are not to do things your own way unless you are specifically given the freedom.

Years ago, as I ministered in one church after another, my ministry started to dry up. It became stale, at least to me. I besought the Lord as to what was wrong. He told me that I was concerned for how I was ministering, not for the people to whom I was sent. Selfishly, out of my own insecurity, even my prayers were for the success of my performance. The people were just the sea of faces, one group much like the next, that allowed me to serve—to ''serve Jesus'' but not necessarily the people. I was striving to do my ministry faithfully, but I had no thoughts about loyalty to the people. I repented and immediately the ministry blossomed more than ever.

Loyalty means that a leader hangs in there even when the going gets rough. When Jesus was about to leave for the garden of Gethsemane, Scripture says of Him, ''Having loved His own...He loved them unto the end'' (John 13:1). Even though they were about to run away and deny Him, Jesus loved them with an unbreakable loyalty.

Some congregations would be spared much grief if their elders could only focus more on the people rather than their own ministries, more on the health and joy of the saints than on arguing over the proper way to minister. Many times they struggle because their loyalties are to themselves and their own thinking.

When such things happen, there is much heartache. Some of the churches which had tremendous promise, have broken apart and disappeared. Such times are not easy for God's people.

Though loyalty is often used interchangeably with faithfulness, there is an important difference. Faithfulness refers to actions. When a person is given a task and then completes it properly, he has been faithful. However, that fact tells us nothing about the set of his heart—his motivation.

Loyalty, on the other hand, describes a heart-set that is positive, honoring the one served and giving without self-serving motives. It is that part of love that "seeketh not her own" (1 Cor. 13:5).

How to Gain Loyalty

Some of the things you can do in your own congregation to rectify any lack of loyalty are:

1. Teach the difference between faithfulness and loyalty.

2. Remind your people that, according to their new nature, they already want to be loyal. Unless they are outright rebels, any disloyal acts come out of ignorance and/or weakness of the flesh.

3. Let them know, in light of their sharpened understanding, you are expecting them to be loyal. They will be what you expect them to be.

4. Be careful about whom you appoint to places of responsibility. Look for loyalty, not just faithfulness.

5. As a leader, practice those qualities of leadership that will help people become more loyal to you. Remember, you are representing Jesus to your people. We are *faithful* to Jesus because He is our Master and Lord. We are *loyal* to Him because He is our Brother and Friend.

Pastors and elders are called to be servants not only of Jesus, but of the members of the congregation as well. They are not just called to a town or a certain ministry. They are called to a people; a people whom they are to carry in their bosom; a people for whom they are to live and if necessary to die; a people with whom they are to fall in love, and whom they are to nurture through good times and bad. They are not to serve "with eyeservice as menpleasers; but in singleness of heart, fearing God" (Col. 3:22).

Loyalty, the holy heart-set, is a must if we are ever to have victory in our personal lives and in our congregations.

The Lord Jesus wants to build the steel sinews of loyalty within His people. Within Christ's kingdom, everyone in one sense or another is subject to someone else. We are all servants. We all have masters over us. To serve the ones to whom Christ has given us, we must put aside our individual rights (Matt. 20:26,27; Eph. 5:21).

Pray for loyalty! Pray for new eyes that see your leader with godly esteem. Pray for the Holy Spirit to set an alarm system to guard your thoughts and the set of your heart.

Settle Your Accounts

Jesus describes the difference between a good shepherd and a hireling. It isn't that the hireling doesn't feed the sheep well or doesn't lead them to green pastures. He is faithful to do his job—until the wolf shows up, then he runs. All too many pastors are running, taking other calls, going to other congregations when the going gets rough, leaving the sheep to the wolves. How will such leaders answer the Lord? And how will they ever stand in the crisis to come?

It is not too late! You can still settle accounts with your masters, whether God or men. The Lord Jesus has paid for all disloyalty. The door of forgiveness and cleansing is still open.

You can also settle it in your heart. To whom has God made you a loyal servant? You can settle it in your will, to serve that leader with a loyalty he can trust.

John the Baptist is a servant who exemplifies a heart being focused on his Master rather than upon his own performance. He said to the Jews, "Ye yourselves bear me witness, that I said, I am not the Christ, but that I am sent before Him. He that hath the bride is the bridegroom: but the friend of the bridegroom, which standeth and heareth Him rejoiceth greatly because of the bridegroom's voice: this my joy therefore is fulfilled. He must increase, but I must decrease" (John 3:28-30).

That's loyalty!

41

How Can Video Be Effectively Used in Your Church?

By Morris Sheats

Morris Sheats served as senior pastor of Trinity Church, Lubbock, Texas, for 14 years. During that period the congregation grew from 100 to 4,000. He was senior pastor of Beverly Hills Church in Dallas, Texas, for 16 months with a congregation of 6,000. A vital part of Sheats' ministry was the initiation and development of a "Learning Center" which housed reading, audio and video libraries. Sheats travels throughout the United States and abroad emphasizing the need for consistent teaching.

Our church was exploding with growth. I was not looking for a 40-hour week, but a 40-hour day! I needed to multiply myself. Yes, the Lord had provided an excellent staff at Trinity Church. But all of us needed more time.

One day I was meditating on the idea of "redeeming the time." Then in my studies, I saw the concept emerging of "buying up or buying back time." How could that be possible?

Video. Teach with video. The answer broke in upon my heart as spring rain covers the earth. The year was 1973.

Carefully and prayerfully, the Lord helped me lay the foundation for a learning center featuring the latest in video equipment.

Someone had told me about the learning center at Oral Roberts University. You could actually go to a listening room and "dial up" the video series you wanted to see. What an idea!

Then I discovered the tremendous expense involved. How could a local church use the same idea but cut the cost? Before long the idea began to come.

Listening Rooms

In my next educational building we built a learning center. Here is how it worked.

People would come in and tell the librarian (we started with volunteers on limited hours) which tape they wanted to see. They would then be assigned to a "listening room." The librarians put on the tape for the person who was then ready to learn God's Word—by video.

The "listening rooms" were small—only four feet by five feet. Each room had a large window opening to a landscaped courtyard which made the small room seem larger than it really was.

In each of the five rooms were an audio cassette player and a small television monitor. Audio and video cassettes could be played on this equipment. The video players were in a remote location and operated by staff to eliminate problems.

Now how do we pay for all this equipment? The total package would cost about $25,000. At a special learning center banquet, God used George Otis to inspire the people of Trinity Church to "take a forward step. Be ahead of your time.'' The people did. The funds were given.

Producing Video Tapes

Now came the tough assignment. Where do we find video teaching tapes? The supply was limited. Our pastoral team recognized we would need to produce teaching tapes. We started.

With a plan to produce at least three hours a week, we designed a schedule. Each man took an area of expertise, and the work began.

Are you wondering about all the equipment needed to produce video teaching lessons? It is not as expensive as you might think. Remember, with video teaching tapes you are not producing material to compete with commercial television. You simply want to "multiply yourself." Quality is important, but your goal is not national television. Your goal is to *multiply* yourself with modern technology.

For example, the first series I needed was "Pre-Marriage Counseling." It would have more of an instructional than a counseling purpose. Any good pastor wants to spend some personal time with a couple he is going to marry. But he is even more concerned that they have a basic knowledge of Christian marriage.

I have always required couples to attend a series of classes before they can be married in our church. But what if the fiance is from out-of-state? Or a couple from your congregation may be finishing college in another city and planning to marry the week after returning home. How can you schedule the instruction without putting yourself and the couple under terrific stress?

Video is the ideal solution! You can tape the pre-marital classes, tailoring the content and style to your own objectives. You probably have resource people with training in the area of marriage and family relationships. A family practice medical doctor in your congregation could add valuable insights.

On the other hand, if you are not ready to produce your own video instruction, you can get excellent material from various Christian counseling services. The material is already on video cassette tape and ready for use. Don't be afraid to begin with something simple and gradually build more depth and quality into your presentation.

The idea is that once you have material on video tape, couples can arrange a convenient weekend sometime before the wedding to view the sessions together. It's amazing how much strain this can take off a pastor's busy schedule!

This kind of instruction provides far better preparation for marriage than if you had pre-empted your schedule for one quick, last-minute "counseling session." With the video teaching as a foundation, your personal time with the couple can be focused and directed to their specific needs.

Now that I have illustrated this familiar scenario and how video can multiply your efforts, your mind is already beginning to leap ahead into so many other areas. The counseling ministry alone can be revolutionized through video teaching.

As a pastor, how many times do you find yourself going over and over again through the same territory—only with different people? Self-condemnation, self-image problems, bitterness, unsaved husbands—chances are you have addressed every one of these needs in some detail either from the pulpit or in a teaching session.

Conserving Time

With proper planning, you can capture this material on video. Then when you discern a person's problem, instead of beginning in-depth counseling, you can make an assignment for them to view a specialized teaching which deals with their need. Two objectives are accomplished through this assignment.

First, the teaching will give the individual a scriptural foundation to deal with his problem. And secondly, the next counseling session will not be scheduled until he has received the video instruction. It is surprising how this procedure eliminates those who are not really serious about getting spiritual help.

Don't misunderstand me. I believe in the need for trained counselors. But if we are not very wise and discerning, tremendous time is needlessly wasted. Video can add countless hours to your schedule in this area alone.

How about those situations in a growing church where you simply *must* be in two places at once? At the close of every service, you are literally torn by two needs. You desperately want to go to the counseling room with those who have come to the altar for salvation. If only you could have just five minutes to give them some warm, personal words of encouragement and exhortation! But the need to stay with the larger group and conclude your message is just as strong.

Once again, video can come to the rescue. Set up a video monitor in the counseling room and prepare a short but very personal word expressing those things only a pastor can convey to those newly born into the kingdom. Then the trained counselors can use your words as a "springboard" for their own instruction.

There are many other similar areas where the same technique can be used effectively. The membership and baptism classes are two examples. Often these are held in the 30 minutes prior to the beginning of an evening service. The pastor must be someplace else, but he can be several places with the use of video.

One important caution: I am not suggesting that with your video presence you replace the teacher or associate pastor who should be in charge of such a session. In group meetings, your video portion should serve only as an introduction or conclusion. But it can be a very powerful way to emphasize your vital concern and involvement.

Space doesn't permit me to tell you in detail about teacher training by video. But just imagine the Sunday school teacher for your seventh-grade boys who had to go on a business trip the night you had that tremendous session on "Ten Ways to Keep the Attention of Junior Highers." If you put it on video, he can see the teaching when he gets home. And furthermore, the same teaching will be in your library for all future teachers who might be faced with the same problems.

Innovating Through Video

Begin to let your creative mind flow. The potential is limitless. Within a year after initiating the use of video in our church, every facet of the ministry began to use it as a tool for training, motivation and instruction.

Before long, we were offering video elective classes for our adults. Children's teachers were putting skits on video to be shown in the Sunday school hour. Our puppet ministry was using it to multiply their ministry. And the choir members began to take greater interest in their appearance after viewing one Sunday morning's bedraggled, sour-faced presentation!

"All right," you say, "I can see the value, but I don't have $25,000 or George Otis."

Let me encourage you. First, you don't have to start on a large scale. And second, the cost of video equipment has actually decreased in the last ten years! Just as God provided a way for me to implement my vision, He will provide for you.

Today, several ministries are producing video series to be used in local churches. All that is required is a video player and a television set. If you will use a 21-inch television and elevate it at least four feet, you can have up to 75 people in a class.

In almost every church, there is an "electronic genius." This person loves to work with technical equipment. He knows how to operate it, or at least can learn to do so quickly.

He often has a superb shopping instinct. Let him begin to sniff out the bargains and help you get this ministry under way.

If you want to start with the simplest system, you can use equipment designed for home use as a start. You can expect to get a small camera with tripod, VHS recorder (VHS is more widely used than Betamax at the present time), and video monitor for under $2,500. Every major city has discount stores handling video equipment. Christian journals and magazines advertise consulting firms that specialize in this field. They can give their expertise to those who want more sophisticated systems.

The important thing is that we, as God's servants, must begin to utilize the technical tools He has provided. They are a vital key to reaching our world. But we must exercise initiative in finding creative uses for them.

Start now! Rely on the Holy Spirit. And don't be surprised if He plants in your heart unique ways to use video which will multiply your effectiveness in the work to which He has called you!

42

How Can Video Extend Your Church's Outreach?

By Charles and Frances Hunter

Charles and Frances Hunter have been in the field of evangelism for over 15 years and authored more than 40 books with sales over 8 million copies. They head video schools in the United States and Canada where their video tapes are sold. The Hunters also are co-presidents of City of Light, Inc., a part of Hunter Ministries in Kingwood, Texas.

When the first video tapes were released, it was a victory for the devil. Now pornographic films could be released for home use and viewed by people of all ages without regard to any kind of restrictions or regulations, but as God can, and often does do so well, He took what looked like a victory for the devil and made it an outstanding tool for Himself.

Many beginning churches do not have qualified, anointed teachers in their Sunday school classes. Video is the answer! You can choose from any number of anointed, internationally known speakers who are experts in many subjects, press a button and your Sunday school classes, small or large, are privileged to hear people they might never be able to hear because their schedules are so busy they cannot accept the invitation of every church.

One of the most interesting things about video teaching is that once the anointing is captured on the tape, it never leaves! You can play the same tape hundreds of times, and the teaching and anointing are still there! All of us are subject to periods when we feel the anointing more than at other times, but these precious moments when it is captured on television never die!

Wednesday nights can be turned from a "ho-hum" service into one of the most exciting nights in the week through video tapes. There are so many well-known speakers who have their tapes available today, that you can choose your subject or speaker with no difficulty. Attendance grows when your church anticipates an exciting speaker with a power-packed message.

Do you spend hours in pre-marital counseling? There was a time when everyone felt that such counseling had to be done on a personal basis. Today pastors are providing two to six hours of pre-personal counseling through marriage video tapes and will counsel on a personal basis only after the couple has agreed to listen to the prescribed counseling on video. Many pastors have discovered that when the video counseling is done, the problems have been ferreted out and solved before personal counseling ever takes place. Most of us know that while each set of problems is unique in itself, the answer to all of them still is contained in the Word of God.

Because of disturbances or interference or a lack of time during counseling, a very important fact may be left out. But on video it is always there, and can even be repeated to the listener as many times as necessary!

Children's church has a perfect answer in programs that are far beyond the reach of most churches. The children in the smallest church in the world can be taught through elaborate, exciting lessons by the use of video tapes.

Children of today are programmed to watch a television screen, so there is no problem in getting them around a TV set. When we are competing for children's attention in a world of professional filming of such programs as Sesame Street, we need to be able to present God in a way which will appeal to a child's imagination more than a worldly program does. Puppets presented by Spirit-filled specialists can hold the attention of any and all children (and adults, too).

In all church services there is always a problem of where we aim our biggest gun. Do we aim it at the unsaved? Do we aim it at the ones who need healing? Do we aim it at the ones who need to understand about the baptism with the Holy Spirit? Do we aim it at the ones who need to understand about holy living and total commitment? Or do we shotgun?

Churches can meet the needs of all levels through video. There can be the beginning class to teach new converts how to become grounded in the Word of God. Then there can be a complete series on the Holy Spirit, explaining who He is and what the Holy Spirit's function is. Then there can be a series on the gifts of the Spirit for the more advanced. Almost any subject which a pastor might desire to teach his congregation, or learn himself, can be found by an anointed teacher on video tape today.

Churches which present a pre-service video teaching on Sunday evenings before the regular service discover that the video attendance comes close to what the usual evening service would be. Likewise, some smaller churches are discovering that Sunday school attendance when enhanced by video will almost equal the Sunday morning service attendance. But the most important aspect to consider is that your people are *growing* in the Lord through video teaching.

One of the newest ideas is a video church concept. At first this might sound like a danger signal to the cautious pastor, a warning that people could be taken out of his church. But what it really offers is an up-to-date outreach for churches who want to mother other churches.

The video church can start in the home of an excited believer who sees a need in his particular neighborhood for some good teaching in the Word of God. They may live 40 or 50 miles from the "mother" church, and we have to be honest and admit that many people will not drive that far for two times every Sunday. So "mother" church starts a video church, and provides them with video tapes of worship in the event they do not have a worship leader; a Sunday school teacher in the event they do not have a good Sunday school teacher; a super church program for children if they are short in this area; and even a preacher for the morning service to bring a message. It doesn't necessarily need to take place on Sundays, so people who want to attend another church can be a video church member also.

The video church collects offerings which are sent to the mother church or disbursed as the mother church directs for local needs or to help pay for the video tapes. The services leave time for individual body ministry among those qualified for body ministry, so there is a warm, personal touch in a video church. Leaders can learn from video how to minister effectively.

Sponsoring churches also send an individual from the home church to help supervise in the beginning if proper leadership is not available. As the new church grows, the mother church may appoint a "live" pastor for the group.

This serves two purposes—it helps get the video church off the ground and it provides an outlet for people who need to be able to use their leadership. The video church concept eliminates the cost of renting a building and high overhead in areas where the starting attendance would be small, or in underprivileged areas where the finances might be lacking.

The video church concept is limited only by the thinking of the mother church and may be developed in many ways. One single mother church could have several satellite churches.

Bethany Assembly of God in San Jose, California, caught the vision of reaching Vietnamese-speaking people during the days when flights of refugees were landing there. Subsequent events resulted in this vision being expanded by means of the video church concept.

Sam Siam, a converted former Buddhist priest, launched a Vietnamese ministry in a chapel provided by Bethel. Soon their Sunday afternoon attendance swelled to 200. But eventually many of those who found the Lord had to move to other localities for employment. These converts clustered in Visalia, Fresno and Oakland.

At first Siam sent these groups audio tapes and visited them as often as he could. Other converts moved to Texas. How could he effectively minister to them? A layman came up with the answer—video cassettes. He helped raise the funds for a TV camera and the first video recorders.

Now Vietnamese in many California cities and cities in other states gather in homes equipped with video recorders to receive regular, systematic Bible teaching by Sam Siam, an Assemblies of God home missionary multiplied by video.

The potential for video is limited only by the imagination of the persons involved. From the toddler to the senior citizen, there are video tapes to make everyone happy. The choice of teachers is unlimited, and you can provide for your entire church the teaching and inspiration of servants of God who might never be able to schedule time to visit your church, but who can bring you the blessing and anointing God has bestowed on them through video. Today filming and technology have improved greatly so that many of the video tapes being offered are on a level equal in quality to the finest professional television. And that's the way it should be. God's people should never have to settle for less than the best.

You can pick and choose, select and reject and find what is exactly right for your own church. And remember, video is not a one-time thing! It can be used over and over again.

How will you put this medium to work in your corner of God's kingdom?

Solving Music Ministers' Problems

43

What Should Worship
Accomplish in Your Church?

By Bob Sorge

Bob Sorge is an assistant pastor at Restoration Temple, San Diego, California. He served for three years as director of music at Elim Bible Institute in New York and has conducted and taught at several worship seminars.

E very Charismatic pastor and worship leader should understand why the Holy Spirit is renewing a concern for worship in our churches today. It is no longer adequate to defend our worship services by saying, "Well, we have always done it this way." It is equally insufficient to consider our worship services "the preliminaries," something to "condition" the congregation in preparation for the truly important part of the service: the sermon.

It is time to consider seriously the vital role that worship plays in the life of the congregation.

There are three general spheres our worship services minister through:

1. There is the *vertical* aspect of worship, the level in which the worshipper communicates with the Lord.

2. There is the *horizontal* aspect of worship, the level in which the worshipper communicates with others in the congregation.

3. There is the *inward* aspect of worship, where the worshipper is personally affected by the worship service.

Each of these areas helps us to understand better the role of worship in the congregation.

Vertical Aspect

The primary reason for worship is to minister to the Lord. The basic posture of the worshipper is, "I will bless the Lord," and not, "Lord, bless me!"

Our congregations know that worship is intended to benefit the Lord, yet they will sometimes be critical of the worship service or worship leader, complaining that the worship did not do as much for them as it did last week.

If we understand that the main purpose of worship is to bless and glorify the Lord, then why are we upset when the worship doesn't seem to bless us? The question is not whether the worship service blessed me; the question is, did it bless God? It is not what I thought of the worship that matters—it is what God thought of it! Did *He* approve? Was *He* pleased with our "sacrifice of praise"?

An effective worship leader will learn the ministry of exhortation, and God's people must be exhorted to discard their selfish motivations in worship. (Worship leader: be the worship leader, not the preacher! Learn how to inspire God's people with a 30-second exhortation that lifts their attention from themselves to the Lord.

The Church has been called to be Levites in the New Testament sense, to minister continually before the Lord. Let's take full advantage of this special privilege!

A second reason for our worship service is to realize the manifest presence of God in our midst. We understand that God is everywhere at all times, but yet there are different degrees to which God manifests Himself. He manifests Himself on one level "where two or three are gathered." But when a group of God's people congregate to sing His glorious praise, He "inhabits" those praises and reveals His presence in a special way among His praising people. (See Ps. 22:3 and 2 Chron. 5:13,14.)

In Exodus 33 the Lord made this promise to Moses: "My presence will go with you, and I will give you rest." Moses' response was, "If your presence does not go with us, do not send us up from here...What else will distinguish me and your people from all the other people on the face of the earth?"

What will distinguish us today as God's people from the people of the world? What makes our church services any different from the Rotary Club or any other social organization? The presence of God!

If we don't have God's presence in our services, we may as well dismiss and throw a picnic instead! The presence of God is the hallmark of the church. When sinners experience the presence of God in our churches, they will be convinced of the reality of our faith and turn to God.

How can we experience this dimension of the glory of God? By encouraging our people to lift up their hearts to God in unreserved adoration and praise. God's response to this level of praise will be glorious!

We also hold worship services in order to provide an opportunity for the power of God to be released in His Church. In Luke 5:17 we are told that while Jesus was teaching, "the power of the Lord was present to heal them." It is in the presence of God that the power of God is revealed. It is true that God maintains sovereign control over the working of His mighty power—we cannot coerce Him into demonstrating His power simply because we have worshipped. But when God's presence is manifest in the midst of the congregation, an atmosphere comes that gives God greater freedom to work according to the counsel of His will. God is not reticent to display His power and glory; we are not ready to receive it!

Pastors recognize that at the commencement of the service most of our people are not ready to receive from the Lord in this dimension. But as the leadership allows the people to spend time in the presence

303

of God, hearts will find a release through the Spirit of God, and the people will become ready recipients of the blessings of God.

We also worship in order to provide an atmosphere or seedbed for the gifts of the Spirit and various spiritual ministries to be manifested. Have you noticed that prophecies rarely come forth until *after* God's people have worshipped for a season? This is not accidental. First we worship, and *then* spiritual ministries begin to operate.

It is not that God is unwilling to speak prophetically to His people at the beginning of the service, but we are not often ready to receive what God has to say! God had much to say to His people, but He waits until we are ready to receive His words.

Worship leaders can encourage the prophetic flow by realizing that they have a prophetic anointing upon their ministry. To be prophetic as a worship leader means simply to be sensitive to the thoughts and desires of the Holy Spirit moment by moment. The Holy Spirit is the true Worship Leader, and when we begin to respond to His promptings we will suddenly find ourselves being filled with His presence and glory.

Finally, in this vertical sense of worship, we worship in order to open up the channels of communication between us and God. Worship leaders must be aware that many in the Sunday morning service have not communicated with God since last Sunday! They have not read their Bibles nor spent quality time in prayer all week.

The worship service provides them with the opportunity to confess their sins, open up their hearts to the Lord, and receive cleansing and renewal from Him. God wants to see our faces lifted up to Him; O, how He wants to hear our voices singing sweet praises unto Him! The Lord longs for His people to overcome their inhibitions in the congregation, that they might with open face and strong voice radiate His praise. Worship leaders, watch your people during the worship service. Ask the Lord to reveal to you what is hindering the people when they seem reticent to enter into whole-hearted praise. Are they tired? Are they being lazy? Are they burdened with guilt or condemnation? Are they struggling with sin and defeat?

The sensitive worship leader will discern where the people are, and then will ask the Lord for wisdom to know how to lead the people into a release in the Spirit.

Worship leaders must continually avoid the tendency to control what happens between the worshipper and his God. Once the people have found that release in their spirits, the leader must in turn release the service to the Lord in order that He might complete that work in the believer's heart that He alone can do.

Horizontal Aspect

The interpersonal dynamics of a worship service are more significant than many realize.

We worship in order to enhance the feelings of unity within a body of believers.

Can you remember experiencing one of those altar services when most had gone home, and a few stayed behind to pray and worship? It was a time when the few folk that remained were worshipping the Lord with everything that was within them. You looked over at the one next to you and realized that he was unabashedly pouring out his soul to the Lord. At that moment you felt a tremendous amount of affinity with that brother because he, like you, was totally committed to the Lord.

A tremendous sense of unity came over the group, and soon everyone was hugging each other!

Show me a church that worships with all their heart and soul and mind and strength, and I will show you a church that is moving with an extraordinary sense of unity.

We worship in order to provide believers with an opportunity to confess and profess their faith before others. Our people find it comparatively easy to confess the Lord in the congregation, during the worship service. But they find it much harder to confess the Lord to their unsaved friends, neighbors, coworkers and relatives. But confessing the name of the Lord in the worship service will increase their boldness and faith to declare His name before unbelievers.

Encourage your people to lift up their voice in the congregation—"lift it up, be not afraid"—and the Lord will increase their ability to vocalize their faith to others.

Another key reason for congregational worship is that we might declare the glories of God before unbelievers. The unsaved *do* visit our worship services, and this is an excellent opportunity for them to see the reality of the glory of the Lord. Psalm 108:3 declares, "I will praise you, O Lord, among the nations; I will sing of you among the peoples." It is clearly God's intention that His praises not be confined to the ears of believers.

For too long God's people have been bashful about the praise of God!

Our people sometimes think like this: "I'm not going to bring my neighbor to the Sunday evening service, because our church gets too carried away in worship and I don't want to turn my neighbor off." But a worship service is the best place to bring an unsaved friend because when God manifests His presence in the midst of His people, unbelievers will be apprehended by the convicting power of the Holy Spirit and drawn to the Lord.

Do your people want to win their neighbors for the Lord? Tell them to bring them to the hottest praise service they can find! Sinners don't need to understand fully everything they hear or see—they only need to experience the reality of our God. We do not need to experience the reality of our God.

We do not need to apologize for or explain His praises, we only need to declare His praises. God intends for His praise to be broadcast around the world!

As a final consideration of the horizontal aspects of worship, *we worship in our churches in order to create a proper mood for the sermon and the remainder of the service.* It has been the experience of countless pastors that when the worship is real and vibrant, it is remarkably easy to preach. Not only is the anointing of the Spirit more evident, but the hearts of the people are more open to hear the Word of the Lord.

It is not coincidental that most churches flow in worship *prior* to the preaching of the Word. Any pastor will deeply cherish the ministry of a worship leader who has learned how to bring God's people to a place of readiness to receive the Word of God.

Inward Aspect

Finally, consider the ways in which worship changes the worshipper within. *We conduct worship services in order to release each person in an uninhibited expression of praise and worship.* Many saints are introverted in their expressions of worship—just as many husbands are reserved in their expressions of love toward their spouses. One of the clear goals of the worship leader, therefore, is to see these introverted worshippers released in their expression unto the Lord.

We recognize that all saints worship differently, according to the unique nature of each personality, but it is pleasing to the Lord when we are totally liberated to worship Him according to our true nature. When someone is very inhibited in a worship service but very extroverted while watching a ball game, it seems they are not being true to their personality in the worship service!

Worship leaders will be frustrated about those who are inhibited in worship service until they realize they can do nothing about that. No amount of coercion or upbraiding or coaxing will cause such people to open up. This is a work that the Holy Spirit alone can accomplish. Leave it up to Him!

The duty of the worship leader is simply to provide people with the best opportunity possible to enter into the glorious praise of God. Whether or not the people take advantage of that opportunity is between them and God.

Worship leaders must cease striving to make the worship service what they think it should be. It is not the worship leader's responsibility to see that the worship is free and vibrant—it is the individual worshipper's responsibility to make God's praise glorious. The command comes to the individual: "Praise *ye* the Lord!"

Worship services also teach and reinforce spiritual truth. The apostle Paul stated it this way: "*teaching* and *admonishing* one another in psalms and hymns and spiritual songs" (Col. 3:16). With many of our choruses we are actually memorizing the Scriptures, and in this manner our children are learning the Word of God. So many of the hymns we sing are rich with theological and devotional content. It is safe to say the songs we sing are teaching our children the theology of the church.

Our songs of worship also provide the worshipper with the means to express the heart-felt attitudes otherwise difficult to express. Most of our people are not poets, nor are many fluent speakers. Many Christians have difficulty putting into English the depths of love and emotion they feel toward the Lord. But in our hymnals we have recorded the words of men like Charles Wesley who were particularly gifted in expressing themselves with the pen. And so the congregation can echo the words of the hymnwriter and find their feelings are provided a vocabulary where choice words are coupled with an enhancing melody, and the song becomes a meaningful expression from their hearts to the Lord.

The wise worship leader will couple contemporary choruses with the hymns of old that have withstood the test of time, in order to provide the people with a full and well-rounded vocabulary of worship.

We become like that which we worship. Therefore, as we worship the Lord we are changed into His very likeness! 2 Corinthians 3:18 is a beautiful verse about worship: "And we, who with unveiled faces all reflect the Lord's glory, are being transformed into his likeness with ever-increasing glory."

When we worship with an uplifted countenance we truly reflect the Lord's glory, and it is then that we are changed little by little, becoming more like the God we worship.

Isaiah saw the Lord in worship, high and lifted up, and he was never the same again. Daniel saw the Lord and fell prostrate in worship.

Our people cannot spend time in the presence of the all-righteous God without becoming righteous; they cannot draw near to our holy God without their lives being purified.

Another clear purpose for worship is to inspire a life of worship in each believer. It is easy to get excited about worship in the midst of the congregation, and too many operate at this level alone. They worship only when they feel inspired to do so. But the Lord is seeking those who will be worshippers seven days a week.

It does not matter how enthusiastically our people worship on Sunday; it is how enthusiastic a worshipper they are on Monday that counts! The Lord wants His people to be like the Levitical singers of the Old Testament who ministered before the Lord 24 hours a day (1 Chron. 9:33).

It can be very frustrating to realize that many people wait for the worship leader to push their "worship button." If he does not lead out with the right song at the right time, they simply will not enter in. At such times God's people need to be stirred from their mental lethargy. They need to be reminded of their obligation to "*make* His praise glorious" (Ps. 66:2).

Most believers understand their duty to offer up a "sacrifice of praise" (Heb. 13:15), but they easily forget and allow their minds to slip into neutral.

Make the people aware that they have succumbed to the "neutral syndrome." They will immediately recognize it, and with some positive encouragement from the worship leader will stir themselves to enter with enthusiasm into the worship service.

Our goal as worship leaders is that the people will learn to worship not only when they are prodded by the worship leader, but they will learn the discipline of a life of praise every day. And the worship service is the place where believers will receive the impetus and strength to live that life of worship.

God is preparing *people*; He is preparing you and me, the church of Jesus Christ. What is delaying the new move of God? The church! Once we are prepared to receive it, the Lord will surely send it. Worship leaders must understand that "praise prepares." Psalm 50:23 in the NIV translation says, "He who sacrifices thank offerings honors me, and he *prepares the way* so that I may show him the salvation of God."

Worship softens our hearts, and sensitizes our spirit to the Spirit of God. Then, when the Spirit moves, we are prepared to follow, no matter how non-traditional or unexpected the new way seems to be.

This is why church leaders have been hearing so much about worship in recent times! If the church will hear the call of the Spirit, and become softened and sensitized through worship, our times of waiting and indecisiveness will change into movement and progress in God.

We must be receptive to know when the Spirit moves in a new direction, and worship fine-tunes our hearts to discern that. If we are accustomed to gazing steadily upon His face in worship, then when He moves we will notice.

With a clearer understanding of why we worship, our services will not drift aimlessly but will move forward incisively toward the goal set before us. Our goal? To be worshippers. Why? To minister unto the Lord, experience His glorious presence, and to remain sensitized to His voice.

This emphasis has not been initiated by the will of man, and it will not be fulfilled through the strength of man. Our worship services must not be characterized by the control of man, but by the leading of the

Spirit.

We must allow God to do His sovereign work in the hearts of those who will respond in true worship. The Spirit is calling His church today to a new level of worship. Are we hearing His voice?

44

How Do You Choose an Effective Worship Leader?

By Jean Coleman

Jean Coleman is co-pastor with her husband, Jack, of The Tabernacle, Laurel, Maryland. She also is worship leader to the body of Christ, composer of worship choruses and conference worship leader and speaker. Her many articles have appeared in *Charisma, MINISTRIES* and other Christian publications.

An effective worship leader often makes the difference between a good church and a great church, just another song service or an uplifting worship experience. Yet there is little taught about this high calling—the ministry of leading worship.

Often the song leader is selected with little thought and even less prayer. "How about Tom? He has a pretty good voice." And Tom is almost casually entrusted with the awesome responsibility of leading the congregation into the presence of Almighty God.

Churches are full of mediocre song leaders when what God seeks is people He has gifted to lead others into worship. It is a definite calling—an anointing from God.

Most of us have a preconceived idea of what a worship leader should be. I always pictured a strapping young man with a booming voice in the role. That would have been my selection if I were God. I would have never chosen a middle-aged woman for the task. But His ways are not our ways, and so He chose me—a most unlikely candidate in the natural. However, God does not look at the outward appearance, but rather on the heart. Above all He is seeking worshippers, and so must we. Unless your worship leader is one who knows what it means to worship in spirit and in truth, he will never be able to bring others into true worship.

Is He a Worshipper?

Your worship leader *must* be a spiritual person who loves the Lord with all his heart, mind, soul and strength. He does not have to be a great singer, a professional musician or a trained soloist. The big question is: is he a worshipper? The Lord is seeking one who will stand before the congregation with his eyes upon Jesus and direct their gaze toward the King of kings.

Is your worship leader a true worshipper? Do not settle for less.

Can He Lead?

Another question is: can he lead? The worship leader must be a leader. The one who is placed before the people of God to lead in worship must not be a novice. He must be a mature Christian whose lifestyle reflects Christ. The fruit of the Spirit must be evident. There must be no sin in his life, for sin separates from God. How can he hope to lead others into the throne room when guilt prevents his own entrance?

Your worship leader should be selected only after seeking guidance from God in prayer. You should require the same qualifications for your worship leader that you would for an elder or deacon. It is a high calling in the kingdom of God. When the worship leader steps to the microphone, the pastor delegates to him the responsibility of the entire service. He sets the tone and directs the flow of the service. Often he will be the one who determines how long to wait upon prophecy, tongues and other gift ministries. How dare we hand the service over to Tom just because he has a good voice. God forbid!

Is He Rooted?

The worship leader needs to be mature not only in his walk with the Lord, but also in his relationship with your church. Too often someone with a good voice begins to attend services and three months later he is on the platform leading worship, although he is not yet truly moving in the spirit of your church.

Each church has its own personality. No two are the same, nor should they be the same. God made churches with individual personalities just as He did people—each one distinct.

Someone who comes to you from another church has to have time to settle in and put down roots. We are always in such a hurry. We don't allow people time to get rooted. We just take them and plop them down in the flower bed of our particular church, and then say, "Quick, bloom!" When someone is transplanted, it takes time for him to get his roots down and become a viable part of your body. You need to allow that person time to grow in your church, and then you can be sure his ministry will flow there.

Is He Musical?

While you are not looking for a singer or a performer, rather for a mature worshipper, there are basic musical requirements he must meet. Your worship leader must sing on key and have both a strong voice and sense of rhythm. He must enunciate clearly so the words of the song can be easily understood and followed.

As a leader he must be disciplined as he ministers, recognizing that the entire congregation is following his lead. He cannot stray from the melody into fancy frills or harmony, because people will try to follow his lead.

I think a worship leader needs to be a kind of spiritual cheerleader. It is his responsibility to get the people excited about the great things the Lord is doing. The last thing you want is a dull person before your congregation. That is death. Your worship leader must be alive, vibrant in the Spirit, fervent for the Lord. Excitement is contagious. It is communicable. And that's what you want! You want your congregation to catch a vision of the presence of the Lord. You want their eyes opened so they recognize Jesus in their midst. And when they see Him, they will worship and adore with every fiber of their being.

Some might tell you it is unspiritual to prepare in advance the songs that will be sung during Sunday morning worship. They are wrong. The worship leader needs to pray and seek God in advance for direction on how He wants to move by His Spirit. His list of songs can always be put aside if the Lord decides to move in a different way, but it is wrong to tempt God by inadequate preparation.

Is He Considerate?

In most cases the worship leader does not minister alone. Others are also involved in the worship experience: the pianist, the orchestra and even the one who handles the overhead or slide projector. A little preparation can cover a multitude of problems that could interfere with the free flow of worship, such as long pauses until the correct slide is located, searching for the correct key or the proper chords, or a song with which the pianist is not familiar. The worship leader has the responsibility to orchestrate the flow of worship.

I turn my attention to Sunday morning worship early in the week, quieting my spirit and visualizing myself entering into His courts with praise, and ultimately into the holy of holies in worship. I listen within to hear the songs the Spirit puts upon my heart. When I have heard from God, I give the list of songs and choruses to our minister of music who makes up a folder of the selected music for each member of the orchestra. The slides are put in order. New songs and choruses are rehearsed in advance. We want to present our very best to the Lord. We desire to play skillfully and do all things well so that our sacrifice of praise will be without blemish.

The pianist is the worship leader's best friend. They must move in complete unity, in one spirit. The pianist must learn to sense the direction the leader is moving and submit to it. The pianist must allow the worship leader to set the tempo of the music, slowing down and speeding up as the leader directs, constantly discerning the flow of the Spirit.

A glance in his direction or a barely perceptible nod of my head is enough to signal our pianist that I am moving on to the next song. A slight turning of my finger says, "Let's sing it again." My hand at my side with palm turned down tells him we're going to stop singing and wait upon the Lord. The orchestra is also finely tuned to my direction so that everyone can worship together in the beauty of holiness. It takes cooperation and real unity of spirit, but it's worth the effort.

We are an "alto church" because I sing alto. It's important that the leader sing in keys in which he is comfortable. There's nothing more distracting than a worship leader straining for the high notes. The church will adjust to the leader's range—high or low. Don't let it become a stumbling block.

Is He Talkative?

The transition from praise to worship is very important. Sometimes a simple prayer or a few words of acknowledgment of God's greatness will carry you over the threshold as praises turn to worship and holy hands are lifted to God.

But be sure it is only a simple prayer or a few words. More than that is too much. A worship leader must beware of much speaking.

Song leaders are not called to be preachers, yet many try to usurp that role. They like to give a little sermon between each song, often destroying the atmosphere of worship that has been established. Even a few words spoken in the flesh can hinder the flow of worship. I've seen whole congregations yanked down from the heavenlies by inept worship leaders.

Beware of a performer spirit in your worship leader. Many people desire to be a worship leader because they like to be in the spotlight—in the public eye. You want the people to be attracted to Jesus, not to your worship leader. When worship is at its best, the congregation sees no man save Jesus only. The worship leader must decrease so that He can increase.

Is He Stuck?

Many people resist new songs. They like the familiar, the song they can slip into like a favorite pair of slippers. Yet the church of God is moving, and we must keep our congregations moving too. They need to sing to the Lord a new song.

A visiting evangelist once told me he could judge the state of a church by its music. If he found the congregation still singing the same choruses they sang the year before, he knew there was something wrong. A lack of fresh new music is a sign of stagnation within a church.

It is the worship leader's responsibility to bring in new music. He should play tapes and listen to Christian radio to stay abreast of the songs of Zion. We began to pray for new music, and God answered by giving us original songs. When God was ministering to our church on change, He gave us the song, "Change me, Lord, into the image of Your Son." Ask the Lord for new songs and He will supply your need.

The worship leader should not attempt to introduce more than one new song at a service. If he tries to give the people too many new choruses at once, none of them will be retained.

New songs should be avoided in the midst of high praise or worship. It is better to set apart a special time to teach a new song so that worship will not be interrupted. When the congregation has entered into worship, the leader must allow them to stay in the presence of the Lord.

When we introduce a new song, we sing it several meetings the first week. We sing it at the mid-week meeting and at all the Bible studies. We have the orchestra play it before the Sunday service begins so that it can work its way into the people's hearts. We try to sing new songs regularly for at least a month. Every week opportunity is given to sing it somewhere. And at the end of that time, everyone is singing it everywhere. It has become a comfortable "old favorite" to the church. It's healthy to sing new songs.

Is He Poised?

Worship leaders are human, and there will be mistakes. There have been times I have completely missed the key or started one song only to find that my pianist was playing another. Occasionally, a wrong slide or transparency is shown. It is important to learn to laugh when things like this happen. If embarrassment is not shown, the flock will stay relaxed. However, if anger or irritation is allowed to take over, tension will spread over the entire congregation. The leader needs to have poise, self-control and the ability to rejoice in all circumstances—even the awkward ones.

A good music ministry will attract good musicians. Be sure that all the ones you involve are spiritual men and women. It is not enough that they be skilled musicians—they must also be able to move in the Spirit. If you lack musicians, pray them in. God delights to give you the desire of your heart.

Be realistic in your expectation of praise and worship in your church. Don't expect more of your people than they are able to give. There are different levels of maturity in praise and worship, the same as in other areas of spiritual growth. Give them a mature worship leader who can lead them into mature worship.

My prayer is: "Lord, save us from song leaders. Raise up true worshippers in every congregation who are called, chosen and anointed to bring Your people into Your presence that they might worship You in spirit and in truth. Amen."

45

How Do You Recruit and Retain Choir Members?

By Bonnie Finley

A choir director and piano and organ teacher, Bonnie Finley is choir director at Key to Life Assembly of God, Tacoma, Washington. She has spent 20 years in the ministry of choir directing.

W hat is the most important quality to look for in a prospective choir member? Ability to sight-read, harmonize or hold pitch? Or is it willingness to follow directions, sing expressively or enunciate clearly?

After 20 years of directing a choir, I am convinced the most important quality a choir member can have is the ability to make and keep a commitment. I will choose a committed person with no music background over an uncommitted but musically excellent person. Someone who misses frequently can actually throw off an entire choir.

Discovering Commitment

Determining who feels this commitment is a challenge. I sit down with prospective choir members and ask a few questions to discover what their commitment is. First, I ask if singing in the choir will work out well with their families. I even get specific and ask, "What will your husband or wife do while you're singing in Sunday morning and evening services, and in Sunday afternoon practice?" "Who will look after your children?" Choir members have been in practice with babies on their laps! Our church provides babysitting now, for infants to three years, but someone must be responsible for older children. Family cooperation is the most essential factor in a choir member's commitment.

To help families cooperate, I only schedule one 45-minute practice on Sunday afternoon. We dropped Thursday evening practice because family and work commitments interfered. I must keep family balance.

Another question I ask prospective members is, "Are you a Christian?" Our choir is part of our church ministry. Members are part of our evangelical function.

Another question is, "Can you come regularly to services and practice?" I have learned that jobs and habits have changed since I started directing. Now people often work Sunday morning or afternoon and can't sing at both services, as well as attend practice. There may be 28 people rehearsing, but fewer during service. This happens regularly, so I developed a system. We rehearse a wide range of music, four-part, three-part, or two-part. If the arrangement we rehearsed won't work because we lack certain voices, I pull out another, or even go unison.

Our choir is used to this last-minute switching. I explain my reasons, and they know they will always sound good. It's no blessing to anyone if the choir sounds bad.

For the last 16 years we were broadcast on radio. We stopped a few months ago for administrative adjusting. But before that, the choir never missed a Sunday morning or evening service. We played an important role in the radio service. Music always sounded good, whether it was the congregation singing with the choir, or the choir alone.

Stress-free Auditions

Prospective choir members must audition, and this can be stressful. If someone is anxious or frightened, I ask them to sing while my pianist plays, then I leave the room. Either I can hear from the next room, or I ask the pianist's opinion. It seems easier for people if their "judge" is in another room.

Another technique is to ask the person to hum the note I hum—to match my tone. If they match me, I know they hear the tones, and will be able to follow other choir members.

Turning someone down after an audition is hard. Usually the situation involves someone new in the church. If they sing for me and it sounds as if it would be difficult for them to sing well with the choir, I ask them to wait for awhile and listen to the choir. I ask them to get used to the kind of music we sing. Usually people discover their own singing inability, and they don't feel rejected.

People who sing well but fail to attend regularly are a problem. After repeated absences or lateness, I ask people to drop out until they can work out ways to come more regularly.

My biggest challenge is tardiness. When practice is scheduled to start, I move people closer, to fill empty seats. This means everyone sits next to a different person every time, if people come late. To combat this, I take roll, discuss problems privately with chronically late members, and give a lot of speeches. It's hard to be strict since we are a voluntary group.

Another big challenge is "helpers," those well-intended people who correct others' mistakes. This breaks concentration and makes everyone irritable. When this happens, I announce I will handle any problems, then I discuss the situation privately with the "helper" after practice.

My ideal image for a choir member is a person whose children are eight or nine years of age and whose families take care of them during choir. Mothers with young children have the hardest time meeting choir commitments because they cope with feedings, naps and illnesses. Yet they are the very people who want most to sing in the choir. They need to be involved in something outside the home that makes them feel good about themselves. Our church provides babysitting.

There are few experiences afforded on earth that are more heaven-like than singing God's praises as part of an anointed choir. So I think it is important to open this door of opportunity to all those singers willing to make and keep the necessary commitment. Of course, the singers must possess minimal musical skills, and the choir's end-product must truly minister to the congregation and lift them into heavenly places.

46

How Should a Choir Rehearsal Be Paced?

By Cheri Walters

Cheri Walters is a 1976 graduate of Oral Roberts University with a degree in vocal music. She has directed children's, youth and adult choirs and ensembles for nine years. She is the minister of music at the First Assembly of God in La Mesa, California.

F resh from a four-day music conference, newly enthused and ready to try something different, I gave my choir members a questionnaire about rehearsals. Included were several questions about rehearsal pacing: Was it too slow? Too fast? Just right? Did they feel we covered too much music or not enough?

I was quite surprised at their answers. The overwhelming response regarding the pace of our choir rehearsals was that it was too slow. My initial reaction was, "They just don't realize how much music we actually cover."

Given that our choir rehearsal is shorter than most (from 8:15 to 9:30 following midweek Bible study), I felt confident that the six to eight songs we usually practiced were enough to keep up a good steady pace. But their answers told me clearly that many of my choir members were not being challenged musically. *Not one* indicated the pace was too fast. I swallowed hard and decided to take them at their word.

First, I made copies of the rehearsal schedules I always give to my accompanists and sound technician, and gave them to the choir members. I reasoned that if they had a list in their hands, they would *perceive* that the pace was quicker, whether it was or not. There is something satisfying, a sense of accomplishment in checking off the items on a list. It shows each choir member, in black and white, that they have done what they set out to do.

In giving the choir members their own copies of the rehearsal schedule, two things happened: First, as I expected, they *felt* they were accomplishing more, and second, to my surprise, they actually were accomplishing more. When they picked up their music at the beginning of rehearsal, they could consult their lists and place each piece in proper order. Also, because they were more aware of what was left to be done, there was less "visiting" between songs. Though small in themselves, these little moments saved added up to time for another two or three songs in rehearsal.

The second thing I did was to spend less time on each song per rehearsal. Instead, I rehearsed each song over more weeks. Some studies on learning and memory indicate that people learn better and retain more of what they learn when it is studied in shorter intervals over a longer span of time. Putting this theory into practice took some advance planning that was difficult at first, but spared me some gray hairs later.

It became necessary to think eight to ten weeks ahead, not only for special occasions like Easter, Christmas or Mother's Day, but for each Sunday's anthem.

I began by penciling in on my calendar the songs for each Sunday, always keeping at least eight weeks ahead. When first getting started, it was hard to come to the point of being that many weeks ahead, but once there, it was just a matter of replacing the song or songs just sung with new ones each week.

As time has passed, the printed rehearsal schedules have grown to include announcements pertaining to the music department and prayer requests for choir members, plus special instructions to the accompanists or sound technicians. Also on the list, opposite each song title, I have added spaces to check indicating: "piano," "organ," "reel-to-reel," "cassette" or "synthesizer" accompaniment.

When using a combination of taped and live accompaniments, I try to intersperse reel-to-reel numbers throughout the schedule, giving the sound technician time to cue up, and avoiding "dead air" during the rehearsal. It is a simple matter of forethought to tailor the rehearsal schedule to fit the needs of the choir, instrumentalists (or orchestra, if there is one) and sound crew, and makes the rehearsal progress more smoothly. More importantly, it says to each individual who has included the rehearsal in his or her busy schedule that I value that time.

The care taken in planning allows me to conduct the rehearsal with more confidence, rather than drifting haphazardly from one song to another, and eliminates a great deal of the frustration busy people feel when their time is misspent.

In summary, there are five things I have learned about properly pacing a rehearsal:

1. Give the choir members, accompanists and sound technicians a written list of everything you plan to rehearse. Tailor it to your own situation with specific instructions regarding instruments or taped accompaniments.

2. Plan music at least eight weeks in advance and rehearse each piece of music only once or twice in a rehearsal, but over a longer period of weeks.

3. Schedule around any delays you can reasonably anticipate (tuning of instruments, changing or cueing of tapes). Your accompanists and sound technicians will appreciate you if you work *with* them.

4. Always maintain control of the rehearsal. Project an attitude of cheerful confidence and thoughtful organization. The choir will be much less likely to feel their time is being wasted if they believe the director

knows what is going on and what needs to be accomplished.

5. Most importantly, don't be defensive about the messages your choir members are sending you. Be secure enough to consider their suggestions positively, without taking each comment as a personal criticism. If they are restless or inattentive, perhaps they need to be challenged.

As ministers of music, we also need to be challenged to keep "pressing toward the mark" in this high calling. We must continually strive for excellence. By keeping open to changes we can make, by learning from our choir members new ways to improve our ministry effectiveness, we will continue to move forward toward that mark.

47

What Should Motivate a Musical Ministry

By Raymond Shepard

A Christian musician, Raymond Shepard has ministered mostly in Charismatic Episcopal churches. He is head of the music department of Liberty Bible College in Pensacola, Florida.

C harismatic churches have been both blessed and cursed by their success. The phenomenal growth of many churches has enabled them to minister musically in powerful new ways. A large sanctuary provides a sense of grandeur, an atmosphere conducive to musical productions. The danger lies in the temptation merely to entertain people while pretending to exalt the Lord.

We musicians need to be careful. It is so easy to fall into the world's pattern of performance, focusing on the audience instead of fixing our hearts and minds upon the Lord, making our music into an offering acceptable to Him. The psalmist clearly identified the only target to which he always aimed his music: "I will sing unto the Lord as long as I live" (Ps. 104:33).

In working with students who see music as part of their call to ministry, I find myself frequently concerned with *attitudes*. I urge these talented young people to ask themselves, "Am I ministering in music to call attention to myself or to Jesus?"

Congregations sometimes contribute to the problem. "O clap your hands, all ye people" (Ps. 47:1) has nothing to do with the secular world's practice of applause. An anointed musical rendition may indeed move a group of worshippers to give what some call a "clap offering" to God. But there's a thin line not to be overstepped by congregation or musician. "There is no place for human pride in the presence of the Lord" (1 Cor. 1:29, NEB). Personally, I have adopted a practice of avoiding applause after a musical offering. Instead, I choose to exalt God in another form—raising my hands, singing in the Spirit, or some other response which is less likely to be misinterpreted as exaltation of those who ministered musically.

The twice-a-year musical extravaganza syndrome can be faulted for leading us down the road away from music to extol the Lord and toward performance to exalt the performers. My experience indicates that at such times key decisions must be made, such as: "Will we recruit a person who loves to be seen and heard at Easter and Christmas, but he or she avoids choir participation the rest of the year?"

I do not condemn seasonal musicals as a form, for they can be exactly what pleases the Lord. After all, He set up a schedule of annual festivals of celebration when skilled choirs and orchestras led Israel in praising God. What I condemn is the carnal appetite for entertainment—the demand for frequent, professionally slick productions.

Few non-musicians realize the tremendous expenditure of time and effort required in preparation for such spectaculars, nor the strains exerted through the undue pressures on the family life of the participants.

The focus of the choir's activity should be musical excellence which produces praise and worship of God. All the musicians David appointed were "trained and skilled in music for the Lord." But none of them could pick and choose when they would minister—"young and old alike, teacher as well as student, cast lots for their duties" (See 1 Chron. 25:7, 8, NIV). Some were assigned to minister at ordinary times, others at great festivals, but none for any kind of an ego trip. The bottom line always must be the goal of glorifying the Lord.

And that also includes the selection of musical forms and styles. Charismatic churches generally do well at adapting music that will relate to contemporary people. Worship will be inhibited if the musical format is unfamiliar, even though the spiritual content of the lyrics is powerful in the opinion of the performer.

The underlying danger in adopting contemporary musical styles, however, lies in also adopting the same attitudes that accompany those styles in the world. Such attitudes include a self-aggrandizing spirit and a disdain for anyone who fails to be enthralled whenever this particular style of music is performed.

Such a spirit can result in tension at best, and conflict at worst. Musical tastes vary widely, and some people, right or wrong, assign more spiritual merit to one musical idiom than they do to another. And some go as far as to ascribe the existence of certain musical patterns (lyrics not withstanding) to the malevolent powers of the underworld.

The musician who wants to lift a congregation into God's presence will be sensitive to the musical tastes (and prejudices) of the people. On the other hand, the self-centered performer will be determined to display his skill in the kind of arrangement he likes, even though he knows it will offend various people throughout the church.

Musicians must set their priorities right. When they do, God will bless their ministry. These priorities will include a desire to please the Lord, a desire to lift God's people into a keener awareness of His presence, and a desire to touch the hearts of unregenerated persons.

How will these priorities affect a choir director's planning? or a soloist's selections? or an organist's practice? or a drummer's restraint? or a music minister's motivation?

When these priorities are in place, dedicated work will follow. The musicians will serve in the Lord's temple as an expression of their love for Him. They will develop their abilities as an offering acceptable to Him. And He will add His anointing.

Wrong attitudes will then be no problem, mutual love will flourish and believers will worship in unity of heart and holiness of life.

48

What Should You Consider When Buying a Piano?

By Jack L. Ralston

Jack L. Ralston is fine arts librarian at CBN University, Virginia Beach, Virginia. He holds the degrees of bachelor and master of music in organ and master of library science. Ralston received his degrees from the Conservatory of Music of Kansas City (now Univerity of Missouri—Kansas City) and George Peabody College (now Vanderbilt University in Nashville, Tennessee). He served 20 years as music librarian at the University of Missouri—Kansas City, before joining CBN University in 1980.

Threw piano at home no longer held its pitch so it was donated to the church. That's the way many churches come to have such a hodgepodge of pianos. Maybe that's what happened in your church, and you've got a problem that needs to be corrected. What can be done about it?

A survey of the piano needs within the church is a good place to begin. The condition of each piano now owned should be assessed and those which are "beyond the pale" should be marked for replacement by proper instruments for making a joyful noise unto the Lord (not just a noise!). The pianos in the music room and sanctuary should be checked as well. The ability of the piano to hold its tune, the proper projection of the tone, and the general condition and the quality of the sound should be checked.

If you are in doubt, have the tuner as well as the musicians check each instrument. If you would be ashamed to have a fine pianist play on your pianos, they probably are candidates for replacement.

A committee should be involved in the selection of church instruments. It is wise to have at least two pianists test a piano before it is purchased. One reason for this is that not all pianists use foot pedals in the same way.

There are four kinds of pianos/keyboard instruments you should know about.

The first is the vertical piano, sometimes called a studio piano. In shopping for a new or used vertical piano the following items should be considered: a full 88-note keyboard; locking fall board; braces for the legs; large casters for easy rolling (or a rubber-wheeled undercarriage); a top which can be propped open; the finish and style of design; the height of the instrument (do you need to be able to see over the top to watch the conductor or see the organist?); the music rack (can it hold several books at a time?).

The second type of piano is the grand piano. The following should be considered: the size desired in length (5'8'' up to 9'); the use of a rubber-wheeled under-carriage which will raise the height of the keyboard but allow the grand to be moved easily across the floor without damaging the carpet or finish; the availability of an adjustable piano stool (particularly important if keyboard is raised); the high and low prop stick for opening the lid; the types of finish and style available to match the place where the grand is to be placed.

The third type is the electronic piano which is actually electro-mechanical. The tone is generally produced by a keyboard-actuated metal bar which has an amplified pickup. Things to consider: the portability of the piano—does it break down into two parts which can be carried easily (use of a hand-truck is recommended over carrying by the installed handles); the use of a self-contained amplifier which will allow the instrument to stand alone without additional equipment; the use of input as well as output plugs so that a microphone can be used with the piano as well as external connection into the church's sound system. The keys should be full-sized standard keys, the pedal should be sustaining, and the volume, tone and vibrato adjustments should be available for quick and easy changes.

The fourth type of keyboard is the synthesizer which is fully electronic. Think on these things: there should be as many full-sized keys as possible (61 minimum, but 88 would be preferable); rhythm and special effects devices such as the automatic arpeggio should be easily operable; volume and tone controls should be accessible while playing; and the instrument must be tunable to the fixed-tune piano and organ.

General considerations which apply to the quality of the piano if it is a stringed type include the length of the bass strings. Generally, the longer the strings, the better the quality of tone attained. The bass tones should be deep and resonant with the overtones being very rich. Middle tones should be melodic and yet sound good when chords are played in that area. The treble should be bright and silvery but not harsh and metallic.

On the grand piano, the three pedals should be a shifting *una corda* or soft pedal on the left, a sostenuto pedal rather than just a bass sustaining pedal in the middle, and the standard sustaining (sometimes called the "loud" pedal) on the right.

On a vertical piano, the left pedal should make the sound softer by moving the hammers closer to the strings without any movement of the keys, the middle pedal may be a bass sustaining pedal, and the right pedal should be the standard sustaining pedal.

When selecting a dealer, check the availability of the particular model you wish to purchase so that it will be possible to play the exact instrument you are purchasing. If it must be special ordered, insist on having the instrument set up in the store so that it may be tested in advance of accepting delivery.

On the purchase of a grand the dealer normally provides without additional charge an in-store tuning and at least two tunings after the delivery (at the interval of six months and one year). With a vertical piano only the tuning in the store and one tuning after delivery are customarily provided.

The price should be negotiated with clear understanding of the delivery tunings, warranty and inclusion of the standard bench. The undercarriages and adjustable benches are generally extra.

Every grand piano needs a fleece-lined cover to protect it against abuse and variations in temperature and humidity. A common practice includes locking the fall board on grand pianos to prevent unauthorized use and damage. With all instruments be sure to protect from excessive heat, coldness and high humidity.

All instruments need regular tuning and adjustment to maintain their best level of performance. Keep a list of problems with the instrument and check after the tuner has worked on the piano to see that the proper repairs have been made.

The piano is the "work horse" of the church music program. In Sunday school rooms, the rehearsal rooms and the sanctuary, this instrument is frequently abused and neglected, but it should not be so.

Children should be encouraged to treat all musical instruments with proper respect, and regular maintenance should be performed on all instruments—even those in the Sunday school classrooms.

Solving Ministry Problems of Women

49

How Are Women Ministers Being Accepted?

By Sam Justice

A professional writer and reporter throughout his adult life, Sam Justice devotes most of his writing to inspirational Christian material which has appeared in *Charisma*, *MINISTRIES* and other Christian publications. He is a former staffer for *Business Week*.

I t was the ceremony of institution for a new rector in the Episcopal Church. The bishop for the New York diocese had completed his portion of the ceremony and the newly instituted priest knelt and said: "Oh, my Lord, I am not worthy to have You come under my roof; yet You have called Your servant to stand in Your house and to serve at Your altar. To You and to Your service I devote myself, body, soul and spirit...."

The bishop then presented the minister to the congregation, saying, "Greet your new rector."

The rector, in this case, was not a male but the Rev. Ellen M. Shaver, first woman rector in Westchester County and, according to Bishop Paul Moore, The first rector in a "normal" church in his diocese. Two other of his churches in New York City have women rectors, but one is a mission and the other, in the words of Bishop Moore, is a "kinky" parish—St. Clements in the New York theatrical district frequented by people in the arts.

The Rev. Shaver, in her first year at St. John's Tuckahoe in Yonkers, New York, is symptomatic of a change touching a majority of denominations in America—from the Assemblies of God to the 35-member National Council of Churches, to the three branches of Judaism. All told, these congregations represent roughly 60 million members.

The only major U.S. churches that do not ordain women are the Roman Catholic Church with some 52 million members, eight U.S. Orthodox Churches with 3.8 million members, the Missouri Lutheran Synod and the Church of God in Christ, each with about three million members.

When a woman senses God's call to the clergy, what are her chances of making it to the pulpit? It depends on denominational affiliation, her qualifications for preaching and pastoral ministry, and perhaps divine intervention. In most denominations, chances are considerably better today than a dozen years ago.

The trails were blazed by the likes of Aimee Semple McPherson, who founded the International Church of the Four-Square Gospel in the first quarter of this century, and attracted throngs wherever she went. She was followed by Kathryn Kuhlman, whose healing ministry made maximum use of television in the 1960s and 1970s.

However, the first woman to be ordained in the United States was Antoinette Brown of South Butler, New York, who was ordained in 1853 by the local Congregational Church (now merged into the United Church of Christ).

Miss Brown attended Oberlin College which discouraged female students, but she persevered and got her degree. She managed to get a church and began preaching God's peace and love as opposed to the "fire-and-brimstone" of that day. She lasted one year, gave up in frustration, became a Unitarian and an ardent champion of women's rights. She bore ten children and juggled a career of lecturing and writing. Before she died in her 90s, she enjoyed the victory of woman's suffrage by casting her vote in an election.

Antoinette Brown's ordination did not open the floodgates. There were no further ordinations until 1888, when the Christian Church (Disciples of Christ) approved ordaining women, followed in 1894 by the American Baptist Churches in the U.S.A.

In addition to Antoinette Brown and Aimee Semple McPherson, there were other strong-willed women who left an imprint on U.S. churches in the first half of this century. Ellen White founded the Seventh Day Adventists and led it for 50 years. Mary Baker Eddy founded the Christian Science Church and became its patron saint. Phoebe Palmer was a strong spiritual leader of the Holiness Church. Alma White, whose husband was a Methodist minister, was active as an evangelist. But in 1901, after church officials frowned on her evangelistic endeavors, she founded the denomination that now is called the Pillar of Fire (today headed by her granddaughter, Bishop Arlene White Lawrence).

These women were exceptions; they had flourishing ministries when established churches were not doing much to make room for women in their pulpits. Then, in the 21-year period between 1956 and 1977, five major denominations—Methodists, Presbyterians, Episcopalians, Lutherans and National Baptists—all approved women's ordination.

Ordination of women is still moving slowly—seldom more than five percent of the clergy of a denomination—and there are many congregations who want no part of women in their pulpits. Women who are to get pastorates are under scrutiny for their sister clergy. If they fail or stumble, it reflects on clergywomen generally.

How do male pastors view this influx of females into what was once their private bastion? This is not a problem in most Pentecostal churches or the Salvation Army, where women have been ordained for years. However, in denominations whose ranks are not growing, the appearance of women in the ministry increases the competition for clergy openings. A general preference for male clergy and the experience they have acquired gives them an edge. The question is how long they will be able to maintain this edge as women clergy become more accepted.

One veteran clergy says, "I don't view women's entry as personal competition for me, but for the younger men coming out of seminary, it could be interesting—and challenging."

Women clergy also are concerned about these problems and have groups such as Women in Ministry, based in New York City, to monitor them.

Clergywomen are discovering one approach to dealing with opposition is to serve as interim or assistant pastors. Many women are entering the clergy streams through these channels. Another entry area showing promise is that of co-pastor, where a husband and wife may serve the same church. In the Salvation Army, this has been practiced successfully since its founding.

Sometimes they serve separate churches, but more often it's the same church. It has many advantages, according to the Rev. Barbara Schlachter. In 1982, she and her husband, the Rev. Mel Schlachter, were called as co-pastors of St. Margaret's Episcopal Church in Staatsburg, New York.

"There might have been some real opposition to a woman rector," she recalls, "had we not come as a team. There was only one woman in the parish who really seemed upset to see me in the pulpit—and she still is."

The Schlachters, both 38, take turns preaching. When one preaches, the other celebrates the Eucharist. Each arrives independently at sermon topics, but there is consultation. Also, there's feedback after sermons: what went over, what fell flat. "But we also try not to let church 'shop talk' dominate our home life. We have to leave room for our children—Erika, 8, and Jacob, 4."

But it isn't easy. In the middle of Jacob's birthday party recently, a bereaved couple who had a death in their family came to the rectory. While they sat in one room being consoled, the Schlachters were running back and forth to the room where Jacob was having his birthday cake and ice cream. The Schlachters work to make sure their children realize they are part of a commitment.

Their first year out of seminary, the Schlachters worked as assistants at St. Andrew's Church, a dying parish in Yonkers. He had been ordained and she was ordained a deacon while at St. Andrew's. Both preached, but she couldn't celebrate the Eucharist. After St. Andrew's closed, she taught at Master's School in Dobbs Ferry for four years, while he served as a prison chaplain at a nearby correctional facility.

In 1977—the breakthrough year for Episcopal women—Barbara Schlachter was ordained and became an assistant at St. Bartholomew's

Episcopal Church in White Plains. Meanwhile, her husband was doing pastoral counseling in White Plains. Their first child was born during their five years there.

In 1982, they were called to Staatsburg to begin their career as co-pastors. The situation not only provided the opportunity for each to preach, but for the family to worship together. The small church in north Dutchess County had some 125 communicants when they arrived. Since 1982 it has doubled and there is excitement on the part of the congregation, many of whom are not Episcopalians.

One problem: both are concerned about the same people and situations in parish. A challenge: learning to appreciate one another's style when it's not the way the other would do it.

They find that sometimes one can handle a sticky situation better than the other. One woman member wanted to organize a church group that would meet in a private home. Both Schlachters felt the activity belonged in the church and he told her so. The woman was hurt. Barbara talked to her and helped her struggle through and finally the wound was healed.

They feel that many who have come to church in the last year and a half were drawn by the husband-and-wife team. The appeal extends to singles as well as to couples. Barbara serves on her church's deployment board, which is concerned not only with clergy placement but issues clergy face.

Another key factor is pastors' wives. Where do they fit in? There was a time when a pastor was called to a church, and the congregation assumed it was getting an assistant pastor for free. She might direct the choir, play the organ, teach a Sunday school class, visit the sick or arrange the flowers on the altar.

Today, with roughly three-quarters of pastors' wives employed, few are available or even interested in taking on the chores that at one time fell to the pastor's wife. When missionaries are being sent abroad, the wife often gets a salary equal to her husband. But no such benefit befalls the domestic clergy wife.

A recent National Council of Churches survey shows that in most cases other family incomes (usually from the working wife) supplement clergy pay. This holds true for the top of the pay scale as well as on the low side. When the clergyman is in the $12,000 to $14,000 bracket, 76.5 percent of wives work. But in the top bracket surveyed—$38,000 to $40,000—78.9 percent of wives also work.

U.S. Labor Department statistics for 1982 show that clergy pay ranks slightly above that for janitors. And NCC studies show that women in the clergy consistently are paid less than male counterparts. This has resulted in making some churches available to women who are willing to take the low-paying pastorates in order to get a foothold on the clergy ladder. While that may get them a first church, upward mobility remains a problem. Larger and higher paying openings consistently go to male clergy and there usually is a longer wait between a clergywoman's first church and her call to a second.

One study shows that while the median salary for clergymen is from $18,000 to $22,000, the median range for clergywomen is from $14,000 to $16,000. Employment opportunities are better in churches reflecting steady growth, such as Pentecostals, Lutherans and Baptists. Declining memberships have resulted in fewer clergy openings for women affiliated with the Episcopal, Methodist, Presbyterian, Christian Church and United Church of Christ denominations.

Methodist clergywomen have the least placement problem because of their unique appointment system as opposed to the congregational call method. Once the woman has been ordained, her bishop is obligated to place her. Still, she must work out acceptance issues in the local congregation. Even in highly structured denominations such as the Episcopal and Lutheran, ordination requires the approval of local or regional governing bodies.

However, in congregational type denominations—Baptist, Christian Church (Disciples of Christ), United Church of Christ and some Pentecostal—ordination can take place with the approval only of the local church body.

Here follows added information on how ordination is treated in the denominations included in this study, plus some denominations not shown in the statistical chart:

Assemblies of God

Began ordaining women at its organization in the United States in 1914. As a result, women's ordination has never been a church issue, according to the Rev. Joseph Flower, secretary of this Pentecostal group. Some women serve as co-pastors with their husbands. Seminary training is not required, but candidates must complete specified Berean Correspondence Courses.

Female candidates are first licensed to preach, then two years later are ordained—based on recognition of service. This is handled by a credentials committee that must sense that the candidate has been "called" by God to preach. By the end of 1983 there were 3,507 accredited women, including 259 pastors, 74 home missionaries, 230 foreign missionaries, with 1,529 in other categories such as evangelists, teachers and inactive, with another 1,425 categorized as retired.

This denomination has 1,992,754 adherents in the United States.

American Baptist Churches
in U.S.A.

First woman to be ordained in A.B.C. was Edith Hill in Kansas in 1894. She started a church and served it for several years. In A.B.C., a candidate is ordained by her local church, but if she wants to be recognized by the denomination, she must be approved by the judiciary in her local area. There are some 37 judiciaries in the A.B.C. In order to be ordained, candidates must have an M.A. in divinity from an accredited seminary.

The Rev. Suzan Johnson, the first ordained black woman to head up an A.B.C. congregation, has described her Mariner Baptist Church on New York's lower east side as "a tough parish in a rough neighborhood." But it is no rougher than the Bronx where she was raised. She says, "You won't find many neighborhoods that frighten me."

Miss Johnson, 27, has been ordained for five years and an acting pastor for six months. She has been a talk show hostess in New York, Miami and Boston. She hopes to bring the "feminine" voice of God to her parishioners. She overcame initial resistance to get her first pastorate and foresees a time when women will share pulpits in all denominations.

Southern Baptist Convention

With some 14 million members in over 36,000 churches, S.B.C. is more localized in ordaining than A.B.C. It has been ordaining women since 1964 at local church level and to date has approximately 20 ordained women pastors. However, in conference this June a resolution was passed 4,793 to 3,460 putting the S.B.C. on record in opposition to ordination of women. But the resolution does not bind their churches, each of which has the power to ordain.

National Baptist Convention
U.S.A., Inc.

N.B.C. began ordaining women 25 years ago, but it's almost impossible to estimate a total because ordination is at local level. Only a small portion of N.B.C. churches actually ordains, but convention secretary W. Franklyn Richardson strongly supported ordination and has a woman on his Grace Baptist Church staff in Mt. Vernon, New York.

"God," says Richardson, "is not necessarily white, male or American. The key to the issue of ordination cannot be based on a narrow interpretation of so-called spiritual limitation of women's role in the church, but rather on whether it is God's will. If God calls a woman to the ministry, how can she be denied entry because of historical experience? I am adamantly against those who deny women the right to preach on the basis of gospel. I won't argue against cultural opposition. When women are denied entry, we lose the benefit of female perspective. Women have an understanding that men don't have. None of us is perfect. We are all broken vessels."

The Rev. Flora Wilson Bridges, executive minister at Grace Church, was licensed to preach in April 1980 and ordained in September 1983. She feels that most of the opposition to women in the clergy comes from women. "It's their low self-esteem. Culture has lied to women for a long time. Much scarring has taken place that will take a long time to heal."

Ms. Bridges preaches twice a month at Grace and gets invitations to other pulpits. Grace has 1,500 members, an average attendance of 900 and is the largest black church in Westchester County.

Christian Church
(Disciples of Christ)

This dual-named denomination began ordaining in 1888 because women were needed on the frontier and it was cheaper in outreach activities to send couples. Many couples are continuing as co-pastors and missionaries. One of their best known early women was Carrie Nation.

This church has 35 geographic regions in the United States and Canada, but ordination is handled by autonomous local congregations. In calling, churches are to consider men only if there are no competent women candidates. Some women now serve on governing boards of the 11 administrative units.

Church of God

Headquartered in Cleveland, Tennessee. The Church of God is one of the fastest growing churches in the United States, claiming an increase of 70.4 percent over the 12-year period between 1970 and 1982. It is second only to Assemblies of God with a 79.1 percent gain. This church does not ordain women, but does license them to pastor churches and to serve as evangelists. They cannot participate in the same order of work that deals with eldership. Women were active since the founding of the church in the United States in 1890.

The Church of God in Christ

The Church of God in Christ, based in Memphis, Tennessee, mostly black, does not ordain women. However, women serve significant roles in the congregations of these churches and those with recognized gifts of leadership are honored by the title "mother." This predominantly black Pentecostal denomination claims three million adherents.

Episcopal Church

The Episcopal Church ordains women in the United States and Canada, but not in the Anglican Communion in Great Britain. In the United States, women's ordination was approved by the General Convention in 1977, after years of controversy. Currently, some 90 diocese ordain, but there are 30 diocese that do not and some 35 bishops are on record in opposition, based on the Scriptures, tradition and "Father" image.

At the end of 1983, of 443 ordained women, 36 are rectors of churches, 43 are vicars, 10 are interim priests, nine are priests-in-charge, six are co-pastors. Some 156 function as assistants or associates (curates), 28 are college and school chaplains, 16 hospital or prison chaplains, 16 teach in colleges or seminaries, 22 are in church-related ministries, 32 in non-stipendiary positions where they have full-time jobs elsewhere, and some 69 are retired, in religious orders, or on cathedral staffs, at home or unemployed.

An additional 294 are deacons. A large percentage of the women clergy are married, most attended seminary, a few have read for orders, many have had careers and came into the clergy after another career or having raised a family.

Their leaders counsel women planning to enter clergy to work with other women in ministry or serve as an interim rector where a church is not yet ready for a woman rector.

The experience of the Rev. Ellen Shaver, mentioned earlier, illustrates the workings of the call process, both from the standpoint of a supervisory body and a local call committee.

St. John's Tuckahoe began setting up a search committee in late 1982, but didn't complete a parish profile until well into winter of 1983. Its first list of 25 candidates, sent to Bishop Moore in April, came back sharply whittled. The bishop eliminated all but six and added nine new candidates, two of them women. The women responded that they were not interested, as did others of the new candidates. The bishop came back in early summer with more names, including that of Ellen Shaver, a curate at St. John's Episcopal Church, Larchmont, New York.

When approached by the search committee, Ms. Shaver was receptive and that led to an interview with a search subcommittee. Its approach: we really don't see a woman as rector of St. John's, but we should do the bishop the courtesy of interviewing her.

Ms. Shaver was impressed by the parish profile, and by the committee's struggle to be honest with what the church was enumerating—both strengths and weaknesses. Her reaction: "This could be it."

The search group was impressed, particularly by her homework on the profile, her probing questions and sense of purpose.

Ms. Shaver's attitude varied during the summer from "This isn't going anywhere" to "This could really happen" to "No chance!"

Later, the search group heard her preach and found her theology sound, her pulpit manner satisfactory and a real warmth between her and parishioners. They recommended that her name be kept on the list of prospects.

In October, Ms. Shaver was notified that the list had been narrowed to three candidates. The three met with the full search committee, which narrowed it to two—Ms. Shaver and a male candidate. A week later, the nod went to Ms. Shaver and the governing body of the congregation, the vestry, approved unanimously.

In her first sermon, Rev. Ellen—as she came to be called—recounted her call experience:

"It occurred to me, as I moved through the search process, that this relationship is a lot like getting married. For as in marriage, the search begins with a period of courtship, during which we learn as much as possible about each other. For me, the process began when I received a letter from the search committee chairman. As I read the parish profile with the statements of goals and what you were looking for in a rector, I remember thinking, 'This could be a match. This could be a new and unexpected thing God is doing in my life.'

"So I wrote back, giving my goals and hopes for such a relationship. Next, I met with four members of the parish and we began to get acquainted. Afterward, I thought to myself: 'Nice people. Challenging parish. But women aren't being hired to be rectors.' I figured that was the end of it. It's like being fixed up for a date, having a nice evening, but doubting that you'll ever hear from the person again.

"Imagine my surprise when I learned I had been moved on to the next step in the process. I began to wonder if God might actually be calling me to this position. In my head, I rejected the possibility. It was a strange time. I had no decision to make about coming to this parish because I had not been invited to do so. I believed there was little or no chance that I would be offered the position. And yet, I kept wondering what God was up to.

"I prayed that I might know God's will. The answer came back very clearly: 'Know that I am God!'

"That was it? Not 'Stay where you are,' or 'Go to the new place.' I was mystified, but the more I thought about it, the more I realized it was the ultimate answer to my prayer.

"I still was not clear what the future might bring, but I knew I was being called to trust God and to be open to whatever was coming.

"So when I was invited to meet with the whole search committee, I accepted. In the short time we were together, we talked about our spiritual journeys. I discovered the committee also was struggling to discern and to be open to God's will. And I began to believe God was calling us to journey together.

"Like courtship, it was a time of discovery and growing hope for our future. Then I was informed the search committee had recommended me to the vestry and the vestry had voted unanimously to call me as rector.

"My immediate response was shock. The impossible had happened. This brings us back to the marriage relationship. When two people decide to marry, they make a covenant with one another. That is, they make a commitment to be with each other in the good times and the bad. They seek God's blessing on their relationship and pray that it will be a sign of God's love in this broken world. They trust that within the relationship they will grow in love and that they will come to recognize the Lord's love for them in their love for one another.

"We are entering that kind of relationship. We are making a commitment and seeking God's blessing on our relationship. We are hoping and praying that we will grow in His love.

"But like all newlyweds, there will be a period of adjustment. We will come to know each other far better in the weeks and months ahead. Being human, there will be times when we get on each others' nerves. But there will also be times when we'll be filled with joy as we discover new things about each other. Some expectations will be met; others will not be met.

"I believe God has called me into this Christian community of St. John's Tuckahoe. And I fully expect to meet our Lord and to know and love Him better as I come to know and love you. May God bless our new beginning."

There are three major Lutheran bodies. The Lutheran Church in America (LCA) and the American Lutheran Church (ALC) which are in the process of merging, scheduled to be complete by 1988. And the Missouri Lutheran Synod remains aloof from the merger.

Lutheran Church in America

To be eligible for ordination, a Lutheran woman must be endorsed by a synod, complete seminary, have one year of internship, and get a master of divinity. She also must be called by a local church which gets her name through the synodical bishop. In LCA, women are getting first calls, but are having problems getting second calls. The church is researching factors surrounding second calls for women. LCA has ordained 319 women since 1970 and of these, 223 have calls to congregations, including assistants. Seminary classes of 1983-84 totalled 1,017 students, of which 372—or 36.5 percent—were women.

American Lutheran Church

With 1,170,000 members and 4,897 churches, the ALC has ordained 157 women. A growing phenomenon in both it and the LCA is clergy couples, often serving the same church as co-pastors.

Missouri Lutheran Synod

With 2,054,000 communicants in 6,147 churches this group does not ordain women.

Presbyterian Church (U.S.A.)

The two main bodies of the church, United Presbyterian Church in the U.S.A. and the Presbyterian Church in the U.S., merged in 1983 to form the Presbyterian Church (U.S.A). It has ordained over one thousand women since 1956 and experienced a 300 percent gain in ordinations between 1971 and 1978. By April 1984, there were 231 women pastors and co-pastors, 251 associate and assistant pastors, 53 chaplains (in the army, hospitals and schools) and 34 missionaries.

Studies reveal that most of the opposition to women in the clergy comes from rationalization by generations of masculine imagery in worship, theology and biblical interpretations. These reasons were found for opposing placement of clergywomen:

1. Traditional role of minister's wife is unfulfilled;
2. Interferes with "normal" family processes;
3. Mobility is tied to location of spouse's job;
4. Theological difficulties;
5. Uneasiness with a woman in the pulpit;
6. She could get pregnant.

All synods have at last one woman in the clergy. Two-thirds of clergywomen serve in congregational positions, most as pastor or assistant. Clergywomen are most likely to be located in an urban area, a suburb or a town. Also, they are more in evidence in resort areas and retirement communities.

Salvation Army

The Salvation Army has been commissioning (ordaining) women officers since it was founded in 1865 in England by General William Booth. It was launched in the United States in 1880 as a result of a letter from 16-year-old Eliza Shirley, a recent emigre from England, to General Booth in which she said the unofficial corps (church) she and her mother had founded in Philadelphia had grown to the point where it needed a commissioned officer. Booth responded with a "landing party" of seven women under the leadership of Commissioner George Scott Railton. They landed in New York in 1880, held an open-air meeting on the Bowery, then moved on to Philadelphia where they established the first permanent U.S. base.

General Booth's daughter, Evangeline, served in the United States as national commander from 1901 to 1934, then went back to England to become general.

Almost half of the Army's 3,500 commissioned officers are women. In fact, in the latest seminary class of 1984-85, of the 45 students in the Eastern Territory, 24 are women. Most of the women officers are married to commissioned officers with whom they serve as co-pastors of equal rank. They are ordained after a two-year training program and commissioned as lieutenants. After five years they can move up to captain and 15 years later to major.

United Church of Christ

All ordination decisions are made by the church's 39 conferences at their association levels, where applicants are examined, but actual ordinations are by individual churches. There are slightly over 1,000 ordained U.C.C. women as against some 10,000 male clergy. Of the women, about one-third have their own churches. They must go through the church's Life and Leadership office for placement. They submit profiles which become available to interested churches.

A candidate must express desire to serve in a congregation. A local search committee decides who will be selected. In addition to those with pastorates, others serve as interim ministers, college chaplains, or as assistants. Five or six women pastors serve large congregations and each has a staff.

Two years ago seminary enrollment was 52 and is projected to rise to 75. There is resistance to women pastors in some local churches. The conference minister (bishop) is the key to where a clergywoman will be placed. Some feel a priority to place women. Of 39 conferences, one is headed by a woman.

A big problem for women clergy is getting a second church. Women constitute 62 percent of U.C.C. membership, but this does not augur support for clergywomen since most of their opposition is from women.

African Methodist Episcopal Church

This black church is based in St. Louis, Missouri, and began ordaining women in 1948, with some 84 women ordained to date, but with no information on number of women with pastorates.

African Methodist Episcopal Zion Church

This black church, based in Charlotte, North Carolina, reportedly began ordaining women in the late 19th century and to date has ordained 65 women. They report that women pastors are serving churches with fewer than 250 members.

United Methodist Church

This church resulted from several mergers and each branch has its own history of women's ordination. In the late 1800s, women were granted license to preach. In 1889, Ella Niswonger was ordained by the Central Illinois Conference of the United Brethren Church. In the early 1880s, Anna Howard Shaw was ordained in the Methodist Protestant Church.

In 1956, women were granted ordination and in 1968 were included in full conference membership of the United Methodist Church. In 1983, some 1,456 women were serving as pastors and 1,183 as elders in full connection, which includes those in appointments beyond the local church and other categories. Women make up a little over six percent of all pastors in the church.

The district superintendent works closely with the Pastor-Parish Relations Committee and the bishop appoints clergy. Several conferences have sought to discover what works most effectively for building acceptance of clergywomen.

Why Are Barriers Falling?

What's behind this shift in attitudes on the part of many churches now removing long-standing barriers against women? Certainly much is said about searching the Scriptures, especially the New Testament, to establish a theological basis for women serving as Christian ministers. Such research is commendable but few, if any, religious leaders would attribute this trend to new theological discoveries about the role of women. Instead, these leaders recognize the same sociological forces moving in the religious field that have been moving in other arenas, opening other areas for women's full participation—in business, in labor, in government.

Obviously New Testament concepts have nothing to do with the changes taking place in women's roles in the three branches of Judaism in America. The Reform Jewish branch has ordained some 60 women rabbis since it approved ordination of women 10 years ago. The Conservative Jewish branch has just recently approved the ordaining of women rabbis. And while the Orthodox Jewish branch has not approved women rabbis, women are moving up to where they are taking on lay leadership roles. They now light candles and do readings, and they are petitioning for authority to read the Torah.

It is evident that changing attitudes toward women in our nation's society are in the process of changing women's roles in religion. Not only are women gaining entry into the clergy, some of their number are upwardly mobile on their denominations' ecclesiastical power structures.

Bishop Marjorie Matthews

The highest position to go to any woman in any mainline denomination is that of bishop, to which a 64-year-old grandmother, who began college at age 47, was elected in July 1980. Bishop Marjorie Matthews, who now presides over Wisconsin's 140,000 Methodists, formerly was a district superintendent in Michigan. She is quick to warn against believing that women clergy have arrived.

"Women have not finally made it," she warns. "We have some very hard work in the future. There are still many, many men and women who have questions about this move."

The candid bishop said, "I never said I wanted to be a bishop. I still believe the Holy Spirit has a hand in seeking leadership in the church. The movement (for election) grew—and it is blessed.

"I have been told by some that 'being a woman is an important part of your qualifications. Lift it up and make it a positive quality.' I hope we can do that. Certainly, there are places where a woman's viewpoint—the sensitivity a woman brings to the ministry—is needed."

50

Should Women Be Paid for Their Ministries?

By Linda Howard

An author of three books and numerous articles for Christian publications, Linda Howard also served as editor of a magazine and is administrative assistant in the youth department of Tabernacle Church in Melbourne, Florida. Mrs. Howard has a degree in managerial science and with her husband authored *Aerospace Technologist* for NASA.

Thee was nothing about the day which indicated to Louisa Hedman that she was about to embark on a career-changing experience. When the phone rang that balmy afternoon, she expected one of her close friends to be on the other end. Instead there was a male voice on the line. She realized that it was her pastor.

It is unusual for the pastor of a thriving church to admit to one of his parishioners that he needs help. But Father Frank Gray, who was pastor of St. John's Episcopal Church in Melbourne, Florida, is an unusual man.

"When Father Gray called me," Mrs. Hedman recalled, "he said that he needed someone to pray for him and that the Lord kept insisting that he call me.

"I was taken aback at first. While I knew the Lord had given me a healing ministry and I'd spent several years in study and preparation, I'd never prayed for a pastor before," said Mrs. Hedman, a soft-spoken woman in her early 50s. "I called a friend. She agreed to accompany me and join us in the prayer."

It seemed to be a simple act of obedience for Mrs. Hedman. She placed no real significance on the incident. But it soon became apparent that she had opened the door to a new career.

The Holy Spirit ministered to Father Gray through Mrs. Hedman and her friend. They prayed for the healing of some hurting memories.

Father Gray was so impressed with the gentle spirit that the women had exhibited and the wisdom they had used in their approach that he recommended them to people who came for healing from mental depression or anxiety.

There were so many people coming for healing and prayer that Father Gray could not keep up with the demands. He desperately needed an associate pastor, yet the church did not think they could afford the added expense.

"I came on staff with the title of administrative assistant," said Mrs. Hedman, "but I was really the assistant pastor."

Mrs. Hedman's ministry staff has grown to include five others—all of them laypersons. For almost 10 years, there were only women who worked with her. Recently, they added a man.

It is a wise pastor who knows how to utilize fully the women members of the congregation who are operating in a ministry. Louisa Hedman's ministry is healing and prayer. There are others, however, who have just as valid a ministry in other areas. It is the principles by which she was allowed to function that need to be examined.

Part of the success comes from the nature of the man who initiated this prayer ministry—Frank Gray. "I've never met anyone like him," one of his friends said a few weeks after he had moved into the parsonage. "There is such an anointing on his preaching and his life."

Perhaps it was the anointing that made Frank Gray different, perhaps it was something else—something inside the man.

"I believe he is a genuinely generous minister," someone observed.

He could be compared to Barnabas in the book of Acts. Barnabas had one of the most successful ministries of his day. But Barnabas was not satisfied. He kept remembering a brilliant, fiery young man he had met in Jerusalem.

Barnabas made a trip to Tarsus and found Saul. He urged Saul to come to Antioch and help with the ministry.

That is the picture of a generous man. Gray is that kind of pastor. A smaller man would have tightened his work-schedule belt and refused to allow anyone to share in his glory. Gray and Barnabas were cut from the same pattern.

Gray also saw to it that Mrs. Hedman served in an apprenticeship position while she was getting her footing. She was allowed to prove herself before she was put on staff. While the prayer team had ministered to him, he did not make any hasty moves. He allowed Mrs. Hedman to ease slowly into the calling God had placed on her life.

The next step is one which is often overlooked—especially for the *woman* who is functioning in a God-given ministry. Gray put Mrs. Hedman on salary, thereby giving her credibility with the other parishioners.

There is a lot of preaching about how Paul earned his own way. Little is said about the situation that he constantly faced because of his avocation as a tentmaker. Many people doubted his credibility because he refused to take a salary

Anointed, qualified women often fall into the provide-your-own-support category of Paul and Barnabas.

Fran has been a Bible teacher for over 30 years. She has taught Bible classes throughout the community as well as in the adult Sunday school class in her church each Sunday morning for over 15 years. When her husband died two or three years ago, she was left with a small insurance policy and the sympathy of her friends.

"How will you support yourself?" a close friend asked.

"I'm not qualified to do anything but teach the Scriptures," Fran said. "I don't know what I'd do to earn a living."

By no means is Fran an isolated case. Many times these highly qualified women teachers and ministers end up as salesclerks in the nearest department store working for minimum wages in order to support their ministries.

While it is certainly true that not everyone is called to be a staff member of their local church, it is important that we remember the most vital part of the "Barnabas Principle," which is: people (including women) with anointed ministries have an essential place within the program of the local church.

51

How Do You Cope
With Telephone Interruptions?

By Nancy Hoag

A homemaker and free-lance writer with nearly 135 articles to her credit, Nancy Hoag has served as a leader in many women's groups, both Christian and secular, and taught in Christian and secular high schools. She has a B.A. degree in English and did most of her post-graduate work in counseling and guidance for women.

I answered the insistent ringing. "I know you're busy but...." The introduction was familiar. I wondered how many had used it in the past week while I'd wrestled at my end of the line, quelling urges to shout ear-splitting admonishments!

Yes, my "friend" was right: I *was* busy. But for nearly half an hour I endured her laments. The dog had run away for the third time; the washer had swallowed her husband's socks; the little league coach had unfairly yanked her son (who was destined to be the "next Babe Ruth"); and her daughter's acne was "the devil's own curse"!

With one eye glued on the clock, I uttered "uh huh's" and "oh my's" to suggest undivided attention but inwardly I fumed! She'd done it again! Furthermore, she hadn't been the only one.

It wasn't that I hadn't experienced years of these sorts of calls. And actually there had been days when a minute or two on the line hadn't seemed such an interruption; in fact, I'd considered it a blessed respite from teething toddlers, a dog who resisted being housebroken—the daily mundanes.

Now, however, my children were off to college, the dog had been escorted to the pound by the local gendarmes and my nest was empty! How I longed—along with Greta Garbo—to be left alone! But I couldn't seem to muster the heart, nerve or gall—whatever it took—to be abrupt and hang up. Instead, I silently whined—then harbored ill feelings toward *myself* for my hypocrisy!

Sometimes I wasn't sure if I felt angrier with my caller or myself! After all, my children had been passed over on occasion (when I knew perfectly well coaches, teachers and entire administrations had goofed.) But lately my ability to empathize had waned. At "40-plus" I felt it was time for new beginnings. I wanted to write. Furthermore, after months of praying and searching, I was convinced the Lord wanted me to do just exactly that. No longer was I to dabble; it was time to press on with fervor!

My inability, however, to convince the others regarding the seriousness of my work resulted in my phone's incessant ringing— followed by my spells of secret seething.

The Scriptures instruct, "Do nothing out of selfish ambition or vain conceit, but in humility consider others better than yourselves'' (Phil. 2:3, NIV). However, they also admonish, ''Anyone who lets himself be distracted from the work I plan for him is not fit for the kingdom of God'' (Luke 9:62, LB).

''If you'll take yourself more seriously, the others will follow,'' my husband suggested. I glowered at him. I had taken Psychology 1—and I didn't recall anything in Prof. Sanderson's course about how taking myself seriously would turn my peers around. Still, my husband might be right.

By mid-afternoon, when the evening paper arrived with a flyer from a local store selling telephones and answering machines, I saw how I might take a positive step forward. Whether or not my friends and neighbors responded as my husband had predicted concerned me less and less as I read the entire ad—and made up my mind.

The man at the counter was helpful. He explained I could record a ''lovely message'' on the tape and encourage folks to call again. Better yet, I might suggest I'd do the calling. By the time I returned home with the black box and blank tapes, I was totally absorbed—rehearsing messages, picturing recipients' faces (and reactions) and dreaming of peace, quiet and productivity!

First, I had to learn to operate the machine. Because I'm not exactly mechanically minded, it took awhile. I twisted a tape, recorded several garbled messages and erased myself completely in the first hour! However, with my husband's help. I eventually worked it through.

Immediately, there were ''ruffled feathers.'' One friend responded, ''I love you but I hate your machine!'' In fact, it became necessary (with several friends) to explain personally I still loved them, too. However, I made it clear I was going to write if I had to cloister myself and have Wendy's deliver the beef!

Eventually several friends and acquaintances began taking me seriously. Some of them suggested their real concern (all along) had been for me. Was it something to do with my middle age, my empty nest or that my husband traveled and left me alone too often? Or had I always been a bit eccentric?

For the most part, they understood, and I began receiving cheering messages about how they hoped I'd ''have a good day,'' too! They also wished I'd meet them for lunch but knew I was writing the novel which would make Margaret Mitchell look like a piker! Lunch could wait. One caller said she believed if anyone could, I would; but at the end of her message I caught a snicker. I chose to ignore it.

My husband had been right. When I decided to take myself seriously, those who were my friends followed suit; those who weren't quit calling. And as a bonus folks selling siding, storm windows and swampland in No-Where-On-The-Map, New Mexico, gave it up! The battle was over, and I'd won!

The apostle Paul said, "Am I now trying to win the approval of men or of God? Or am I trying to please men? If I were still trying to please men, I would not be a servant of Christ" (Gal. 1:10, NIV). I rest in the belief I am serving God—doing what He has called me to do.

At last, I'm taking both God and myself seriously. As far as I'm concerned, that's the best answer to peer pressure.

52

How Do You Please Your King?

By Joyce Simmons

Joyce Simmons is the author of *Shared Joy Is Double Joy* and four children's books. She traveled for 10 years with her husband in evangelistic ministry before becoming a full-time homemaker.

As I was growing up I remember thinking that I would never want to be either a missionary or a pastor's wife—or be in the ministry in general. As it happened, I met and married a man with whom I shared the first 10 years of our married life in full-time evangelistic ministry. During those 10 years our home was a customized Greyhound bus, which we shared with 14 other members of the Lowell Lundstrom Ministries. We traveled 300 nights of the year holding rallies and city-wide crusades.

During this time I searched for the talents I considered necessary so I could do my best for the Lord. I needed a good singing voice, so I spent hours a day singing and practicing with my vocal tapes. Somehow I never seemed to find the quality of talent I sought to attain. The harder I tried to do moy "part" for the ministry the more frustrated and discouraged I became. If God had truly chosen me to be a part of a ministry, surely He should have provided me with some amazing, visible talents.

As I traveled from town to town I met countless pastors' wives who were also striving to do feats and wonders to impress people in the church and even their own husbands. They battled with low self-image. They were depressed and discouraged—and there were signs of tension and anxiety within their homes.

It was when our oldest son reached school age and I decided to remain at home so that he could go to public school that I realized God did have a special ministry for me. My ministry was to be that of a modern day "Barnabas"—an encourager to my husband and children. The kindness, compassion and love which I could show to them and others was as important and fulfilling a ministry as I could wish for!

To my friends I could be their inspiration when failure lurked outside their door; I could be their encourager when they faced difficult circumstances.

What a full-time ministry! How can I equip myself to accomplish it? Through encouraging myself daily in the Lord. By trusting in God's ability to show Himself through me as I strive to grow and mature in *His* love. In this way I can bloom and be fruitful where He has planted me.

Many clergy wives live visible, co-serving lives alongside their husbands, but just as many others serve in the background—they provide quiet strength. They bind marriage and families with strong spiritual ties.

God wants each of us who are married to ministers to grow where He has planted us, and to become what He intends. Being what He wants us to be does not always mean filling a place of prominence nor does it necessarily mean being like another minister's wife.

An old fable carries a message:

"A king went into his garden and found to his disappointment dying trees and shrubs and wilted flowers on every hand. Asking the oak the cause of its withering away, the oak told the king that it was dying because it could not be tall like a pine. Turning to the pine he learned that it began drooping because it was unable to bear grapes like the vine. And the vine explained that it was dying because it could not blossom like the rose.

"To his surprise, the king found the heartsease blooming as fresh as ever. Upon inquiry as to why it was not dying as were the other plants around it, the king received this reply: 'I took it for granted that when you planted me here you wanted heartsease. If you had desired an oak or a vine or a rose you would have planted such. So I thought since you had put me here I should do the best I can to be what *you* want. I can be nothing but what I am, but I am trying to be that to the best of my ability.' *The king was greatly pleased.*"

As women in ministry, every one of us is called to greatness, even if it is only in our own home. God calls each one of us to make indelible impressions on our children whose attitudes are molded and shaped within the walls of our homes. And He calls us to be a source of strength to our husbands who face difficult and challenging situations. No matter what our talents, every one of us can be an effective encourager.

But this does not come simply because our husbands are called to the pastorate or mission field. First we must seek after God's love, and we must allow Him to fill us to overflowing—for love cannot flow from an empty cup!

The capability to provide encouragement comes as a result of time spent in God's presence in prayer, which brings strength, and in the Word, which brings wisdom and knowledge.

Prayer and personal Bible study establish the foundation on which you build greater love for others. This love goes beyond natural love. It comes from the very heart of God. It allows you to be patient and understanding when your husband's hours are long and irregular; or when he brings home unexpected guests; or even when he volunteers you for some new committee. This love helps you realize our worth is in God and gives you freedom to be yourself and use your abilities and gifts (even if these don't include singing or piano playing).

To give your love, smile and tenderness to your family or to someone in need is truly the greatest of all ministries. As you freely give these priceless gifts, you will receive that special kind of fulfillment that comes only from serving God with a heart of love.

Be an encourager to everyone as you seek to produce wholesome fruit in God's garden—the fruit of your *personal ministry*. By this you will please the King.

53

What Constitutes a Balanced Ministry?

By Linda Howard

An author of three books and numerous articles for Christian publications, Linda Howard also served as editor of a magazine and is administrative assistant in the youth department of Tabernacle Church in Melbourne, Florida. Mrs. Howard has a degree in managerial science and with her husband authored *Aerospace Technologist* fo NASA.

W ould-be women leaders come in all sizes, shapes and forms. Two of the most popular are the forceful Matriarch and the sweet Finger-winder.

The forceful Matriarch is usually built like a truck and sounds like a misplaced baritone. "I have a word for you directly from the Lord," she insists with unblinking eye. "When you leave here, your needs will be met." As the Matriarch begins her rehearsed speech, I get the feeling that not only are my needs not going to be met but it's going to take three weeks of repentance to get her domineering message out of my craw. The more insistent she becomes, the more I know my biggest problem is how to find the nearest exit.

Then there is the sweet Finger-winder. She is a soft, cuddly cat with barbs hidden in the pads of her feet. Her ploy is to have things done the right way—her way. By winding everyone around her little pinkie, she can get things done properly. The only problem is that even baby Christians aren't small enough to fit around someone's little finger.

Her ministry drips of sweetness and light. Words which ooze from her lips sound soothing and smooth but the pricks of her claws are always felt even when they seem safely retracted into her paw.

Insipid ministries are never balanced.

What constitutes a balanced ministry? Paul gives that answer in 1 Corinthians 14:6. "But now, brethren...what shall I profit you, unless I speak to you whither by way of revelation or of knowledge or of prophecy or of teaching (instruction)?" There should be a balanced four-pronged delivery: revelation, knowledge, prophecy, instruction.

They seem to be divided into two groups. Revelation and knowledge apply and relate to the entire group. They are an enormous blanket of warmth in the middle of a snow storm. Prophecy and instruction meet the needs of the individual. Like the pricks of a needle extracting a splinter from an infected finger, these words go deep into selected and personal problems and help to bring healing.

The revelation of the Word of God is a supernatural interpretation of the Scripture which is given by inspiration of the Holy Spirit. It is not a teaching which is learned but *received*. It isn't enough to be a parakeet pronouncing the truth given to someone else. Left-overs in ministry never sound alive or vital. Revelation comes through prayer and divine interruption into our lives. Regurgitated Word has no string of reality.

One of the first signs of the death of a ministry is when a leader no longer shares from the vantage point of revelation. Iverna Tompkins once stated that she had been teaching for so many years, it would be easy to draw from her thousands of sermons instead of seeking a "new word" from the Lord.

Knowledge, the second prong, is facts and figures learned by study and digging deep into the Scriptures. Other books, commentaries and Christian publications can also give us interesting insights into the daily lives of the Bible characters. Too often we fill the gaps of our knowledge with opinions that are no more than dirty sludge right off the top of our head.

I once overheard a popular speaker comment with amusement about people's reactions to her ministry. They always mentioned that they loved the way she could ad-lib. "I hate to burst their mirage," she said, "but those off-the-cuff remarks come from hours of study and preparation. Though I've been teaching for over 20 years, I still spend hours getting ready to speak."

Prophecy is somewhat akin to revelation. 1 Corinthians 14:3 is a description of prophecy as it relates here. "One who prophesies speaks to men for edification (instruction in moral knowledge) and exhortation (to excite by words of advice) and consolation (to set at rest)" (NAS).

While I was speaking in a small class of women, a middle-aged woman began to cry. Because I did not know this lady, I was in the dark about the source of her tears. After the teaching session, she came up to me. "How did you know?" she asked. There was a strange feeling of warmth and mutual understanding in her voice.

"I'm sorry," I confessed. "I don't understand what you're talking about."

Suddenly she blushed. "Of course, you don't know," she laughed, realizing her mistake. "You couldn't know how much your teaching met my needs. But the Lord knew and He ministered a healing salve in an area of my life that has been festering and painful for over 30 years."

Like a healing poultice, the word of the Lord applied at a proper time meets the need of the individual. Often the message is so personal it is the person receiving the word who recognizes it as prophecy, not the speaker.

Instruction is close to knowledge. Taking what is known and applying it to a specific problem, usually results in step-by-step instructions on how to eliminate a situation.

I was impressed with the teaching of a young woman who conducted a weekly Bible class I attended for about a year. Each week she challenged the women with biblical truths. Methodically, she presented the Word in such a way that each of us identified with the spiritual principle she wished to establish. Our hearts were convicted by the Holy Spirit as she dug into the Scriptures, comparing verse with verse. But she never left us without an answer—a way out of our spiritual dilemma. As astutely as she exposed our hearts, she came with answers that we could use to come into repentance.

No matter what our position in the body of Christ, everyone needs the push of a balanced ministry. Young Christians should be instructed in seeking the Holy Spirit for growth. Mature Christians face ministry problems which require a blueprint plan of survival.

Insipid teachings have robbed the church of this needed direction. Some women have shied away from public ministry for fear that they will become a stumbling block through imbalance. It is exciting to realize that every teacher can become profitable to the body of Christ by giving what is needed—the balanced word of revelation, knowledge, prophecy and instruction.

54

How Should Hospitality Be Handled in the Parsonage?

By Nancy Hoag

A homemaker and free-lance writer with nearly 135 articles to her credit, Nancy Hoag has served as a leader in many women's groups, both Christian and secular, and taught in Christian and secular high schools. She has a B.A. degree in English and did most of her post-graduate work in counseling and guidance for women.

I don't recall the reason but I do recall being certain I had one! Blue Monday, bills or the rainy season? Something. At any rate, when the call came from a friend who wanted to "come right over" with her distraught neighbor, I nearly dissolved. Certain that Doris hadn't detected my despair, I responded as cheerily as I could manage for the mood I was nursing. "Absolutely! Come right over," I insisted.

Within minutes the doorbell rang. And before the hour was up, I had evidenced God's faithfulness. Even as I'd opened the door, I'd relaxed; my guests seemed to do the same. For, as requested, I had received. He'd imparted His nature to me. Tension lifted and a smile replaced my grimace. My new friend shared why she'd come and I began to be glad she had. Tears followed—and eventual prayer. As I watched each woman's summer laughter on the way out, my spirit soared. But the greater bonus came in the next half hour when my phone rang for a second time. It was my friend, Doris.

"I just want to tell you Pam has never, ever felt so warmly welcomed into anyone's home before," she rejoiced. Then she added, "She actually cried on the way home. Said you made her feel as if she'd 'come home.' Couldn't believe you'd actually respond to a complete stranger that way!"

The experience carried me for months—until several weeks ago, when my hospitality was put to the test again. And again on my own I would have failed. But the Lord stepped in.

"Honey," my husband asked over dinner one night, "you know in a couple of weeks we're running a training session at the office? I'm bringing 20 or 25 folk here for the week." He paused and I knew immediately what was coming. "What would you think about my having them all here for dinner one night?"

I gulped, talked myself into remaining calm, thought about "my work" and "my deisre" to be about it—instead of cooking for two days—then responded, "Sure, Honey, I'd love it!" Instantly I remembered Pinocchio's nose and touched my own.

For two weeks I wrestled. Yes, I recalled the former situation. In fact, other reminders came to me: God had given us our home; it had been returned to Him for His use; and both my husband and I were eager for people to come sense the presence of the Lord and be blessed! But this week? "No!" I moaned as the time drew too close and I tossed myself to sleep. Finally, when I couldn't whimper alone any longer, I called my closest friend for sympathy. I was shocked when I received admonishment.

"Nancy, too few wives these days would say 'yes.' But that's one of the things that separates us from the world's ideas!"

"I know, " I wailed. "But it's such an awful time. I'm so busy."

"Too busy to bless your husband?" she asked.

"So you think I should do it," I groaned, resignedly, wondering if I might have called someone else.

"I think you should," she responded.

"And not just for Scotty, either. You should do it for the others, too. Just being in your home will bless them." She paused. "I mean it." Then before I could muster up another excuse, she added, "Wait a minute and I'll find that lasagna recipe you wanted. It's perfect for a crowd."

As I took notes and mentally shopped for cheeses and meats, I gave up. But before I crawled into bed I turned to the Lord and said, "You know I do *not* want to do this. But I do want to bless my husband; and I want to bless his friends, too. So, Father, I'm trusting You to give me Your nature, again—to make me happy to have guests—to give them, and my husband, a good evening."

Our company was due at 6:00 on Wednesday but by Tuesday the Lord had done His work in me. I began preparations that morning: shopped, polished, arranged flowers, baked enough desserts for two trays and shined every faucet and piece of glass in the house.

At 6:00 they arrived. And it was wonderful. By the end of the evening I'd noted my husband's happiness, the Lord's presence and a change in our guests. They'd come through the door, stiff and formal. I wondered if it was because my husband was "the new boss." But as the evening progressed, they relaxed. Soon we resembled a family reunion. Our guests took seconds, poured my coffee, laughed and shared. One told me about his new baby. Another was proud of his wife—in college and managing at home, too. A young man who handled cooking detail at home said my lasagna was even better than his own. And one girl, about the age of my oldest, hung around the kitchen and stirred my "motherly instincts." When the last person said "goodbye" with a handshake for my husband and a hug for me, I praised God! He'd done it again! Then I wondered, human that I am, if I'd ever entertain so many again. And if I did, were there secrets to learn—beforehand? A plan I might tuck away to avoid panicky prayers and tremors? I turned to my pastor's wife for answers.

I was certain Ruth had served dinner to half the congregation. "We do have so much company," she laughed. "Our boys ask, 'Who's coming for dinner tonight?' They actually expect and enjoy it!" So does Ruth.

"He's given me the 'gift of hospitality' and I'm glad. Some don't have this particular gift," she added, and I wondered if she's a mind reader as well as a perceptive hostess. "We should learn to enjoy whichever gifts we have and stop feeling guilty about the ones we don't!"

"Also," she continued, "my husband protects me. That's one of our 'secrets to success.' " Another secret: she plans simple meals. "I always pray there'll be enough—and pray over the dishes, too. No matter how many 'extras' show up at the last minute, there's enough—always." If she has advance notice, she prayed she'll fix a favorite and usually discovers she has! "Sometimes I have plans but the Lord sends a check in my spirit—so I don't fix that! I usually find out my guest(s) couldn't have eaten what I'd planned."

One day, on the "spur of the moment," there were five extras. "If I stay relaxed, it works out fine but I pray to be relaxed." Occasionally, someone calls and says, "Hey, we're bringing pizza!" at the very time her husband's invited extras. One "coincidence" became a party—pizza, chicken, "the works!" As Ruth rejoiced and shared the fun of that occasion with me, I remarked it might well have "finished me."

"But I've always enjoyed it," she smiled. "I like doing things without much planning. ("Whew! I detest it!" I thought but hesitated to reveal myself even to the pastor's wife—until I remembered: Stop feeling guilty.) And keeping the house in some sort of order helps. I never let it get away from me."

"But what about the actual cooking?" I asked—admitting I just don't like it all that much.

"Well, Merv cooks, too. In fact, he's a good cook! He likes helping me—even with clean-up. Perhaps I'd resent it if he didn't help, but he's always there. Of course, he'd rather cook!" We shared laughter and attitudes not unlike her husband's.

"One time I was pregnant and had the flu. Merv wanted to bring home a couple he was counseling but I was sick all day." So her husband cooked the entire chicken dinner and had everything prepared before their guests arrived.

"I always wanted to be a minister's wife," she smiled as she returned from answering the door to a pre-school friend. "As I grew up I was very much aware of my minister's wife—so caring and loving. I could go there anytime." As a result of that relationship, Ruth decided she wanted to be "just like her."

"So far," I said, "it sounds so positive, I wonder if I'm going home determined or discouraged.''

Wait,'' she laughed. ''There've been times when I've said 'no.' Sometimes I've known: no way could I bring myself around to it.'' But she's felt good about it—knew she'd done all she could do on a particular day. ''It's not necessary to run yourself ragged. I do what I can; I'm honest when I can't.'' There've been times when someone's just caught her when she's exhausted. ''If I don't feel like entertaining, I accept that about myself and feel free enough to say, 'I'm tired.' It doesn't happen often. But again, that's where my husband's protection comes in. He never tells me he's bringing somebody; he asks.''

Driving home I reviewed my conversation with Ruth and thought of my hesitancy to be like her—then recalled: Whatever our gifts—however we feel about our guests—our God is a hospitable God and He desires us to be the same. We may not always ''feel'' hospitable but we can always turn to Him, tell Him, and expect to be filled. He's just waiting for us to ask. The Bible says, ''Ask, and it shall be given you...For every one that asketh receiveth'' (Matthew 7:7,8). When guests knock at our door, we can knock at His. And He will give us what we need—to entertain strangers.

55

How Can a Pastor's Wife Juggle Her Schedule?

By Betty Jane Grams

Betty Jane Grams and her husband, Monroe, are missionaries to Latin America with the Assemblies of God. Mrs. Grams is also a teacher and lecturer and has authored two books, *Women of Grace* and *Families Can Be Happy.*

A recent survey indicates that approximately 70 percent of pastors' wives are working outside the home. How does a minister's wife manage to juggle her home, her children, her mate, her ministry and her job and still maintain her sanity?

In this day of the two-salary home, the divisive spirit of the age, the staggered schedules of jobs, women must be flexible in their time, their attitudes and emotions to be able to roll with the punches.

As missionaries to Latin America for 32 years we have the opportunity during our furlough time to be guests in the homes of nearly 150 pastors during the course of a year. I am amazed as I visit in these homes to find the adjusting of schedules and the give-and-take to which pastors' wives are adapting.

I have memories of juggling schedules and making it all fit together as I finished my undergraduate work plus teaching missions and Spanish six hours at a Bible college on one of our furloughs. I left home at 6:25 every morning with a friend. The lunches for each of us were fixed at night and standing in a row in the refrigerator. My husband got the children off to school before driving to the university to finish his graduate studies. On weekends he ministered at churches.

The laundromat was nearly empty at midnight so that was a good time to wash clothes while I studied. In the morning we stacked the baskets of wet clothes into the car early to take them into the college laundry to toss into the dryer before the first class. Then between each successive class I would exchange the dried ones for wet, fold and stack, arriving home at 3 p.m., just in time for the children to come from their schools.

Supper together, study, get ready for classes, and the days whirled into a full year of working, studying, teaching and organizing. Three happy children were proud when their minister mommy graduated valedictorian. All had helped.

Recently I received a letter from a talented, busy pastor's wife who serves as leader of the women's department for a large area. She asked, "With six children to clothe and educate, how can I help supplement our finances without hurting our home or minimizing my ministry with my husband?'' This is a hard question to answer.

Possibly a reassessing of our priorities would help us see that some of the factors which push women out of the nest into the working world are pressures that could be avoided. The pressure to keep up with the Joneses! The pressure to drive a bigger, better, fancier car. Wanting to upgrade the carpet. Or the contemporary ERA pressure that everybody's doing it to be fulfilled.

Sometimes there's more month than money. Women must weigh the pros and cons in making the decision about working outside the home for a salary. Years ago the congregations would bring in a quarter of beef, a side of pork, fresh vegetables, eggs, fresh cow's milk and baked goods. We now live in a more commercialized society, so it's each to his own, and oftentimes the finances just don't stretch. There may be special financial needs such as having college-age children which seem to make it imperative for the woman of the manse to seek supplemental outside employment for the costly tuitions.

Some pastors' wives are finding employment and fulfillment in the Christian day schools which are being opened in conjunction with their churches. Others serve as secretaries or nurses, or in a wide variety of secular jobs.

New Kind of Commitment

At a recent wedding, I listened as the pastor read the ceremony and the pledges. I heard a new section included on the economic necessity of a two-salary home, asking the bride and groom to be elastic in their demands on each other and also being helpful as well as faithful. It was a new twist for me, to include those thoughts in the ''and hereto I plight thee my troth.''

Later the pastor was teaching on the meaning of a good marriage and said he's learned to help at home since his wife works. He got a good laugh when he said he knows how to empty the dishwasher.

One pastor's wife, who was a full-time church music director, said one way she kept her sanity was to set aside one day when the whole family helped. She divided the house with sections assigned to each child and parent. They could manage to clean the house in one hour and then go out together for a special meal. This was togetherness time.

Since I have directed music, led choirs, helped with radio broadcasts, taught in Bible schools and been a full-time minister alongside my husband, I have learned through the years to delegate my tasks to others. If someone else can do it, I let them.

The idea of family chore-sharing is not new. In my girlhood home my mother helped attend the office for my daddy. This meant that he was obliged to help at home. He did the dishes. Each of us children learned early that if we all helped out there was time for choir, youth meetings, music, sports, friends and that after-school job.

Children can learn to do many things. This reinforces their sense of worth and lightens the family load.

Delegate to others the tasks they can handle. Keep a notebook with a list and mark it off as each task is concluded. Tasks and time can be juggled to fit.

A good thermometer for a pastor's wife is Proverbs 31:27, LB: "She watches carefully all that goes on throughout her household, and is never lazy." So in adjusting to growing children who have staggered schedules, a pastor's busy commitments, and our own well being and peace we need to learn new skills. We need to learn to streamline the daily tasks, and rearrange and simplify part of our living.

Peace

To be able to juggle home, family and work, a woman must rely on the peace of God to undergird her body, soul and psyche. Agnes Sanford writes as a minister and wife of a pastor about the gift of peace in her autobiography *Sealed Orders*. She says that everything she did with either her mind or body could be done with half the energy and half the time when the Holy Spirit invades both the conscious mind and heart, and the subconscious soul, spirit and inner intelligence of mind and body. She says, "I could write and not be weary, and cook and not faint. I could now serve a dinner in half an hour instead of in an hour and a half."

A spiritual woman must rely on the peace of God for continual renewal. We are more alert and more efficient as the Holy Spirit invades our being with the gift of peace—"the peace of God which passeth all understanding shall keep your hearts and minds through Christ Jesus."

Praising the Lord brings the constant presence of the Holy Spirit into our everyday lives and facilitates our ordinary work with precision and speed. My mother used to say that she had learned to overcome problems and needs by living with constant praise in her life to the Lord.

Pastors Can Help

One half of all wives in the general population are employed. This poses new problems for personal spirituality, and for our churches and pastors to make adjustments to include all these women in scheduling and consideration.

Today's pastor must be conscious of the needs and schedules of the congregation when planning times of services. There has been a decided shift from an agricultural society where we had to wait for the men to come in from the barn, clean up, eat a quick bite and get to church, which meant that in our first parish we were waiting for some of our deacons to amble in at 9 p.m. for an 8 p.m. meeting. Today everyone lives with distances to drive and staggered schedules. Wise pastors will analyze the way to make church meetings fit the family needs.

Some churches are practical enough to have an early Sunday evening service from 6 until 7:45. This gives the whole family an opportunity to attend church and still have time together at home before starting back to the heavy schedule of school and work on Monday.

We visited a Catholic Charismatic service that started at 9:30 p.m. The church was full of both men and women who had come from their jobs, shops, offices and businesses. Young people had come after their outside school activities. All were worshipping together.

In another church we were scheduled on Sunday for a 4:30 p.m. Bible teaching hour. As we inquired about this arrangement, we were informed that most of the people worked in an early Sunday morning fleamarket. They had recently found the Lord, and the pastor, realizing their need for training, had revised his Sunday school schedule to meet the needs of the people. Choir, evangelism, children's meetings, teaching classes all were juggled into the afternoon to fit into the schedule of that busy market.

The wise pastor will consider the value of women and be flexible enough to include them in schedules. The Holy Spirit is given to the handmaidens to be part of today's burgeoning church.

Today's woman has great potential, preparation and spiritual vitality for the kingdom. Women are growing in the gifts and want to participate in the life of the church.

56

Why Is Age 35 a Time of Crisis?

By Betty Malz

A newspaper columnist, author, wife, mother and church organist, Betty Malz leads a busy life attending to her own activities and helping her husband who is a certified marriage and family counselor and vice president of Trinity College, Ellendale, North Dakota. She has written four books, two on the national best-seller list, and also authored numerous articles for various Christian publications.

When a woman hits age 35, there emerges a lonely little 5-year-old girl who needs to be held closely, rocked, stroked, patted and petted, admired and treated with tender *intimacy.* Sometimes this need surfaces overnight, sometimes gradually, but happen it does. No one but her own husband can meet that need, fill that void, the empty vacuum in the secret, lower corner of her heart and emotions.

Why write such a chapter? I must! Four young women either called, came to see me or wrote to me, in just six days, crying, begging for help: the common denominator, they were all approximately 35 years old.

I prayed for an understanding heart. When you want to know how to get to Bismarck, you find someone who has been there *and back,* not just someone planning to go, or one who is also on the journey to Bismarck. I do understand. I have been there and back, not once but twice.

My first husband was an energetic promoter, a successful businessman who worked long hours. He died following open-heart surgery.

I am now married to an educator who is vice president of a college. He used to serve me only his leftover charm each evening. I once accused him of depleting his last ounce of charm before he left the campus to head home.

Four women in six days with the same basic need? There is an answer.

Recently I spoke at a convention of women in Oklahoma City. I sat beside a beautiful, shapely young woman who poured out her heart weeping almost uncontrollably: "My husband is youth pastor in Tulsa. He is consumed with gaining the senior pastor's approval, and has become extremely popular with the kids, because his every waking hour is invested in entertaining them. I tried a part-time job to prevent boredom, but nothing satisfied. I needed to be admired by my own husband, have him touch me. I tried to join him in every activity, throw myself into his work. I was just one in a long line of the charmed mice filing in parade, trailing behind the Pied Piper. About the only time

I get to 'touch him' is by doing his laundry. It seems we are playing a game of 'God and Moses'—he is God, I am Moses. Moses never saw God's face, only his "hinder parts." I only see his back as he goes out the door to do some wonderful thing for someone else, not me."

A young farmer's wife called me on the phone. I did not recognize her voice because she was so depressed. "All my husband has for me anymore is his leftover energy, his dusty body and his sleepy mind. At the end of an 18-hour day, he falls into bed, sometimes without even kissing me goodnight. I tried climbing up on the tractor, riding with him all day, just to look at him, to be with him. Instead of his realizing I wanted a touch, some intimacy, he began barking commands at me. Above the roar of the motors, he talked at me, not to me. I emerged not a close wife, but another hired hand. He hasn't seen my eyes since last winter. I need warmth and attention, not just sex."

I took a sobbing young wife for a two-hour drive in the country while she breathed out her woe to me: "My husband is a wealthy, young, successful doctor. No one believes my *need* because they cannot realize that the things they visibly see, I don't need. I am barren, hungry for tenderness, just a touch—for him to stop me in the hallway and without words, just hold me because he wants to be near me. I tried to explain this to him, and he said, 'What more could any woman want? I don't chase women, I don't drink, I don't smoke. You have your own car, a fabulous home, two cute kids, money and anything it can buy. What you need is a job.' "

She went on to tell me, "I tried to get involved in charities, but it drove a wedge between us, and robbed my children of the time they needed with me. I tried a part-time job and started my own little business, but I became tired and even more empty at the end of the day, and the gap between my husband and me widened.

"I do not want to be away from the responsibility of my children, but I have been a mother for 15 years. I am tired of being the hub around which my family rotates because I work for them all.

"I am tired of being the supporting, absorbing factor which helped my husband finish medical school and become successful. Won't *my time* ever come?

"I keep thinking—hoping—that someday soon he will notice me, hold me close for a few minutes. He's reached a high goal. When will he help me reach my small goal, just to be cherished, to know tenderness and to have his intimacy? It wouldn't take that much time, as he passes by me, at the table, during television, just before falling asleep. What can I do? When I tried to explain my basic need, he called it nagging, categorized it as 'criticizing.' "

What can you do: write him a tender, loving *letter* in which you state your needs, listing them tenderly but frankly.

You can take the initiative to show intimacy. When he is sitting quietly, place yourself in the middle of his lap so he can't get up, place your hand over his mouth so he can't debate or talk you down.

Pray for him: "Lord, make him happy, bless him, satisfy him with earned success, give him an understanding heart where I am concerned."

Mail him this article to read in his private, quiet time.

Clip cartoons that express your need in humor, mail them to his business address, or to your home, letting him know that you invested time and effort to get his attention.

Don't talk too much. The reason some men don't listen is because they hear too much of your voice too often. Sad to say, but some women must have been vaccinated with a phonograph needle.

Going home to "Daddy" (your father) will not cure your condition either.

If by now he hasn't taken serious consideration of your need, write a meaningful, expressive letter of appeal to an unbiased friend who cares for you both. Ask that middle party to meet your husband, read the letter to him and discuss your need prayerfully.

It works!

Three of the four young women have reported back to me already this week, and it's only Tuesday. "It works," they told me.

Where's the fourth story?

A young, attractive, career girl, 35, called. She had not taken seriously either love or marriage, but had invested herself in becoming an executive. But she had not escaped the Plateau 35! She now yearned for warmth, intimacy, to be held by a husband—one of her own. She could not understand her friends who were crying to me. She wished she had their problems, their children, their unthoughtful husband to cope with. How could those complaining women be so blind?

I have watched married Christian women in this age bracket become closet drinkers, even alcoholics, trying to fill the void their husbands could fill.

Failure to meet this unseen need has resulted in the disaster of divorce, or in seeking affection from other men.

Or a woman can become a religious fanatic, so heavenly minded that she is no earthly good, chasing the convention, retreat, study-group circuit trying to substitute Jesus, the source of her soul's need, for her husband's lack of tender intimacy. We are spirit and flesh. Only Jesus can meet our spiritual need, but only a loving mate can meet our natural desire.

The other tragedy is a futile substitute, food and eating. Many women at this age become obese because they try to satisfy the hunger, the yearning for intimacy from their mate with the overeating of morsels for the stomach. It becomes a vicious cycle. They lose their self-esteem when they become depressed and fat. The reason: "We tend to think of ourselves as the most important person in our life thinks of us."

Only one person can satisfy the hidden need in the corner of a woman's heart—her own husband.

P.S. FOR MEN ONLY: If you are offended by this, consider the possibility that you may be more concerned about your "image" than you are concerned about your wife or her needs. This was not meant to point out neglect in busy men, but to reinforce the fact that you have the ability to meet the most basic need your mate will ever have. Your response to that need can solve an emotional, psychological problem for your partner, your other half, the person who is your best witness of success, since she also bears your name.

Section VII

Solving Home Group Problems

57

Are Home Groups a New Fad?

By C. W. Howard III

C. W. Howard III is assistant director of Career Planning and Placement, Old Dominion University, Norfolk, Virginia, and was recently elected president of the Mental Health Association of Tidewater. He has pastored two churches, assisted in organizing another church, served interim pastorships in 13 churches and spent 25 years as a professor of psychology. Howard also has conducted leadership groups.

Almost every major renewal in the Christian church has brought with it a return to small groups and a rapid increase of such groups in individual homes for prayer, Bible study and a sharing of faith. And it's happening again. Small groups were a common ingredient in the important movements of the Holy Spirit throughout church history. They characterized early Pietism, the Wesleyan Revival and the Holiness Revival of the late 1800s.

Wesleyan Small Cell Groups

John Wesley's small cell groups played an important role in England's great Wesleyan Revival two centuries ago. Wesley formed his "class meetings" to help converts become established in the faith. He soon saw dramatic results. According to Howard Snyder in *The Problem of Wineskins*, to those who criticized the method, Wesley replied, "Many...happily experienced that Christian fellowship which they had not so much as an idea before. They began to 'bear one another's burdens,' and naturally to 'care for each other.' "

Wesley did not feel bound within the walls of the institutional church. He preached a clear message of personal salvation through Jesus Christ and consistently emphasized a life filled with the Spirit. He also urged an active social consciousness.

As thousands began to attend his revival meetings, Wesley said he was impressed by God to divide the people into small groups of twelve, each with a leader. In these small groups people came to know each other better and to experience true Christian fellowship.

Wesley's secret lay in his desire to be thoroughly biblical. He was a man of God's Word. He sought biblical answers to life's problems, but he also appealed to experience and reason. His cell groups provided a biblical answer to the needs of the many converts.

Today most small groups are still beneficial to Christian growth and experience. But biblically based small groups differ from the many encounter groups, sensitivity groups and other such groups in the church which focus primarily on what man can do for himself, rather than providing him with standards for judging his conduct. Such groups generally have humanistic goals.

Biblically Based

Small groups can be a vital part of the church only if they are biblically based, with scriptural goals and methods, where members can grow in the fellowship of the Holy Spirit.

This kind of small group is more than a superficial, social fellowship. When a church group gathers only for socializing, as a civic club or neighborhood get-together, no matter how enjoyable and helpful the friendly socializing may be, it is no substitute for the fellowship of the Spirit.

Although true fellowship is a gift of the Holy Spirit, churches should ideally afford an environment in which this fellowship can take place. The Bible, however, says very little about how churches should be structured to afford such an environment.

From the concept of the fellowship of the Holy Spirit, we may define a church structure as: a gathering together under the Holy Spirit; in a way that encourages communication; where there is an informality and intimacy that permits freedom of the Spirit and where there is provision for Bible study in the context of community.

One structure satisfies this definition: the small group. Christians who gather in small groups will most likely experience the fellowship of the Holy Spirit.

Never a Substitute

But small groups must never become a substitute for the larger assembly. Meeting only in small groups can lead to cliques or to a group becoming too subjective or self-serving.

Nor must the small group be looked upon as a panacea. Man's efforts cannot cause the church to be more faithful in meeting needs or problems unless the Holy Spirit guides by His indwelling power. In order for the Spirit to guide, group members must be open to God and others. And that openness thrives best in an environment of supportive love and fellowship with other believers.

Although the structure of large corporate groups and small fellowship groups may vary according to different cultures and circumstances, both groups are essential to the biblical idea of the church.

Group Features

Small groups have certain distinctive features:

1. Flexibility in time, place, purpose, order, length and frequency of meetings.

2. Mobility of meeting place. As pastor of a church in Argentina with many small groups, Juan Carlos Ortiz decided to find out just how well his large Pentecostal church in Buenos Aires could manage under persecution conditions. He closed the church building for a month. The result? Because of its structure as a body and its ministry

through informal contacts and small cell groups, the church kept on functioning normally.

3. Openness to various kinds of people. A small circle which devotes itself to prayer and an intimate sharing of spiritual support will draw a person in and welcome him. The small group usually does not operate a budget, elect officers to oversee its administration, or promote an idea or product. It is, therefore, free to welcome a person into the circle for his own sake.

4. Personal rather than impersonal in communication. Small groups of about eight to twelve people gathering informally in homes provide one of the most effective structures for communicating God's Word in modern society.

5. Growth by division. As a group grows, it can break into more small groups. A network of small cell groups has a great effect on society through its continual cell division and multiplication.

6. Effectiveness in evangelism. In a small group an unbeliever can hear the Holy Spirit's voice convicting him of sin and wooing him to commit his life to Jesus.

Robert Raines reports he has "watched proportionately more lives genuinely converted in and through small group meetings for prayer, Bible study and the sharing of life than in the usual organizations and activities of the institutional church."

7. Adaptability in the institutional church. The small group is part of, not a subsitute for, the church.

Christian Obedience

Small groups must have an objective rather than subjective purpose. Personal spiritual growth is a worthy outcome, but if that is the main focus, the groups may turn inward. The objective purpose of small groups involves working to achieve goals. These groups exist for service and facilitate Christian obedience in the world. With the purpose of obedience and service in mind, small group members focus on Bible study. Something special happens in a small group Bible study. The Holy Spirit gives the unique gift of *koinonia* which brings greater involvement to Bible study.

Snyder says the fellowship of the Holy Spirit is that special quality which makes small groups effective. It is "the deep spiritual community in Christ which believers experience when they gather together as the church of Christ."

Develop Gifts

Snyder feels the local church should "expect, identify and awaken the varied gifts that sleep within the community of believers." The Holy Spirit has the divine option of giving all or only some of the gifts noted in the Bible to a church group. And He will grant all the gifts needed for the church's edification.

Small groups function in part to encourage the development of spiritual gifts. Gifts are given primarily for and within the community. Small Spirit-led groups, where members discover, share and reinforce common values, provide the context for stirring up spiritual gifts.

Church members depend upon each other for using the gifts, because no one member possesses all the gifts. Also, according to Scripture, the ordinary gifts are needed more than the showy ones. Miracles may only occur now and then, but members must express acts of mercy on an on-going basis. A proper use of gifts should lead to a life of self-giving, not self-centeredness.

Spiritual Environment

The first Christians knew an unusual unity, oneness of purpose, common love and mutual concern. This was more than either the immediate job of conversion or the knowledge of shared beliefs. It was an atmosphere, a spiritual environment, that grew among the first believers as they prayed, learned and worshipped together in their own homes (Acts 2:42-46; 5:42).

The early Christians maintained a pattern of small groups and large groups, meeting together in homes and in the temple. Small groups provided the intimate community life which gave richness to the large group meetings.

Common worship in large groups and understanding and living out one's commitment to Christ in smaller groups are still part of the church's function today. It is important to maintain that small-group, large-group pattern.

58

How Do You Start a Home Inquirer Group?

By Robert E. Coleman

Robert E. Coleman is director of the School of World Mission and Evangelism, Trinity Evangelical Divinity School, Bannockburn, Deerfield, Illinois.

Home inquirer groups represent one of the most promising avenues of evangelism in our day. Such small, informal meetings are open to unbelievers where they can hear the Christian faith discussed in an undogmatic and friendly way.

Steps for Starting Group

1. *Secure a good leader.* Like everything else, the secret for this work is in its leadership. It is imperative that the one selected for this ministry not only be qualified in every way to bring people to a vital Christian experience, but that he or she be one gifted in making friends and teaching. A pastor can fill the position, but it is much better to have lay people do it. Perhaps a couple could take the assignment together. They must see that everything is in order for each meeting, preside over the discussions and maintain a spirit of reverence with honest inquiry and informality.

2. *Select a strategic home for meeting.* The group should meet in some neutral location where attendance does not carry the connotation of membership in the church. A church member's house usually lends itself well to this situation, but it should be in a desirable location with adequate room for meeting and for parking cars. At other times, the meeting might be held at a restaurant or hotel. The important thing is that the place encourage the attendance of those who are not committed to Christ, and yet still preserve the opportunity for wholesome discussion.

3. *Extend personal invitations to people.* The church can announce the meetings in the bulletin, and make it known that all are welcome, but in all probability only those who receive a personal invitation will come. The lady of the host house can extend invitations to her friends to come, and persons in the groups can seek to contract their unconverted friends and invited them to the meeting. The idea is to get some to come to this meeting who are outside Christ and the church. Aim at having as many or more unconverted people there are true Christians.

4. *Make persons feel right at home as they arrive for the meeting.* The responsibility for creating this friendly atmosphere rests largely

392

with the leader and the host. The leader must be at the place of meeting early to greet people as they arrive. The meeting should begin with everyone being personally acquainted. If the meeting is preceded by an informal breakfast or dinner, which is often the case, the time of introduction will be moved forward accordingly.

5. *People should be seated so as to see each other.* The best way is to form a circle of chairs or to be seated around a table. The leader takes his place in the circle as merely one in the group.

6. *The meeting itself should make its purpose inviting and intimately relevant.* Where the objectives of the gathering are clearly understood and implemented by the group, everyone present should feel before it is over that the meeting was designed with their need in view. Usually this can be accomplished in about an hour and a half, though it will last longer if more time is given to fellowship before or after the meeting.

Meeting Time Allotment

7:30 p.m. *The leader explains something about the purpose of the meeting and the procedure to be followed.* It should be made clear that no one is to be put on the spot, that this is a free discussion of opinion, and that everyone is encouraged to be perfectly frank in expressing feelings. Moreover, no one is expected to agree with the majority opinion, or for that matter, the position of the church. However, for those who would care to make a commitment to Christ, they should know that the opportunity to do so is always present. This will help clear the air and put the uncommitted more at ease.

7:35 *Leader calls on someone to pray.* After prayer, if anyone has come in who is not well acquainted in the group, proper introductions can be made again. Appreciation may be expressed to the host in whose residence the group is meeting.

7:40 *The subject is presented, either by a brief statement or by reading a passage of the Bible.* In the case of the first instance, a group member can make the presentation in five to ten minutes. The talk should conclude with the question in point, for example, ''What does it mean to be converted?'' or ''How does God answer prayer?'' In the case of a straight Bible study approach, the issue can be presented by simply reading a portion in the Scripture. There are many ways it can be done—one person reading the whole passage, or everyone participating by reading responsively in unison or taking turns reading verse by verse.

7:50 *The subject is opened for discussion.* Here the leader must display his or her true gift of leadership by keeping the discussion objective and yet open for every opinion. There needs to be a feeling of complete honesty and freedom. Everyone should be encouraged to make some contribution, and no one should be allowed to dominate the discussion, including the leader. The leader is to see to it that the discussion keeps moving within the subject, and as far as possible, without controversy. One of the simplest ways to get the ball started is to ask each member of the group to comment briefly on the subject, stating his or her own experience. The leader might need occasionally to stimulate the discussion by asking such questions as: What do you think is most significant point in the passage? Why? Would you mind putting it into your own words? Have you ever had any experience like this? How would you apply this principle to your life now? Do you see here any promise of God? Any warning? Any command? What does this show us about Christ? If questions arise in the group and are not answered, the leader should not feel obligated to settle them by virtue of superior training. Rather, the leader will try to get the group itself to discover the answer by further study. Perhaps members of the group could be appointed to look into the matter and bring back a conclusion at the next meeting.

8:30 *The discussion ends, and someone summarizes the views presented.* The leader or someone else can do this. It might be a good experience to rotate this duty among group members.

8:40 *Any announcements are made relative to the next meetings—* its place, time, topic, chairman, etc.

8:45 *The meeting closes with prayer.* People can share prayer needs. Occasionally at this time someone under conviction may ask to be remembered in some special way. Perhaps it would be good to ask several to lead out in prayer, or just have a period of silent meditation followed by a closing prayer. Vary the procedure. The rule is to be led by the Lord.

9:00 *Refreshments can be served, if desired.* Fellowship is not the purpose of the meeting, but it is certainly a byproduct of it. So make the most of the opportunity to get better acquainted with others.

7. *Seek out again those who show a deeper interest in knowing personally the Savior.* Probably the best fruit of the inquiry group will be seen in private conversations after the meetings. Again the initiative here rests with the leader, and only one who follows through with the advantage gained in these meetings will likely see the expected harvest.

59

How Are Churches Using Home Groups?

By MINISTRIES *Panel*

Panel members:

Ray Bade is director of video-cell evangelism for The Happy Church in Denver, Colorado.

John English is home group coordinator for Tulsa Christian Fellowship in Tulsa, Oklahoma.

Linda Lees assists her husband, Don, who is director of the home group program for The Tabernacle Church in Melbourne, Florida.

Bill Scheidler is director of pastoral ministries for Bible Temple in Portland, Oregon.

Tay Wallace is a section pastor for Grace World Outreach Center in Maryland Heights, Missouri.

Small home groups—suddenly they are everywhere, like mushrooms all over the yard the morning after a summer shower. It's been a quiet, unheralded phenomenon in church life, totally different from the roar and rattle of a decade ago when impulsive pastors mobilized fleets of buses to race frantically toward new statistical heights.

Those buses may have been harbingers of the age of super churches. On Sundays the crowds throng to acres of blacktop and swarm into tiers of pews in mammoth auditoriums. It's awesome!

But what about the caring, loving interaction Jesus insists is the core of His disciples' identity? "By this shall all men know that ye are my disciples, if ye have love one to another" (John 13:35).

In their book, *The Search for America's Faith,* George Gallup, Jr. and David Poling report that 52 percent of the Christians polled said small groups provide the "support system" for their faith.

How did these groups come into existence and what are they doing? To discover the answers, *MINISTRIES* contacted directors of home group ministries in five strategic localities across the country. The observations of this panel-by-telephone are based on their day-to-day experiences.

The panelists are (from the West to the East): Bill Scheidler, director of pastoral ministries at Bible Temple, Portland, Oregon; Ray Bade, director of video-cell evangelism at Happy Church, Denver, Colorado; John English, home group coordinator of Tulsa Christian Fellowship, Tulsa, Oklahoma; Tay Wallace, section pastor of Layman's Outreach Ministry of Grace World Outreach Center, Maryland Heights, Missouri; and Linda Lees, assistant to the director of the home group program of the Tabernacle Church, Melbourne, Florida.

MINISTRIES: **When and why did your church begin its small group ministry?**

Bill Scheidler: It has been about ten years. The reason for doing it was to give better pastoral care and oversight to the flock as it got larger and became more and more difficult for us to keep track of individuals—how well they were doing and their needs. We now have about 85 percent of our church body of 2,300 participating in approximately 80 home fellowship meetings, with some 25 or 30 in attendance in each group.

Ray Bade: We've been involved in home groups for just about a year. We have our home meetings for an evangelistic outreach. We're trying to reach people in Denver who would not normally come to a church, but they might come to someone's home. So far, we have 13 groups with about 10 people in each. We call them Happy Hours. We are called the Happy Church, and by the term Happy Hour, we want people to know that the only true happiness is in Jesus. They might think that we're going to have booze there, but we will give them "new wine" from the Word of God.

John English: For the past seven years we have called our groups households—"Ye are the household of God" (Eph. 2:19). We had Bible study groups for years before that. We see a difference between a Bible study in the home and a church in the home. About 80 percent of our 800 people are involved. If our doors were locked on Sunday at the main church, it would make no difference. Our congregation would simply continue business as usual because we have functioning house churches that meet every need of the people.

Linda Lees: We now have 31 groups whose present structure was established in September 1982. Before that, we had four or five loosely structured groups. We felt that because the church attendance was so large (around 1,000 to 1,200), it was not possible to meet the needs of every person—they "get lost"—and it was not possible to build relationships. Small groups would be like a family setting where people would support and care for one another and keep tabs on one another through the week.

Tay Wallace: It was the same story with us. Being a growing church, we were finding that the needs of some of the 3,500 people were going unmet. By having home groups we could not only minister to each other, we could have personalized groups to reach to the St. Louis area as an outreach of our church. We have 110 groups in our laymen's outreach ministry with about 900-1,000 members and 150 visitors attending each Thursday night. This ministry has been in place for a little more than a year.

MINISTRIES: How are leaders chosen for your groups?

John English: One of our leaders' jobs is to watch the maturing level of each person. Over a period of one to two years, they will notice which ones are potential leaders. The leadership couples then challenge these other folks to become leaders. We do that with a presentation of what we want the church to be. If they accept that, we enter them into a six-month training program.

Linda Lees: We have overseers with one to six groups under them. When they see potential leaders, they notify my husband who directs the home group program. And these people are invited to attend training sessions.

Tay Wallace: At first we ran into a problem. Our staff drew up a list and we called these people in and laid it all out to them. But then we realized we had contacted our key people who were overly involved and trying to compensate for a congregation that really wasn't active. They couldn't do it; they were just overloaded. So we opened it up to our congregation and took applications. We taught a training course and we took those people who had a real heart for the vision—people who were excited, able to communicate, to lead, to challenge others. A lot of them were young Christians and some were problem people who turned into some of our greatest leaders. They were problems because they just didn't have anything to do, so we turned them loose and these people proved to be excellent leaders.

Bill Scheidler: We try to have a home leader and an assistant home leader in every home meeting so that when time for division comes, one will take one half and the other will take the other half, so the people will be familiar with them.

Ray Bade: We have a school of ministries and a lot of our leaders come right out of that program. There are seven courses available to help develop people to have leadership potential for our home cell groups.

Tay Wallace: We now have a 24-week lay school program and we observe them in that class. We believe in using people with qualities of leadership who are excited about the vision—dedicated, mature Christians who have also served in other areas of the church. We ask them if they want to be a home leader. If they say yes, then they put them through more training.

John English: The couple who runs the group is able to train and reproduce themselves. I don't do the training. Every time a group is generated, the couple is equipped to do everything in the ministry. They know how to reproduce. We have had one couple who reproduced themselves four times, and they soon will have a fifth group.

MINISTRIES: **Do you have women in leadership?**

John English: Yes, it is usually the wife of the leader. We do not put women in charge of home groups.

Linda Lees: We have one woman in leadership but she does not do the teaching. She's the coordinator for the group; a man does the teaching. In my case, I am not assistant director. My husband is the director of the home group program and I'm the assistant to the director. I do the leg work, the detail work. I fill in if I have to but he meets with the staff and keeps them apprised of what's going on, of any problems or successes. I keep the files and make contacts. I work with the church office staff on anything they might need from us.

Tay Wallace: We have women in leadership as home cell leaders. I'm the only woman pastor on staff at the time.

Bill Scheidler: We use husband and wife teams. We've never had any single women or individual woman lead a group. Sometimes the woman is a little more outgoing and so forth and takes a more active role. But basically it's assigned to the husband and wife team, and the husband in particular.

Ray Bade: Probably half of our group leaders are women. Maybe more.

MINISTRIES: **Do you try to have homogeneous groups—that is, similar in economic situations and so forth—or do you use geographical guidelines?**

Tay Wallace: We are both geographical and homogeneous. We're finding the need to get people together in the same class—same professions—and we're starting to do that with our businessmen. We also have groups for singles, women, youth and older adults.

Bill Scheidler: Portland is divided up into five pastoral districts, and over each one of those we have a pastor who oversees that district with a senior deacon. That district is broken down into a certain number of home meetings. We appoint a deacon or a home leader over each cell group. The groups meet twice a month on a regular basis—the first and third Tuesday of the month. The second Tuesday of the month the elder or pastor over that district meets with all of his home leaders for training and development.

Ray Bade: Our groups usually meet once a week. We have them in homes; we also have them at places where people work. There's a place called the Federal Center in Denver where three of them meet during the lunch hour. There are two at a nursing home as well.

Linda Lees: We don't use geographical guidelines unless the person who needs a group does not have transportation and needs to be close to his or her home. The main purpose is to identify the members' gifts so they can start to use them in the kingdom work. Each group has its own particular personality—in one of the groups some of the members take in foster children; they just seem to have a heart for that. There are three groups that lend themselves to the young people; two are college and career and one is high school. One of the groups is for older singles. They all meet in homes except one large group that did not wish to split, so they use the church fellowship hall. All our groups meet once a week on various nights.

Tay Wallace: Our groups meet in homes on Thursday nights. About once a month we ask them to choose another location among their members. We don't want one leader to be burdened with opening up his or her home every single Thursday night, so they just change locations. It gives the group an opportunity to go door to door and evangelize different sections of their neighborhood. Every contact who comes into our church—first-time visitor, recent convert, a person reached through the hospital ministry or street-witnessing, or someone who comes for counseling—goes through our home leaders. We mail the leaders a postcard with the person's name, and within a week they are visiting that person. While they go on those calls in their neighborhoods, we ask them to make the most of the time and go down the row of houses, knock on doors, introduce themselves and invite the neighbors to a non-threatening Bible study. We like to say we are a "nuclear explosion" in our neighborhoods, bringing light and help.

John English: We believe the groups should be an image of the Christian family where you have youngsters living with oldsters. We disbanded our singles' ministry and asked them to become committed to the home groups so we have older folks, marrieds, singles, junior and senior highers, and young children.

MINISTRIES: **What arrangements are made for small children during group meetings?**

John English: Every group decides among its members how to handle the children. Some groups want the children in during the worship then take them to another part of the house. Other groups want the children in for the worship, and then have someone come in and have a teaching session. Other groups simply let members of the group take care of the children on a rotating basis.

Tay Wallace: We prefer the children do not attend the regular Thursday night meetings. But some groups have a children's meeting in the basement or in another room.

Linda Lees: There's only one group I know of where the small children come to the home group. The rest who have small children hire their own babysitters so they can go out that evening.

Bill Scheidler: Most home meetings just have one or two little ones and the older children can be woven into the fabric of the home meeting. They can read Scriptures, they can give their opinion—we try to involve them as much as possible so they grow up with the sense that they belong, they're involved, they're participants, they're important.

MINISTRIES: **Do all groups use one curriculum or does each group set up its own?**

Bill Scheidler: Each group determines what it wants to do. We give guidelines and suggestions. Once in a while, if we want to have a special emphasis through the home meetings, we have done that. For instance we've run a series on prayer. We encourage them to have one meeting that's more of a formal nature with a Bible study and the other semi-monthly gathering with more of an emphasis on fellowship.

Tay Wallace: Our leaders all teach the same lesson. It's written by one of our assistant pastors. Our group meetings have to be different from our church services; we discovered they were competing.

Linda Lees: Our group leaders are free to do as they wish as long as it is biblical, and as long as the overseer feels it is the right material. Some of the groups will take a Christian book and read the chapters during the week and discuss them at the next meeting. Sometimes a leader may feel he should use the evening for ministry or praise and worship, and he'll drop the lesson for that week. They try to go by the leading of the Holy Spirit.

Ray Bade: We have been taking video machines to the homes along with half-hour video teachings of Marilyn Hickey's ministries. They have been using that as the curriculum.

MINISTRIES: Do groups handle their own finances in any way?

Ray Bade: They take an offering and bring that offering into the church once a week. That offering helps us pay for the video tape. Any money left over is used for a missionary outreach, for example, buying food or Bibles for an area like Ethiopia.

John English: We look at these trained laymen as pastors in these small groups, so they are able to help, able to have a bank account—money in reserve, if they want. We don't require anything of them.

Linda Lees: I know of one group that saves money. Individual members save their change at home in a jar so they can respond to a need. I know of a recent need: a baby was about to be born and the couple didn't have insurance, so the group brought their money in and paid for the hospital bill.

Tay Wallace: Our groups take up an offering Thursday night and give people an opportunity to give to the church; that money goes into the general fund. If a group member is having a financial need, then that group might take up another offering to meet that need. One group decided to start a savings account on a weekly basis, and if a need came up, to pull from it. One district of St. Louis might have five or six home groups which gather regularly. They pray for their area. They might have a project with a needy family, so they'll pool their resources and give to that needy family. At Christmas our city group held a concert for a lot of the poor people in the city. The group brought clothing and groceries and gave them to the poor.

Bill Scheidler: We do take an offering in the meetings—it all comes into a central saints' relief fund. We have this fund as a separate account in our church and its primary purpose is to help minister to the needs of the saints—someone who can't pay his house or electric bill. The elders can help evaluate that need.

MINISTRIES: **To whom do the group leaders submit, and what about discipline?**

Tay Wallace: The group leaders submit to the district leader, and the district leader is under a section pastor. As a section pastor I have five district leaders and I talk with them every week. We spend time together weekly, and they talk to their home leader every week on the phone. They concentrate on getting a report of the meeting and any significant happenings. They encourage, teach, train, pray and correct. If a leader is in error, the district leader, under a pastor's direction, will find out why his group isn't working. If the district leader doesn't get anywhere, the section pastor and district leader talk to the leader and it's usually resolved. We have two services Sunday morning and we meet between the services with our leadership. We train our leaders at that time. Once a month the senior pastor trains the group leaders.

John English: Discipline is handled within the group. If it is a problem greater than the leaders can handle, then they come to me or other pastors.

Bill Scheidler: The group leaders submit to the pastor over their particular district. Generally speaking, because of the strong teaching in the church here on discipline, order, structure and the like, by the time someone becomes a leader we don't have that much of a problem. Over the last ten years, I can count only three or four incidents.

MINISTRIES: **What benefits have accrued to your church and the kingdom of God as a result of the small groups?**

Linda Lees: I would say healings in relationships. People are becoming spiritually whole so they can serve each other out of their wholeness rather than out of their sickness.

Bill Scheidler: I think a main benefit is that it produces a family spirit. People's needs are being met. There's a sense of rest, peace and contentment in the body. There's a real health in the body, and when people are healthy, of course, they reproduce themselves. It's raised the healthiness of the whole church.

John English: Thanks to these groups, the people in our church are no longer spectators, but they have become participants. And it is difficult to get to know 1,000 people in one or two hours in a Sunday morning church service. But in the intimate confines of a home, you can get to know each other intimately, become involved in one another's lives and begin to express your developing gifts.

Tay Wallace: People aren't getting lost in numbers anymore. When there's a need, it surfaces. In a large congregation it's easy for people's need to go unmentioned and unnoticed. When people are plugged into the home groups, if there's a need, a pastor knows about it within the week. As far as the benefits to the kingdom of God, we feel we're not only going out into the world winning people to Jesus but we're fulfilling the other half of the Great Commission. We're able to disciple people and teach them who they are in Christ, put them in active duty and send them out to recruit more people.

Ray Bade: We have written a letter to everyone in Happy Church in the zip code area of a home group. Now there is an opportunity for fellowship as well as an evangelistic outreach through these cell groups.

MINISTRIES: **What advice would you offer a church that is thinking about starting small groups?**

Ray Bade: I would think the most important thing is to develop a plan and know exactly how you are going to do it before you start doing it. Have some guidelines already set out. Know the direction and vision of where you want to go and what you want to attain through your home cell program.

John English: What we did was simply train the lay leaders to be able to reproduce themselves, and then we put them out there. We trusted they would have the ability to hear what God was saying to that particular group. Our objective was to wean them onto the Lord, not to continually have them under our wings.

Linda Lees: Rather than go into an area and start a group, we let people come to us and tell us they want one. We build out of a need rather than trying to start groups mechanically. But I would say let them begin by choosing the man with a gift of administration to head the program.

Bill Scheidler: The main advice I would offer is, don't get discouraged if you feel God has led you to do it. With all new efforts there is a great deal of enthusiasm, and then the enthusiasm wanes. Often on that downward cycle churches abandon the new program. But if they press through that time, they will experience the fruit of it. Too many people allow their home meeting programs to die because of that cycle.

Tay Wallace: It has to be birthed out of the heart of the pastor; it cannot become another sideline of the church. To succeed it really has to become the heartbeat of the church. The pastor has to believe in it. It's not a numbers game. It's not a gimmick to bring quick church growth. It's loving and helping people. And out of the love and concern for the people comes growth. Your pastoral staff has to share the vision of the pastor; they have to make it their vision too. You have to pour yourself into your leadership with time, good resources and energy. You must give yourself to it to make it a success.

60

How Does a Support Group Work?

By Harvey A. Hester

Dr. Harvey A. Hester is director of the Melbourne Counseling Center, Melbourne, Florida. A licensed marriage and family therapist, he is a clinical member of the American Association of Sex Educators, Counselors and Therapists, and an alcohol and drug abuse counselor.

L ast month my wife, Yvonne, and I took a cruise to celebrate 25 years of marriage. Our two daughters, Sharon and Ann, came along with us on the ship which departed Miami and then touched various ports-of-call in the Bahamas and Mexico. We took the girls along because Yvonne and I are no longer two people—we have become family.

Like most professional counselors, I spend the majority of my time working with troubled marriages—or with problems stemming from trouble in marriage. Therefore I feel that 25 years of living with the same woman (and she with the same man) is significant in today's world.

On the cruise a number of people—many of them into their third or fourth marriage—discovered we were celebrating our 25th anniversary. They were genuinely curious as to how (and why) we have "stuck it out" so long.

Although marriage for the Christian leader is never a bed of roses, neither is it something Yvonne and I have had to "stick it out." When we entered into marriage we expected it to be positive, rather than something we'd probably regret. That mind set has made a lot of difference.

That's not to say we've not had a lot of ups and downs. There was the time, shortly after we were married, when I accused her of listening to her father rather than listening to me. We had strong words about that.

There was another time, after I had finished seminary and was pastoring a church, when she had enough of my telling her what to do and what to think. Her temper flared and she verbally blasted me, her pastor-husband.

There have been other times—lots of them. But the major problems in our marriage have emerged over the last few years—since, ironically, I received the baptism in the Holy Spirit. As I look back on it, I realize much of our married life before then was lived on a superficial level. We argued about doing rather than being. Walking in the Spirit has opened us to each other in a new and frightening way. That openness could have destroyed our marriage.

However, this same Holy Spirit has also provided resources to over-come the problems—and has given us wisdom and faith (gifts of the Spirit) to enter wonderful new levels of knowing and loving each other.

Primary among the resources God has given has been my support group—a small group of families to whom my wife and I have committed ourselves in a deep, personal relationship.

Not everyone needs professional counseling. But I am convinced every Christian leader needs a support system.

Like most ministers, I knew I needed help if I was to overcome the problems in my marriage. Yet like most ministers, I was reluctant to open myself to anyone. I had some deep needs. Yvonne had deep needs. While we both had individual friends we could share with, we needed a more solid foundation. We needed a place where we could grow in our relationship.

God provided us with this place. We have a home group that meets every Monday night. While we are committed to studying the Word, this is not our purpose for getting together. While we are committed to pray—and spend great amounts of time praying for each other—this is not our *reason* for getting together. We get together to share pains and problems, concerns and joys.

I minister to a number of pastors in my counseling office. Very few of them have such a place of refuge—where they can hurt and grow. If they did, I suspect most of them would not have to come to me for professional help.

I have discovered that in order to grow, a minister needs at least three elements.

First, he needs a place of safety. Neither Yvonne nor I would ever share our deepest needs if we did not feel it safe to do so. Since I am a professional counselor, people expect us to have it all together. That sounds good, but it isn't always so. We, too, have our times of frustration. As a result we need a safe place to work things out.

In my counseling I often recommend to my clients the books by John Powell. Powell asks tough questions. "Why am I afraid to love?" "Why am I afraid to tell you who I am?"

The answer is simple: if I tell you, if I expose myself to you, you might not accept me. You might laugh at me or ignore me or reject me. I have these same fears, which is the reason Yvonne and I remained closed to other people for a number of years. It's tough to be honest about your problems—unless you have a safe place to get honest.

Recently Yvonne and I had a crisis in our marriage. In fact, it was so big, for the first time I began to consider how I could get out of the relationship. That Monday night the group was supposed to meet at our house. During the day I discovered Yvonne had changed the meeting to the home of another family in the group. I knew what she was doing. She was setting me up and didn't want it to be in our house where our children might hear her angry accusations—and my even angrier reaction.

My first impulse was to run. Yvonne was going to "expose" me in front of the group. I dreaded it. Yet, even though I feared the confrontation, I found myself thanking God that my wife had such a group to whom she could turn for help.

It turned out to be one of the most painful—and most blessed—evenings of my life. I experienced truth flavored with love. And even though the furnace was hot—I was safe.

The second element necessary for growth is nourishment. I need to be fed—not just milk, but meat. Our group is out of milk. We offer up beef jerky to chew on.

I don't need criticism or judgment. I get that from my enemies. I need direction. I need to be given that which allows me to grow. One night after I exploded and told the group their advice sounded like manure to me, one of the ladies calmly reminded me that manure was fertilizer—and it makes things grow.

The final element necessary for growth is encouragement. Just when you think you cannot continue, you find the strength. My friend, Brooks Watson, who is a professional engineer and developer, said to me on that fateful evening, "You have no choice, Harvey, but to listen and love."

Those words helped put my entire life back into perspective.

I need a place of safety to share myself. I need others who will force me to look at myself and my motives. I need others who will not placate me but will encourage me to walk through the valley—fearing no evil.

For a number of years the thrust of my ministry has been to help wounded leaders—especially pastors. This group of hurting, lonely people often has no place of refuge because, unfortunately, the church often kills off its wounded. As a result our churchy culture is so structured that the pastor and his family are often the loneliest people in the congregation—and have no place to go for real and meaningful help.

Last month a pastor from another state brought his wife and came to Melbourne, where I live, to spend three weeks finding the help which was unavailable in his own church—a church, by the way, which prides itself on being "family." He had developed a relationship with another woman in his congregation and his wife had discovered it. But since they were afraid to tell anyone in their church about it—for fear of rejection—the couple had to travel several thousand miles to find help. In this case, not only did I minister to them professionally in my office, but I used my support group as a "model." If he does not develop his own support group when he returns to his pastorate, he will soon be back in the same trap.

Both of them had been cut off. Neither had anyone with whom they could share their hurts. The "affair" was not the problem—it was merely symptomatic of something far deeper in both of them. Simply being in the presence of people who accepted them for who they were gave them new hope and new direction in life.

Although this was "business as usual" for my home group, for those receiving ministry it was a new and exciting experience.

Pastors and their families are human. They have their own needs. Too many times they are placed on a pedestal and warned they should not fall—or even show signs of cracking. The pressure is too great—and many wind up leaving the ministry.

Adultery, alcoholism, abuse, emotional problems—these are no respecter of persons. God's "called" are affected also. Where do they go? To whom can they turn?

I believe the Scriptures are clear. We are to turn to each other for in doing so we turn to the body of Jesus Christ.

Fifteen years ago I spent time working with Carlyle Marney, the founder of Interpreters' House at Lake Junaluska, North Carolina. Marney ministered to wounded leaders. He took his theme from *Pilgrim's Progress* and the sign over the Wicket Gate, which said, "No matter what you have done, you will in no wise be cast out."

For many pastors that was too big a bit to swallow. They could believe God would accept them. But they had trouble—and for good reason—believing God's people could do likewise.

Twenty-five years of marriage is significant. But I don't want to take on the next 25 without help. My support group fills that need.

61

How Does a Pastor Benefit From a Closed Group?

By Jamie Buckingham

    Jamie Buckingham, senior minister at The Tabernacle Church, Melbourne, Florida, is one of the most widely read Christian writers of his generation. He is an award-winning magazine and newspaper columnist and has served in editorial positions for *Guideposts* magazine, *The National Courier* and *Logos Journal*. At present he is on the board of directors and is editor-at-large for both *Charisma* and *MINISTRIES* magazines, and is an editorial consultant for Wycliffe Bible Translators. He has authored 33 books.

Q: I understand you promote home groups in your church. How many do you have?

A: We have 31 small home groups. Although all meet weekly, the structure of each group is different. Some are prayer groups. Others are Bible study groups. Some major in evangelism, reaching out, growing, then dividing to form new groups. Others, such as the one I am in, are relationship groups and as such are "closed."

Q: Does it bother your church members that you, as senior minister, belong to a "closed" group? It sounds almost cliquish.

A: It bothered some when we first got started. At that time I was the pastor of the church and some people were jealous that I belonged to a group they couldn't join.

Gradually, however, the people have become comfortable with my being in a group. In fact, I think they feel safe in having a spiritual leader who submits his personal life to a small group. They accept what I have been saying for years—that one person can effectively interact with just so many people on any level. A long time ago I decided I must do as I hear God leading me and let Him justify the course of action. At the same time I strongly urge all our people to find a group in the church which will meet their personal needs as our group meets mine.

Q: Are you the leader of your group?

A: Although I am the spiritual overseer of The Tabernacle Church, I am not the leader of our home group. When I meet with our elders, I am looked up to as the leader. But when I am with our home group, Jackie and I are simply one of the five couples who are in relationship together. The others in the group are business or professional people. Every pastor needs to belong to something he's not required to lead.

When it comes to the governmental affairs of the church, I voluntarily submit to the church elders. But Jackie and I submit our personal lives to the men and women in our home group. From them we receive correction, direction and encouragement. If Jackie and I hit a personal impasse during the week, we often put the argument on "hold" until Monday night and then submit both sides to the group.

We have been meeting together for almost seven years and by now we are free to discuss even the deepest personal problems. Those in the group are not only our close friends, but they are our "extended family" with whom Jackie and I can be honest about all our feelings and facts.

Q: You say you meet weekly. What do you do?

A: Despite my heavy travel schedule, I give top priority to our Monday night meeting. We usually meet at 6:30 p.m., rotating between the five homes. Normal fare is a covered-dish supper followed by our sharing time together.

Our leader, Gene Berrey (actually he prefers to be called a coordinator), is the manager of a public utility company. After supper we spend time "checking in," allowing each person 5-10 minutes to talk about the deep things in his life at that time. If one family is going through a particular crisis, we might spend the entire evening ministering to that couple.

Recently one of the wives blew up at her husband, saying she was fed up with the way he was spending more time with his secretary than with her. It was a critical situation and we stayed until almost midnight talking that one through. We wound up in deep prayer together, and husband and wife both agreed to make the proper concessions so healing could occur.

Everything is not serious ministry. We often go out to eat together, celebrating birthdays or anniversaries. We take at least one seven-day summer vacation together. For the last several years we've done this in Gene's three-bedroom mountain cabin (now that's real togetherness), and we take occasional week-end group trips.

Only one couple in the group has teenage children (the rest of our children are grown) so we basically interact as adults.

My grown daughter and her husband belong to a similar group in our church. Although their group is made up of young couples with small children, their basic concepts are the same (they also take vacations together, etc.) but they adapt differently since they have different needs. Their meetings are similar but they usually get baby-sitters.

Q: Does "closed" mean others are not welcome in your group?

A: We do, on occasion, invite visiting couples (usually some minister and his wife who may be visiting me) to sit in on one of our Monday night meetings. We do this primarily to allow them the opportunity of seeing how we function, or to minister to them in some deep area of their lives. This latter purpose is especially true of several missionary couples our group is vitally interested in.

However, the transparency we have developed across the years as we air out our deepest feelings is often a threat to others who are unfamiliar with this kind of catharsis. The presence of others, even our friends, sometimes inhibits the group as well. One of the men who is angry with his wife, or who is terribly burdened over a wayward child and feels the fault is his, would not be as willing to open up before strangers as he would before his own family.

For this reason we rarely have visitors, and then only on consent of all in the group.

Q: You mentioned you were a "covenant" group. What does that mean?

A: Our group has met together for seven years. During this time we have come to know each other well, loving and respecting each person. This has taken time but as we grew closer we realized we had indeed entered into some kind of deep commitment, or covenant, of the heart. We were, in a true sense, "family." What is mine is theirs also.

A couple of years ago we debated building our homes together in "community." We also spent several weeks praying about some kind of written covenant. We opted against this but we did agree we had entered a relationship that had some of the characteristics of marriage in that there was no "back door." We look upon each other as true brothers and sisters. Our children are all spiritual cousins. We pray daily for each other, are in close personal contact during the week (some of us play racquetball together), and we keep all conversation in the group confidential. We have not taken any vows, but we do feel the Lord has made us "friends" for life.

Q: Do you feel every pastor should belong to such a group?

A: I remember, sadly, sharing with the pastor of a large church about my group, and the safeguards it provides for my own personal life. There is nothing I can do which would break the relationship. This means I can go to our group—or perhaps to a couple of the men in the group—to seek help on things like my inordinate sexual yearnings, my deep personal fears or any anger I may have.

The pastor sat across the table from me, weeping. He said he wished he had such a group around him. But his only relationship was with his elders and staff—and they were afraid of him. In fact, the relationship was so impersonal none of them dared call him by his first name.

The following year his elders dismissed him, having discovered he was involved in long-term sexual immorality. Not only did he have no one he could have been honest with ahead of time, but when he fell he had no friends to pick him up.

I thank God for friends who know *all* about me—who have seen my wife and me in violent (and on one occasion, physical) arguments, who have called my hand on numerous occasions, who have seen me cry over personal failures—yet who love me and stick beside me regardless.

Yes, I wish every pastor had such a group. If so, there would be far fewer casualties in the ministry.